Beyond Effective Go

Beyond Effective Go

Part 2 -
Striving for High-Quality Code

Corey Scott

First paperback edition June 2024

Book Cover by Siew May Tan

Cover Image by Arek Socha on Pixabay

Illustrations by Siew May Tan & Corey S. Scott

Edited by Rachael Churchill

ISBN 978-0-6455820-4-8 (Paperback)

ISBN 978-0-6455820-8-6 (eBook)

www.coreyscott.dev

To my children, S & O,

I hope you discover a vocation you love doing as much as I love programming.

About the Author

Corey is a passionate programmer who's been programming ever since his dad brought home a brand new Apple IIe.

He believes that programming is a craft and, as such, it should be shared, celebrated, and debated.

He also believes that all professional software has three equally important audiences, the users, the programmers, and the business, all of which have different and competing needs that must be met.

While he has written software in many languages over the years, Go is his current preferred language for writing large-scale backend services and convenient automation tools.

Acknowledgments

The people who helped review and shape this book and to whom I want to offer my sincerest thanks:

Siew May T.

Anthony M.

Chia Hsiang C.

Tien N.

Vishal K.

Binbin T.

Tony W.

Contents

Chapter 5
Optimizing for Code UX

Chapter 6
Advanced Unit Testing Techniques

Chapter 7

Improving your Development Productivity 201

Chapter 8

Examining Unusual Patterns for Go 239

Chapter 9

Preface

When folks ask me, "How do I learn Go?" I tell them the first stop is the Tour of Go from the **go.dev** website. Then, I tell them that while they are ready to program after the tour, they should also read the Effective Go article. I also warn them that they likely won't absorb all of the wisdom in the article right now, but they should add a reminder in their calendar to re-read it in six, twelve, and twenty-four months.

However, when folks come to me and say, "I've been doing Go for a while and want to get better, where do I go now?" I don't have a concise answer to this. So I decided to take a shot at collecting the community's best practices, the Go-isms, and all my hard-won experiences into a book, which became this series. These books are my humble attempt to help you become more efficient and more effective while using Go as the language to provide tangible customer value.

You may have noticed from the book's subtitle that it is part of a more extensive collection of work. I have decided to release the content in parts to ensure it is available to you without being delayed by the lengthy process of writing, editing, and publishing (and everything else).

If you are interested in the other parts or want to provide feedback, then please:

- Drop by my website: **https://coreyscott.dev/**

- Reach out via GitHub: **https://github.com/corsc/**

- Or message me on Twitter/X: **https://twitter.com/CoreySScott**

Book Structure and Formatting

The first question you probably had when picking up this book was why it starts at chapter four and where the first three chapters are. The first three chapters form Part 1 in the series. They are titled Chapter 1—*Understanding Concurrency, Parallelism, and the Sync Packages,* Chapter 2—*Applying Go Concurrency: Primitives, Patterns, and Tools,* and Chapter 3— *Achieving High-Performance Code.*

In this book, each chapter is comprised of five sections:

1. **The introduction**—Outlines the chapter's goal and highlights the key concepts that the chapter will cover.

2. **The code listing**—This section is a powerful tool for your learning journey. It includes a link to download the code used throughout the chapter. You are encouraged to refer to it often as it often provides more context beyond the code highlighted in the book.

3. **The main content**—This is where all the knowledge is.

4. **The summary**—This attempts to summarize the chapter by highlighting the key concepts.

5. **The list of questions**—This is a vital part of your learning process. It allows you to gauge your understanding of the chapter's content. They are designed to encourage you to actively engage with the material and test your knowledge.

Throughout this book, we have used the following style conventions:

- Regular text - This is the default style and will be used for any content not covered by the other styles in this list.

- **In-line code** - This style is used for code that appears within regular content.

- Code Blocks - This style is used for blocks of code.

Chapter 4

Exploring Software Design Principles

Introduction

There are as many ways to program as there are programmers. However, every programming language is created with an ideology, preferences, and style built into it, and Go is no different. While it is possible to write Go programs in an object-oriented, interface-providing, Java-like style or to use Go to write in a functional Node.js-like style, neither approach is effective or efficient. This chapter will explore the software engineering, design, and patterns we should use to be effective Go programmers.

There will be three main idea threads running throughout this chapter:

1. We will introduce principles to consider during software design and construction.

2. We will introduce proven approaches or patterns that can apply to software design.

3. We will outline a standard vocabulary to debate software design.

Before we dive into these concepts, please remember that they result from the hard-won wisdom of our industry over many years—in the case of the design patterns, decades. They are, however, not the solution to every problem but rather something to be selectively applied if and when they are the best option.

The following topics will be covered in this chapter:

- Exploring Software Design Principles
- Object-Oriented Design Patterns

Code

To get the most out of this chapter, you will need a recent copy (1.13+) of Go installed and your favorite IDE.

The full versions of all code examples and other related material can be found at:

https://github.com/corsc/Beyond-Effective-Go/tree/master/Chapter04

Exploring Software Design Principles

Software design principles are standards or practices to be considered when constructing software. They are not rules; we are not wrong when we don't use or intentionally go against these principles. The key is to be aware of these ideas and apply them pragmatically. If a particular principle can be applied, and it will improve the code and make your life easier, then do it!

Sometimes, these principles will get in the way of the initial implementation of a particular feature. Please ignore them during the initial implementation, wait until the feature works, and then refactor the appropriate principles into the code. My personal motto is:

> Make it work, make it clean, then (maybe)
> make it fast.

For me, this is the order of precedence. Code has to work, or it provides no value. Ideally, it should be clean—e.g., well-factored, readable, and maintainable—but we can survive if it's not. As for speed, most code doesn't need to be fully optimized, and we should only spend time optimizing the code that needs it.

I have included the most pertinent principles for effective Go in this chapter. There are many others. You should seek to find and understand as many software design principles as possible. You will find that some principles apply to almost all languages; you will find that some will make Go better and some worse. You will even find that some principles conflict with others. Those presented here will give you a great start on your journey.

Minimalist and composable

Sometimes referred to as the "Unix Philosophy", this ideal prescribes that a program should only perform one task and be easily composable, such that several components can be easily composed to solve more significant problems.

This idea can and should apply to not just programs but packages, structs, and functions.

This philosophy is evident in the Go standard libraries, such as within the **encoding/json** package. The package itself provides a minimal API for the processing of JSON data. Inside the package, we find the **Marshaler** interface, which looks like this:

```
type Marshaler interface {
    MarshalJSON() ([]byte, error)
}
```

This interface is also minimalistic and defines only one feature, the ability for an object to output its JSON representation in bytes. If this interface had not been designed with this principle in mind, the designer could have easily assumed that, in many cases, users would need to marshal and unmarshal their data, and instead defined an interface like this:

```
type JSONObject interface {
    MarshalJSON() ([]byte, error)
    UnmarshalJSON([]byte) error
}
```

Instead, this package separates these two features into two interfaces that we can compose or use separately.

So these ideas are great for shared libraries, but how can they apply to your singular-purpose code? Let's tackle this by first looking at the minimalist aspect. Have you ever heard the advice "avoid common or util packages"? These packages often result from trying to reduce code duplication, which is an excellent idea that we will dig into later in this chapter. However, such packages are inherently not minimalistic and contain unrelated code. Because of the wide variety of code in the package, the package's purpose is unclear.

If, instead, we were to make multiple smaller packages out of this code and give them purpose-specific names, then the purpose of the packages would be more apparent. This, in turn, increases our ability to reuse the package. A great example of this from the standard library is **crypto/rand**. This package serves one purpose, creating cryptographically secure random numbers, and it only has three public functions and one variable. Without the Unix Philosophy, these features could have been part of the **crypto** or **math/rand** (where the insecure random number generator lives) packages, but this would have increased the scope and decreased the specificity of the purpose of these packages.

Now, let's look at composability. This aspect is both deceptively simple and extremely difficult. How often do you think you use the interface **io.Reader**? Because many functions and methods use this ubiquitous little interface, we can compose lots of our code without incessantly casting or performing type conversion.

To achieve the same level of composability in our own projects, we need to look for opportunities to use or reuse small interfaces when passing data through our modules. When dealing with bytes or strings, adopting **io.Reader** instead of a concrete type or a custom interface will help immensely. In other cases, like when passing around large data objects, we may find that instead of passing the data object around and having tightly coupled code, we can introduce an abstraction in the form of an interface. This would not only reduce the coupling of the code but also increase the composability of the packages. Take, for example, the following function:

```go
func recordUserLogin(user *User) {
    fmt.Printf("UserID %d logged in", user.ID)
}
```

You will notice that this function does not need the whole **User** object and, by extension, does not need to be coupled to it. We can change the function to this:

```go
func recordUserLoginByID(user IDer) {
    fmt.Printf("UserID %d logged in", user.GetID())
}

type IDer interface {
    GetID() int
}
```

With this change, we have not only decoupled from the **User** object, but since we can use any object that implements our simple interface, we have greater flexibility when composing this function with other parts of the system.

The DRY principle vs. the KISS principle

The *don't repeat yourself* or DRY principle's primary goal is reducing duplicate code. This reduction of duplication is intended to make code easier to maintain, because every line of code has a non-zero maintenance cost.

When code is thoroughly DRY, each algorithm or piece of logic would only exist in one place, and therefore changes would only need to be made once. These are compelling arguments and definitely something we should keep in mind. However, strict adherence to this principle can be detrimental. In fact, the DRY principle frequently conflicts with another fundamental principle, the *keep it simple, stupid* or KISS principle.

Consider a situation where we're adding a new feature and, about halfway through this work, we realize that we need some logic from another package. To strictly follow the DRY principle, we'd stop what we're working on and extract the shared logic into its own package. After extracting the new package, we'd return to implementing the new feature—only to discover that we didn't actually need the logic we extracted. What do we do now? Do we undo the package extraction or leave it and have to maintain the extra package? There is no correct answer to this question. If the logic can stand independently, I would follow the minimalist idea and make it a sub-package of the original package. This way, it still belongs to the original package but could be easily upgraded to a shared package if needed.

Let's consider a slightly different and likely more common scenario: instead of needing the extracted code, we discover that its original functionality is not precisely what we needed. To complete our new feature, we need to expand the capabilities of the extracted code to enable this variation. As a result, the extracted shared code is now more complicated in both UX and implementation than the original. Additionally, any subsequent requirements requiring us to add more complexity to the extracted code will only worsen this problem. If, instead, we intentionally duplicated the similar code, there would be less coupling in the codebase overall, and each copy would be more straightforward and able to evolve independently.

I am not trying to imply that we should not follow the DRY principle, but rather that we should be pragmatic about its application. A reasonable way to balance the DRY and KISS principles is to consider the relationship between the packages using the shared logic. If they are strongly related, then any changes to one are often going to be needed by the other, so the fact that the logic is shared allows us for easier maintenance, and the coupling brings us value.

There is one more approach you should consider. Instead of stopping work on the new feature to extract the package, we continue implementing it by copying and pasting the shared code.

With this approach, we can complete the new feature faster and get our unit tests in place to confirm this. Then, with our unit tests to ensure that all of our features continue to work, we can refactor and remove or leave the duplication depending on how much the copied code was changed. With this approach, we are not distracted by the DRY or KISS principle (or any others) while implementing the feature, and only once it is implemented we refactor from a position of greater knowledge and test-provided safety.

Aspects to consider when applying the DRY principle

When contemplating refactoring based on the DRY principle, we should first ask ourselves the following:

- **Who will own the shared logic?** Does the logic belong to the package or module where it currently resides, or is it generic enough to be extracted into its own package? If it belongs in its current package, how does adding this feature to the public API of the package change the package as a whole? If the logic is generic, then where does this new package belong? Should it be a child package of one of the existing packages or at the same level? A common mistake here is to dump this logic into a **commons** or **utils** package; please don't do this. For a more extended discussion on this point, jump to *A little copying vs. a little dependency* in Chapter 5.

- **What is the relationship between the current usage of the logic and the new one?** Any ties should influence how the code is organized. Similar packages should exist together, and any shared packages should be in the same location. On the other hand, if the newly added and previous logic are not closely related, we should consider not applying the DRY principle.

- **Now that this code is being used more broadly, what is the proper abstraction?** When code is written for a particular purpose, it is named and abstracted for only that purpose. When extracting the code, we may need to choose more abstract naming. We should reduce its dependencies where possible. Additionally, we should improve its underlying quality to ensure it's appropriate for this more prominent role and ensure its long-term viability.

- **What does the extraction imply about the surrounding code?** When extracting the logic, could we be forced to extract other objects, like data-transfer objects or interfaces, as well? How much of the original code are we going to need to extract? If we are forced to extract much of the original package, we should consider refactoring the original to be more generic and handle both cases.

Any principle that reduces the effort required to maintain code is worth keeping in mind, and the DRY and KISS principles are both definitely capable of this. The critical aspect to remember is that reducing lines of code is not the goal; improving code maintainability is.

Delegation

The Delegation principle has two main goals. The first is to reduce duplication, and the second is to improve the cohesion of the code. It achieves these by delegating the processing of a request to another, more appropriate object. Let's look at an example. In the code below, we are testing if two user objects are equal:

```go
func Example_noDelegation() {
    userA := &User{
        Name:  "Bob",
        Age:   16,
        Email: "bob@example.com",
    }
    userB := &User{
        Name:  "Jane",
        Age:   23,
        Email: "jane@example.com",
    }

    if userA.Name == userB.Name &&
        userA.Age == userB.Age &&
        userA.Email == userB.Email {
        fmt.Println("Users A and B are the same!")
    } else {
        fmt.Println("Users are not the same")
    }

    // Output: Users are not the same
}
```

This code works fine but does not comply with the delegation principle as the comparison logic belongs to **main()** rather than **User**. This will severely limit both the discoverability and reusability of this logic, often leading to duplication and inconsistencies. Instead, we should refactor our example and delegate the comparison to the **User** type itself like this:

```
func Example_delegation() {
    userA := &User{
        Name: "Bob",
        Age:   16,
        Email: "bob@example.com",
    }
    userB := &User{
        Name: "Jane",
        Age:   23,
        Email: "jane@example.com",
    }

    if userA.Equals(userB) {
        fmt.Println("Users A and B are the same!")
    } else {
        fmt.Println("Users are not the same")
    }


    // Output: Users are not the same
}
```

The resulting code now has greater cohesion, meaning the logic for testing equality is now coupled or owned by the object. So where does the reduction in duplication come in? The next time we need to test the equality of two users, we can call the method on the **User** object instead of reimplementing or extracting the original logic.

Depending on your programming background, you might ask why we added a method to the **User** type. Or *What is wrong with an **IsEqual(a *User, b *User) bool** method*? These are valid questions; creating an **IsEqual()** function would have achieved the same code reduction. However, such a method would have different discoverability, and it is then possible for the **IsEqual()** method to become separated from the **User** object. By adding the **IsEqual()** as a method to the **User** type, we are avoiding these suboptimal outcomes.

In our previous example, the delegation was direct and non-optional, but there is another approach called optional delegation. With optional delegation, we delegate when possible and fall back to a default implementation otherwise. To demonstrate optional delegation, we need a new example; assume we are sending data in bytes over a TCP connection. A naive implementation might look like this:

```go
func Send(conn net.Conn, data interface{}) error {
    // convert data to bytes
    payload := []byte(fmt.Sprintf("%s", data))

    _, err := conn.Write(payload)
    return err
}
```

In this implementation, the conversion of the input to bytes will only work for basic types and, in some cases, might produce a different result than we want. We can improve this approach and allow the data to use optional delegation by introducing an optional typecast and leaving our original implementation as the fallback:

```go
func Send(conn net.Conn, data interface{}) error {
    // convert data to bytes using optional delegation
    var payload []byte
    if encoder, ok := data.(ByteEncoder); ok {
        payload = encoder.Encode()
    } else {
        payload = []byte(fmt.Sprintf("%s", data))
    }

    _, err := conn.Write(payload)
    return err
}

type ByteEncoder interface {
    Encode() []byte
}
```

With this approach, we are not reducing the usability of our **Send()** function by requiring all data to implement our **ByteEncoder** interface. Instead, we are letting the user decide.

We can see more examples of this form of optional delegation in the standard library, including in the **encoding/json** package that allows custom marshaling and unmarshaling and how the **sql/driver** package converts data for sending to databases.

Favor composition over inheritance

Given that Go does not support inheritance, this point is more prominent than it is for other languages. If Go's lack of inheritance has ever worried you, don't stress, we can use composition in place of inheritance, and in many cases, we are better for it.

Firstly, we should ask ourselves, what were we trying to achieve with inheritance? There are typically two common answers to this.

First, we want to use inheritance to reduce code duplication. This is done by moving the shared code into a parent or abstract type. When using composition, we can achieve the exact same outcome by moving the shared code into another struct and then composing that struct like this:

```
type bird struct{}

func (b bird) Fly() {
        // not implemented
}

type Duck struct {
        bird bird
}

func (d Duck) Fly() {
        d.bird.Fly()
}
```

Composition even allows us to extend this further. We can reduce the coupling between our two types by introducing an interface and injecting the shared code as a dependency.

If we really wanted our code to look like inheritance, we can even use Go's support for anonymous composition and implicit delegation and change our example to this:

```
type bird struct{}

func (b bird) Fly() {
```

```
        // not implemented
}

type Duck struct {
    bird
}
```

You will notice that the **Fly()** method is no longer needed, just as it would not have been needed with inheritance.

The second goal of inheritance is to define a family of object types that should be interacted with in the same way. Often this would take the form of either an abstract method or an "implements" definition that defines the contract we want the object to adhere to. In typical Go style, we can achieve this but with less required formality. We still define an interface that outlines the interactions we expect; however, to ensure our struct implements the interface, we would either have to compose the interface into the struct or add a compile test like this:

```
// Use the compiler to ensure Duck is a talker
var duckTalker talker = Duck{}

type talker interface {
    Talk() string
}

type Duck struct {}

func (d Duck) Talk() string {
    return "Quack!"
}
```

This may seem odd, but it is a convenient way to document our expectations and prevent regression of our API without relying on our users to do it for us.

At the start of this section, I promised you that, in some ways, we would be better off with composition than inheritance. These ways include:

- **Composition allows for multiple "parents"**—With single inheritance, you can only derive from one parent. With composition, that relationship can be whatever we need it to be.

- **Composition is often more natural**—When we utilize composition, the interaction between the components is explicit and clear. When we use inheritance, there is more indirection and magic. For example, with inheritance, when a user calls a method on our struct, it can be implemented either in our struct or in one of its parents.

- **Composition has less resistance to change**—Composition makes it easier to respond to requirements changes. Any changes tend to be more localized, and when the objects are loosely coupled, the potential for shotgun surgery is significantly lessened.

- **Composition is more dynamic**—Composition occurs at runtime, which means it can dynamically respond to conditions, including user input or runtime configuration.

As you can see, we are no worse off because Go does not support inheritance. If you are concerned about how to get by without the Gang of Four's Object-Oriented Design Patterns, don't worry. We will look at some of the most common patterns later in this chapter.

Accept interfaces and return structs

Like many of Go's ideals, behind the pithy statement is a wealth of knowledge and some surprising advantages. On the surface, this ideal looks like an incomplete version of the "Code to interfaces and not implementations" idea that exists in other languages, whose goal is to achieve loose coupling by depending on abstractions and thus maximize the flexibility of code.

The primary goal in the Go is the same, but the implementation is different. Let's dive deeper by examining the two parts separately. Firstly, accepting interfaces.

Accepting interfaces

The intent of accepting an interface is to reduce friction and increase the usability of the function. Consider the following example that requires a struct as an input:

```
func SendEmail(user *User, subject, message string) error {
    // implementation removed
    return nil
```

```
    }

    type User struct {
        EmailAddress string
    }
```

To use this function, users must first build the input struct. This results in extra effort and potentially more work for the garbage collector, as this object will likely be discarded after the function call. Conversely, by accepting an interface, we no longer require that the user create a new object to call the function. They are free to pass in any object that satisfies the interface. Applying this idea to our example gives us the following:

```
    func SendEmail(recipient Recipient, subject, message string) error {
        // implementation removed
        return nil
    }

    type Recipient interface {
        GetEmailAddress() string
    }
```

After these changes, we gain an additional bonus. The coupling between the user's code and our function has been reduced.

The advantages of accepting interfaces continue beyond there. Accepting interface inputs also increases both the testability and encapsulation of our code. To show this, we are going to need a more meaty example. Consider the following function that validates and saves the supplied **User** object:

```
    func CreateUser(repository *repo.UserDAO, user *user.User) error {
        err := validateUser(user)
        if err != nil {
            return err
        }

        return repository.Save(user)
    }
```

This code looks pretty straightforward, but the problems start to become more apparent when we try to write a test for this code like this:

```
func TestCreateUser_happyPath(t *testing.T) {
    // mock the database
    db, mockDB, err := sqlmock.New()
    require.NoError(t, err)

    mockDB.ExpectExec("INSERT INTO user").WillReturnResult(sqlmock.NewResult(1, 1))

    // build the repository
    repository := &repo.UserDAO{Database: db}

    // build inputs
    testUser := &user.User{ID: 1, Name: "Amy", Email: "amy@example.com"}

    resultErr := repository.Save(testUser)
    assert.NoError(t, resultErr)

    assert.NoError(t, mockDB.ExpectationsWereMet())
}
```

What is this test actually testing? It should be testing only the features provided by the
CreateUser() function. The **CreateUser()** function validates the supplied input and calls the
repository to save the user. However, we spend over half the test mocking the database. In fact,
our **CreateUser()** function and any tests of it should have no knowledge of the database, as this
is the responsibility of the repository. An easier way to spot this problem is to ask yourself, if we
swapped out the SQL database inside the repository for an object store like DynamoDB,
would the test for our **CreateUser()** function have to change? Yes, they would and they
shouldn't need to.

The encapsulation of the database has leaked into our tests and, as a result, made our tests more
complicated and coupled to the repository's implementation. To address this, we first switch
our input to an interface like this:

```
func CreateUser(repository UserRepository, user *user.User) error {
    err := validateUser(user)
    if err != nil {
        return err
    }

    return repository.Save(user)
```

```
}
```

```
//go:generate mockery -name=UserRepository -case underscore -testonly -inpkg
type UserRepository interface {
    Save(user *user.User) error
}
```

Then, after creating a mock implementation of our interface, our test is reduced to this:

```
func TestCreateUser_happyPath(t *testing.T) {
    // mock the repository
    repository := &MockUserRepository{}
    repository.On("Save", mock.Anything).Return(nil)

    // build inputs
    testUser := &user.User{ID: 1, Name: "Amy", Email: "amy@example.com"}

    resultErr := repository.Save(testUser)
    assert.NoError(t, resultErr)
}
```

After these changes, our test has no knowledge of the database and is solely focused on testing our function.

After convincing you to use interfaces instead of structs for inputs, you might be surprised that I am not recommending doing the same with outputs. After all, many of the same advantages apply, and this approach is often what other languages do.

Returning structs

From many perspectives, returning an interface and an object that implements the same interface are equivalent. In the following example, both functions return an object that implements the **UserDAO** interface:

```
type UserDAO interface {
    Load(ID int) (*User, error)
    Save(user *User) error
}
```

```
func NewUserDAOInterface() UserDAO {
    return &UserDAOImpl{}
}

func NewUserDAOStruct() *UserDAOImpl {
    return &UserDAOImpl{}
}
```

As both return variables satisfy the same interface, they can be used in the same way, as shown in the following example:

```
var userDaoA UserDAO = NewUserDAOInterface()
var userDaoB UserDAO = NewUserDAOStruct()
```

This is possible due to a language feature called implicit interfaces. Using this correctly will lessen our workload and allow users to decouple from our functions if they want to.

Firstly, lessening our workload. When we return a struct, we do not spend the time defining and maintaining the interface and keeping it in sync with the underlying implementation. Additionally, we are not tempted to provide a mock implementation of the interface. Defining a mock implementation in this package so that you can apply the DRY principle and reuse both the interface and the mock in other packages is a mistake. If we did this, we would have test code outside of a test file—which is not only messy but could accidentally be used in production. These should be auto-generated, so the cost of creating and maintaining multiple instances is trivial.

Secondly, if we were to provide an interface, we would discourage our users from correctly decoupling from our code. If users adopt our interface instead of defining their own, there is an increased likelihood of encapsulation leakage. This means that our interface leaks beyond the code that uses it, which increases overall coupling. Also, when users define their interfaces and abstractions, they can reduce the interface to only their requirements. This serves to document their requirements concisely, and any tests and mocks would then be appropriately decoupled from our code.

This approach might seem strange, but, as you can see, the best outcome for our users is for us to provide less.

The singles principle

When I first wrote this section of the book, it was titled *The single responsibility principle* until it was correctly pointed out that I had extended the single responsibility principle beyond Robert C. Martin's original intent. Hence, a new principle was born: *the singles principle*.

Given that the singles principle (SP) was inspired by the single responsibility principle (SRP), we should first take a quick look at SRP.

The single responsibility principle was coined by Robert C. Martin in 2005, and it states:

> A class should have only one reason to change
>
> —Robert C. Martin

While Martin used the term *class*, this principle can and should be expanded to include all software components, meaning it applies to our functions, structs, packages, and modules.

The singles principle, however, encompasses SRP and extends the singular aspect even further to promote focused discrete components.

> All components should be focused and discrete
>
> —The singles principle

The underlying goal of SP is to keep our software architecture simple. SP encourages us to design our software components, functions, structs, packages, and modules so that each component has:

- A single purpose
- A single responsibility
- A single level of abstraction

When our software architecture is simple, it is inherently easier to understand; our ability to compose and reuse the components increases, and our code is far easier to test.

Let's dive deeper into these points, starting with *a single purpose*.

A single purpose

When a component has a single purpose, then its reason for existence is clear. It does one thing and only one thing.

When a component has a single purpose, then it is:

- **Easier to understand**—To understand both the intent and the implementation, we only need to read the code for the component. There are no distractions and nothing unrelated.

- **Easier to test**—By limiting the component's purpose, we also narrow the usage scenarios. By extension, we are left with fewer test scenarios.

- **More likely to be reusable**—This one can be counter-intuitive; however, by decomposing our code into smaller chunks that serve a narrower purpose, we can discover areas of logic reuse.

So how do we ensure our component has a single purpose? We can apply something I am calling the "comment test". The comment test consists of two steps:

1. Write a one-line comment for the component that describes the component completely.

2. Examine the comment you wrote for words like *and*, *or*, *all*, *various*, or *several*. These words all suggest that you have multiple purposes. Additionally, if it was difficult to describe the entire scope in one comment, then it is likely too broad.

Try it out on this struct diagram:

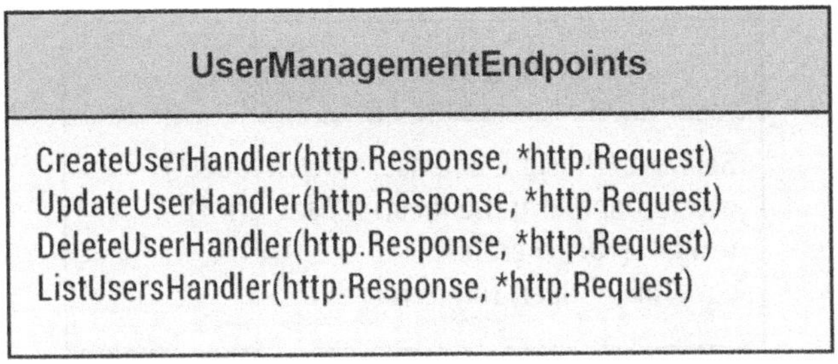

<table>
<tr><td align="center">UserManagementEndpoints</td></tr>
</table>

```
UserManagementEndpoints

CreateUserHandler(http.Response, *http.Request)
UpdateUserHandler(http.Response, *http.Request)
DeleteUserHandler(http.Response, *http.Request)
ListUsersHandler(http.Response, *http.Request)
```

Figure 4.1—User management endpoints struct

You probably wrote a comment similar to this:

```
// UserManagementEndpoints provides HTTP handlers for all User management
```

You can see from this comment that our struct has clearly more than one purpose. We can fix this by decomposing it into one struct per endpoint. However, when doing so, we should also consider the next aspect of the singles principle: *responsibility*.

A single responsibility

The goal of single responsibility is the very essence of the SRP, as defined by Robert C. Martin. In 2014, Martin published a clarification of the SRP that focused on the "reason for change" section, in which he outlined that the focus should be on people. By this, he asserts that only one person (or group of related people) should be able to influence a single component.

Let's revisit our previous example. You will remember that we decomposed our monolithic struct into one struct per HTTP endpoint. This change enabled us to pass the "single purpose" test. But what happens when we look a little deeper at the private methods of our struct? Our struct diagram actually looks like this:

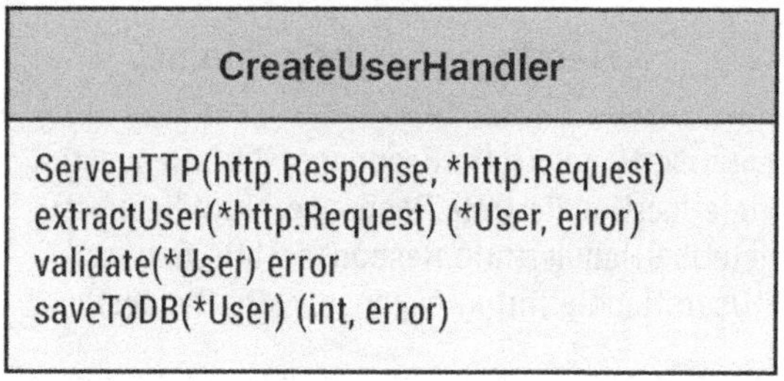

```
┌─────────────────────────────────────────────┐
│              CreateUserHandler               │
├─────────────────────────────────────────────┤
│ ServeHTTP(http.Response, *http.Request)      │
│ extractUser(*http.Request) (*User, error)    │
│ validate(*User) error                        │
│ saveToDB(*User) (int, error)                 │
└─────────────────────────────────────────────┘
```

Figure 4.2—Create user handler

As you can see, we are handling multiple responsibilities, including extracting the **User** from the HTTP request, validating the supplied **User**, and saving the **User**. Each of these three responsibilities is independent of the others. As such, if the person responsible for defining the HTTP format of the request decides to make a change, it should not necessitate a change to how we validate or save the user.

The same goes for a change in the database structure. Such changes should not require changes to the request or the validation.

In small projects, the "person responsible" might just be you. But that's not a reasonable justification to abandon this goal. Any expansion or maintenance of this system will still benefit from sticking to the "single responsibility" ideal.

Another appealing benefit of this approach is reduced complexity. If we follow this goal and decompose our struct into separate responsibilities, testing and maintaining each component becomes simpler. And, by extension, we see a reduction in the likelihood of bugs. If we were to decompose our struct like this:

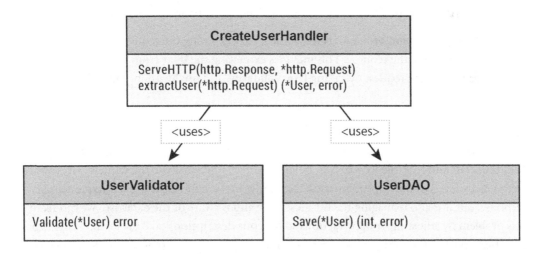

Figure 4.3—Create user handler decomposed

Now each component has one responsibility. Each component can be tested in isolation, making for smaller and simpler tests. Additionally, we can ensure that the interactions between the components are correct as the tests validate and enforce the contracts between them.

It can sometimes be challenging to identify when a component serves multiple responsibilities or, inversely, when we have decomposed our components too far. To help us with these situations, we should consider our final point, the level of abstraction.

A single level of abstraction

When applying the singles principle, we are encouraged to decompose our problems so that each component serves a single purpose and contains only a single level of abstraction. Achieving this single level of abstraction is harder to intuit than our goals of *single purpose* and *single responsibility*.

We can delve deeper into this by returning to our **CreateUserHandler** example. Previously, we had three structs; these were:

- **UserValidator**—This struct is responsible for validating that the supplied **User** was correct and complete.

- **UserDAO**—This struct is responsible for saving the **User** into the database.

- **CreateUserHandler**—This is responsible for extracting the request details for coordinating the request. This includes extracting the **User** from the HTTP request, validating the request by calling **UserValidator**, and finally calling **UserDAO** to save the **User**.

As you may have guessed after reading that last description, we have a problem with the **CreateUserHandler**. While its goal is singular—namely, to coordinate the request—it is aware of too many levels of the implementation. Not only does it handle the HTTP request and response, but it is also managing the business logic and is aware of the database. We can rectify this problem by adjusting our abstractions so that our descriptions take the form: "This struct does [feature] and then delegates to [dependency]". Applying this to our example, we get the following:

- **CreateUserHandler**—Extracts the **User** from the HTTP request and then delegates to **UserManager**

- **UserManager**—Validates the supplied **User** and then delegates to **UserDAO**

- **UserDAO**—Saves the supplied **User** to the database

When we draw this new set of components, we can see the dependency pyramid has changed into a waterfall like this:

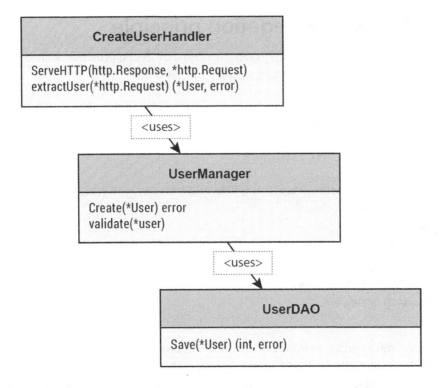

Figure 4.4—Create user handler decomposed into a waterfall

You can also see from this diagram that we've minimized and simplified the dependencies between our components. This shows that we've achieved our goal of one level of abstraction per component.

As we have seen, to adequately address the singles principle, we need to ensure that each component has a single purpose, a single responsibility, and a single level of abstraction. This is not easy to do, especially during the initial implementation. There is nothing wrong with coding an implementation, complete with unit tests, and then refactoring. Any such refactoring would be from a more informed perspective, and that little bit of extra knowledge can make finding the optimal software architecture significantly easier.

The interface segregation principle

The *interface segregation principle* (ISP) is another software design principle defined and popularized by Robert C. Martin, which states:

> Clients should not be forced to depend on methods
> they do not use.
>
> –Robert C. Martin

This principle seems straightforward, reasonable, and even easy, and yet it is not uncommon to see interfaces that look like this:

```
type CityModel interface {
    Save(*City) (int, error)
    Update(*City) error
    LoadByID(int) (*City, error)
    LoadAll() ([]*City, error)
}
```

At first glance, this interface seems reasonable, and it is easy to imagine the implementation being a single struct. Such a struct is even likely to comply with the single responsibility principle. After all, **Save()** and **Update()** are likely to share some logic, as will both of the **Load()** functions.

However, this interface is considered a "fat interface" because it is improbable that users will require all or even most of these methods. In fact, users of this interface will often only use a single method each. If users adopt this interface, they will cause themselves additional complexity and work. Readers of the code would be forced to waste precious time figuring out which methods were used and which were not.

Additionally, any time this interface was mocked or stubbed, more code would have to be written or generated to create methods that are never called.

Let's expand on our example. The following code shows how our **CityModel** is used by an HTTP handler that loads and returns a city by its ID:

```go
type LoadCityByIDEndpoint struct {
    cityModel CityModel
}

func (l *LoadCityByIDEndpoint) ServeHTTP(resp http.ResponseWriter, req *http.Request) {
    id, err := l.extractIDFromRequest(req)
    if err != nil {
        resp.WriteHeader(http.StatusBadRequest)
        return
    }

    city, err := l.cityModel.LoadByID(id)
    if err != nil {
        resp.WriteHeader(http.StatusInternalServerError)
        return
    }

    l.renderCity(resp, city)
}
```

You can see from this code that we are only using one method of the interface. For our code to comply with the ISP, we need to reduce the interface to only the method we need, like this:

```go
type CityByIDLoader interface {
    LoadByID(int) (*City, error)
}

type LoadCityByIDEndpoint struct {
    loader CityByIDLoader
}
```

After this change, we have also improved our software architecture in two additional ways. First, we 've loosened the coupling between our **LoadCityByIDEndpoint** struct and the struct that provides the **LoadByID()** feature—giving both structs a higher degree of freedom to evolve separately.

And second, we have explicitly defined the requirements of our **LoadCityByIDEndpoint** struct. When our requirements are defined in such an explicit and minimalistic fashion, the interface also documents our requirements. Such documentation also makes our structs easier to understand, maintain, and test.

You might be concerned that the interface segregation principle conflicts with the singles principle. Given that the ISP is pushing us towards minimalistic interfaces, and the singles principle is asking us to have components with a single responsibility, how can we achieve both at the same time?

Roles versus responsibilities

We need to introduce the term *role interfaces* to understand the interplay between the ISP and the SP. When we apply the ISP and create a thin, explicit interface, the resulting interface outlines the role required by that component. For this reason, such interfaces are referred to as role interfaces.

On the other hand, when discussing the SP, we were not talking about roles but rather responsibilities. Responsibilities are generally larger than roles as they group related functionality together to address a single purpose and abstraction level.

Returning one more time to our **CityModel** example, in the following diagram, you can see that we can implement one interface per role and, at the same time, still have a single struct that provides a single responsibility:

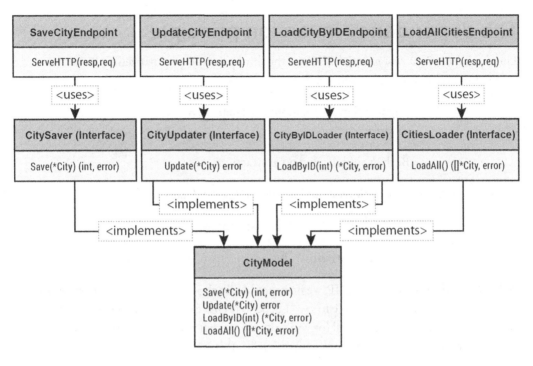

Figure 4.5—One interface per-role

As a result, our components are loosely coupled, so they can be maintained and evolved separately. However, we have not created excessive components or suffered from complexity or duplication issues.

As we have seen, the primary goal of the ISP is to prevent unintentional coupling by reducing interfaces to their bare minimum. It is essential to remember that this coupling doesn't only occur between a component and its dependencies. It can also happen with function and method inputs. Because of this, we must keep the ISP in mind when also applying the *Accept interfaces and return structs* principle that we discussed earlier in this chapter.

The dependency inversion principle

The *dependency inversion principle* (DIP) is the third principle popularized by Robert C. Martin that we're going to examine, and it states:

> High-level modules should not depend on low-level modules.
>
> Both should depend on abstractions.
>
> Abstractions should not depend upon details.
>
> Details should depend on abstractions.
>
> –Robert C. Martin

To be able to dive deep into the DIP, we first should talk about dependence and perspective; let's start with an example. If I were to say "I depend on my car to get me to work in the morning", it would only be natural for you to conclude that my car is a dependency of mine. If we were to code this up, it might look something like this:

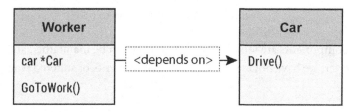

Figure 4.6—Worker depends on Car

From this perspective, I do, indeed, depend on my car. But is it really necessary? Is it the only way I could get to work? If I were to take a different perspective, and instead of being specific about how I get to work, I abstractly defined my requirements, the relationship would look like this:

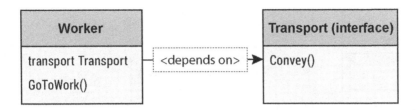

Figure 4.7—Worker depends on Transport

Instead of being prescriptive and specific, I have inverted the perspective and am being permissive and abstract. By being permissive, I have successfully decoupled the act of getting to work from how it happens. This loose coupling not only makes it simpler for us to test each of the components in isolation from each but offers us a very clean extension point. For example, we can now add any number of new **Transport** implementations and not have to change our **Worker** implementation and risk introducing bugs to it.

After expressing the dependency relationship in this seemingly inverted manner, we can revisit Martin's definition and see how his principle can be applied to Go.

Firstly, "*modules should not depend on each other but rather on abstractions*"; as you know, Go has no official or visible implementation of modules. However, this does not mean modules cannot exist. As programmers, we are prone to solve problems by breaking them into smaller, more manageable pieces, which we then compose together to solve the larger problem. These smaller pieces are our modules. Each module can be a single package or a collection of packages working together to achieve this common purpose.

The goal of creating modules in this way is to make the boundaries of these modules depend on abstractions, to ensure the modules are loosely coupled. This loose coupling will allow the different parts of our codebase to evolve independently.

To keep the boundaries of our modules clean, we need to consider the location of our interfaces. In other programming languages, the typical approach is to define the interface alongside the implementation like this:

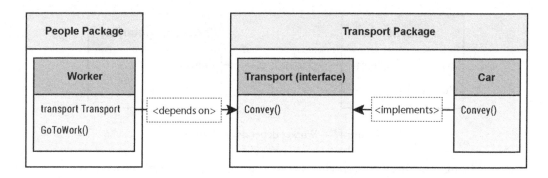

Figure 4.8—Interface alongside the implementation

Typically this approach goes along with the idea that defining the interface in a common or shared place reduces duplication. Indeed it does. However, it also increases the coupling of the code and pollutes our module boundaries. Consider that, in our simple example, if one of the users of the **Transport** interface required another method to be added to the interface or a change in the parameters of that method, all users would also be forced to change.

In Go, we can move the interface definition away from the implementation and instead place it in the package where it is used, like this:

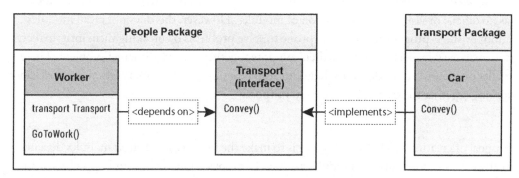

Figure 4.9—Interface defined where it is used

This approach protects our **People** package from changes needed by other users of the **Transport** package and keeps our module boundaries clean. When our module boundaries are clean, our modules are more self-contained. By extension, users of our module are not forced to adopt other dependencies to use our module.

Returning to the second half of Martin's definition, *"abstractions should not depend on details; details should depend on abstractions"*. We can comply with these statements by applying the same approach we have discussed above, but instead of modules, apply it to structs. To recap, this means expressing our member variables and method parameters as abstractions using local interfaces.

This style is, strictly speaking, a violation of the DRY principle that we examined earlier; however, the advantages we receive as a result of the loose coupling are significant. Thanks to the clean separation, we can test, maintain, and extend our components independently, and we may even find opportunities for reuse that would not otherwise have been possible.

Application of the DIP in this manner is an example of one of the Go Proverbs as outlined by Rob Pike, which states:

> A little copying is better than a little dependency.
>
> —Rob Pike

As with others, this proverb and the design principles we have examined in this section permeate through the design decisions and ideologies in the Go language and the standard library. They are the pragmatic application of hard-won lessons learned by our industry across many languages. They are also why many of us were drawn to Go as a language.

My biggest mistake when adopting Go was blindly applying my previous languages' approaches, ideas, and software engineering style to Go code. While I've since learned that this is not the way to write great Go code, we should still pay attention to the ideologies of these other languages. As we will see in this next section, despite Go not strictly being an object-oriented language, some of the Object-Oriented Design Patterns can and should selectively be used in Go.

Object-Oriented Design Patterns

Writing software is not so different from cooking. There are many ways to achieve our desired outcome, but if we want to achieve predictable results, we are best to follow a recipe. Have you ever baked a cake? The general steps are:

1. Mix the sugar and butter

2. Mix in the eggs and other wet ingredients

3. Mix in the flour and any dry ingredients

4. Stick it in the oven

This generalized recipe can be used as the basis for many different types of cakes we want to bake. These steps cannot, however, be used to bake other things like a lasagna.

Software patterns are exactly the same. They are generalized recipes to address a specific problem; they are not the solution to every problem. Also, like cooking recipes, software patterns are designed to give us a common language to use when discussing and planning our design. For example, if we were discussing an object and we needed to ensure that only one instance of it was created, we could say "Let's use the singleton pattern" without discussing the exact details of the implementation.

This section discusses only four patterns: **Singleton**, **Factory Method**, **Observer**, and **Adapter**. There are many more, but these four were chosen because they are the most commonly used in Go.

The singleton pattern

The singleton pattern is one of the most widely used design patterns. It aims to restrict the creation of multiple instances of a class and provide a single point of access to it. This pattern is often employed to reduce the cost of creating and maintaining resource-intensive objects and promote the reuse of that single instance.

Usage

Typical usage scenarios for this pattern include:

- **Connection pools**—Take, for example, a pool of database connections. Opening and maintaining these connections has a high performance cost, and the maximum number of connections we can make is limited. It is, therefore, preferable that we only have one connection pool.

- **Caches**—Assume we implemented an in-memory cache. We want to have only one instance of this cache, to limit memory consumption and to improve its efficacy.

- **Application config**—Config is often loaded from a file and parsed. This is a costly operation. As such, to ensure that we only perform the load once, we can use a singleton.

Implementation

For our example, we will apply the Singleton pattern to a **Cache** object. First, we define a private global variable to store our **Cache** instance and a **sync.Once**:

```
var (
    instance   *Cache
    initConfig sync.Once
)
```

We are using **sync.Once** to ensure the population of our global variable is thread-safe and only occurs once. Now, we provide a public accessor function like this:

```
func GetCache() *Cache {
    initConfig.Do(func() {
        instance = &Cache{
            items:     map[string]interface{}{},
            createdAt: time.Now(),
        }
    })

    return instance
}
```

As you can see, our **GetCache()** function will instantiate the **Cache** instance when needed and return the single, shared instance of the **Cache**.

What is different in Go?

Traditional object-oriented implementations of the Singleton pattern use a private or static constructor to enforce the singular construction that forms the intent of this pattern. Go, as you know, does not have these features. As a result, we have two options. One is to use a simple implementation, like the one above, and trust ourselves to interact with this object "properly". Or, we can enforce the strictness with a more complicated implementation. In such an implementation, we would have to:

1. **Move the singleton to a separate package**—ensuring nothing can access it directly.

2. **Switch the return value to an interface**—removing the ability for direct instantiation.

3. **Ensure that the returned object is private**—also preventing direct instantiation.

To see this more strict version, please refer to **https://github.com/corsc/Beyond-Effective-Go/ tree/master/Chapter04/02_design_patterns/01_singleton/02_strict/**

The factory method pattern

The purpose of the factory method is to provide a framework for creating objects in a way that is flexible, scalable, and easy to maintain. The pattern achieves this by defining a function that is responsible for creating instances of objects from a group of related objects. By centralizing the creation logic in a single function, the factory method pattern simplifies object creation and makes it easier to manage and maintain code over time. This approach removes code duplication, complexity, and a common source of bugs that often occurs when the group of objects is used in multiple places.

The best way to identify when to apply this pattern is to look for the combination of object creation and a collection of conditional statements, like a **switch** statement or a series of **if** conditions.

Usage

In the following example, we can see an example of conditional object creation:

```go
func SingSolo(favorite string) {
    var beatle Beatle

    switch favorite {
    case "John":
        beatle = John{}

    case "Paul":
        beatle = Paul{}

    case "George":
        beatle = George{}

    case "Ringo":
        beatle = Ringo{}
    }

    beatle.Sing()
}
```

When we see code like this, we should ask ourselves two questions:

1. Will there ever be more object types (e.g., new **case** statements)?

2. Will we need this conditional object creation elsewhere?

If we answer yes to either of these questions, we should apply the factory method.

Implementation

The implementation of this pattern is pretty straightforward. We must extract the object creation logic into a separate function with only that responsibility. Let's start a new example to add a little more complexity than our previous one. We are going to define an abstraction called **DocumentFormat** that has two methods, **Header()** and **Bold()**, like so:

```go
type DocumentFormat interface {
    Header(string) string
    Bold(string) string
}
```

Now, we can implement this interface twice, once for Markdown format and once for HTML format; you will find sample implementations for this in the code for this chapter.

With our abstraction and implementations in place, we now apply the factory method to the creation logic like so:

```
func NewDocumentFormat(format string) DocumentFormat {
    switch format {
    case "md":
        return Markdown{}

    default:
        return HTML{}
    }
}
```

And that's it. As long as we ensure all creation is done via the **NewDocumentFormat()** function, our code will be fully decoupled from the implementations of the **DocumentFormat** interface.

You can find the full implementation in the code for this example: **https://github.com/corsc/ Beyond-Effective-Go/tree/master/Chapter04/02_design_patterns/02_factory_method/ 02_example/**

What is different in Go?

Traditional object-oriented implementations of the Factory Method use a static method to contain the creation logic. This approach is driven by the object-oriented nature of the languages and the need for discoverability of the constructor method. Go does not have this restriction, and, as such, our factory method works just fine as a function.

Additionally, some implementations of this pattern used private or protected constructors to enforce the decoupling between the created objects and the user of the factory method. As we saw with the singleton pattern, we can achieve the same result by moving this code to a separate package and ensuring the created objects remain private. However, it's arguably a more appropriate Go style to trust users to behave nicely.

The observer pattern

The purpose of the observer pattern is to allow one or more objects, referred to as *observers*, to listen to events that occur in another object, referred to as the *subject* or *observable*. This pattern allows the subject to remain decoupled and unaware of both the number and implementation of the observers.

Usage

This pattern forms the basis of many "event-based" systems; typical use cases include:

- A component that listens for user-triggered events
- A component that listens and reacts to a data stream

Implementation

For our example, we will implement the **Celebrity/SuperFan** relationship from a fictional social media system.

First, we define our Subject object, the **Celebrity**:

```go
// This is the subject
type Celebrity struct {
    fans    []chan Post
    mutex sync.RWMutex
}

// Subscribe/add to list of observers
func (c *Celebrity) Follow(responseCh chan Post) {
    c.mutex.Lock()
    defer c.mutex.Unlock()

    c.fans = append(c.fans, responseCh)
}

// Unsubscribe/Remove from the list of observers
func (c *Celebrity) Unfollow(responseCh chan Post) {
```

```
        c.mutex.Lock()
        defer c.mutex.Unlock()

        for index, observer := range c.fans {
            if observer == responseCh {
                c.fans = append(c.fans[:index], c.fans[index+1:]...)

                // close the channel and stop the watch loop
                close(responseCh)

                return
            }
        }
    }
```

You will notice that we require the observers to provide a channel when they subscribe. This allows subscribers to control how much buffering they want.

Now we can define a method to notify all of the listeners:

```
// Notify all observers
func (o *Celebrity) Upload(post Post) {
        o.mutex.RLock()
        defer o.mutex.RUnlock()

        for _, fan := range o.fans {
            // optional write so that observers cannot block this method
            select {
            case fan <- post:
                // successfully notified observer

            default:
                // skip observer that isn't ready
            }
        }
    }
```

In this implementation, we use a lossy or optional write to the channel to prevent slow consumers from causing deadlock. The use of optional writes here is not compulsory, but is strongly recommended. It should also be clearly documented so users know they may miss events with due to insufficient buffering or slow event response. Users should also be warned not to close the channel as this will cause **Post()** to panic. If you do not trust your users to abide by this, then you need to add panic handling to the channel write and to the channel close in **Unfollow()**.

And finally, we can define an Observer object, the **SuperFan**:

```go
type SuperFan struct {
    eventCh chan Post
}

func (s *SuperFan) Watch() {
    for post := range s.eventCh {
        fmt.Printf("Celebrity has posted %s", post.Content)
    }
}
```

In this example, we have implemented the observer as a struct. This is not necessary. It is also unnecessary for all observers to be the same type; the only requirement is to provide a notification channel by calling the **Follow()** method.

What is different in Go?

In traditional object-oriented implementations of the observer pattern, event notification from the subject to the observer is performed via a function call. It is possible to implement the pattern the same way in Go; however, there is a downside. Should any observer be slow in processing the notification, it would inhibit sending notifications to the other observers.

The adapter pattern

The adapter pattern aims to modify a struct's API from one form to another. The goal is to allow the use of an object in places where it would otherwise be incompatible.

This pattern consists of three parts:

- **A target interface**—This is the interface that we want to use.

- **An adaptee object**—This is the struct we want to use with the target interface, but it does not implement the target interface.

- **An adapter**—This is the struct that wraps the adaptee and makes the adaptee conform to the target interface.

Usage

This pattern is handy when dealing with legacy and third-party components where changes to the target interface are impossible or disincentivized. In these situations, you often have components that provide the functionality you need but not in the format you need, and you cannot refactor them. Another benefit of this approach is to give a more flexible or convenient UX for users. A great example of this is the relationship between **http.Handler** and **http.HandlerFunc** from the common library.

Implementation

For our example, we will explore a situation where we are in the progress of migrating between two different loggers.

Firstly, this is our **OldLogger** interface and a function that requires it:

```
type OldLogger interface {
    Error(message string, args ...interface{})
}
```

```
func LegacyFunction(logger OldLogger) {
    // implementation removed
```

}

Now, compare the **OldLogger** implementation with our **NewLogger**:

```
type NewLogger interface {
    Error(message string, tags ...Tag)
}
```

You can see how our **NewLogger** has a different signature. To enable us to use **LegacyFunction()**, we define an adapter that wraps the **NewLogger** and implements the **OldLogger** interface like this:

```
type oldLoggerAdapter struct {
    newLogger NewLogger
}

// implement OldLogger interface
func (o *oldLoggerAdapter) Error(message string, args ...interface{}) {
    // adapt from OldLogger requests to NewLogger format
    o.newLogger.Error(fmt.Sprintf(message, args...))
}
```

Now we can use our **LegacyFunction()** with the adapted **NewLogger**. The above example is a regular, traditional use case for this pattern; in the next section, we will see how this pattern can be used unconventionally to solve a very Go problem.

What is different in Go?

The implementation of the Adapter pattern in Go is very similar to that from other languages. We can, however, use Go's support for anonymous embedding to save us a bunch of work.

Examine the following diagram in which we have a **User** struct and a **UserForLogin** interface:

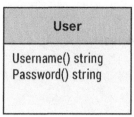

Figure 4.10—User struct and UserForLogin interface differences

You will notice that the **User** struct is missing the **Token()** method. With anonymous embedding, we can make an adapter very cheaply. The code is only this:

```
type UserLoginAdapter struct {
    User
}

func (u *UserLoginAdapter) Token() string {
    // implementation removed
    return ""
}
```

This same approach can also be used to override existing methods. Now, take a look at the following diagram in which we have two packages, **version1** and **version2**:

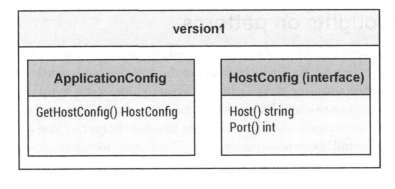

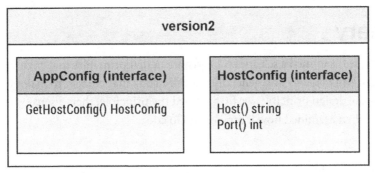

Figure 4.11—Multiple packages with the identical HostConfig interfaces

As you can see, both packages contain an identical interface called **HostConfig**. Even though the interfaces are identical, if we tried to use the **ApplicationConfig** struct from **version1** in the **version2** package, Go would fail to compile and complain that the function signatures are different. However, we can get around this restriction with an adapter like so:

```
type configAdapter struct {
    configVersion1 *version1.ApplicationConfig
}

func (c *configAdapter) GetHostConfig() version2.HostConfig {
    return c.configVersion1.GetHostConfig()
}
```

This is possible because of Go's support for implicit interfaces. Given **version1.HostConfig** implements the same methods as **version2.HostConfig** it is implicitly converted and requires no more code.

Final thoughts on patterns

In this section, we looked at four object-oriented design patterns. We discussed when, where, and how they can be used. We also highlighted how Go ideologies and features influence both the implementation and usage of these patterns. When considering the use of patterns, there are two essential things to remember: firstly, they are a tool, something to use only if and when it's appropriate; and secondly, there are many more than just the four we have presented here. When we seek out and master more patterns, we will have more tools available next time we code.

Summary

In this chapter, we examined a selection of software design principles that align with Go's language design and ideology and generally make for code that is easier to maintain and extend. For each software design principle, we first defined the principle, then discussed its underlying intention, and then examined how it applied to Go code.

In the second part of this chapter, we introduced the idea that design patterns, like software design principles, are generalized recipes or solutions to problems we face every day. We then examined four of the more commonly used object-oriented design patterns.

Hopefully, many of these principles and patterns are familiar to you, and as such, this chapter served as a refresher and an illustration of how these ideas can be applied to Go. If not, stick a bookmark in this section and reexamine it again from time to time. These principles and patterns will provide a quick solution to many of your daily tasks and a common language to discuss these problems and solutions with your colleagues.

Questions

1. What is the Unix Philosophy, and how does it apply to Go?
2. What is the intention of the DRY principle?
3. What is the intention of the KISS principle?

4. When the DRY and KISS principles conflict, which do you think takes precedence?

5. How does loose coupling improve code?

6. Why is strong cohesion important?

7. How does the singles principle help improve our code organization?

8. Where should interfaces be defined and used? (Hint: on the provider or the consumer of the feature?)

9. In what situations would the singleton pattern be a good solution?

10. In what situations would the factory method pattern be a good solution?

11. In what situations would the observer pattern be a good solution?

12. In what situations would the adapter pattern be a good solution?

Chapter 5

Optimizing for Code UX

Introduction

This chapter will examine software design ideas that focus on improving our code's usability by adding clarity, consistency, and predictability.

These attributes are more important than performance, cleverness, or innovation. Code usability is second only to providing customer value. This chapter's underlying intent is to arm you with a selection of concepts and the ability to selectively apply them.

This chapter has many concepts; some might elicit a lightbulb moment, and some may even evoke disagreement. I have benefited from each of these concepts and ask only that you consider trying them before deciding to adopt or reject them.

It might take a while to realize, as it did for me, but Go has a particular way of doing things, both intended and beneficial. This chapter is my current understanding of writing intuitive and straightforward Go code.

The following topics will be covered in this chapter:

- What is Code UX?
- Achieving Clarity
- Striving for Consistency
- Becoming Predictable
- Dealing with Conflicting Goals

Code

To get the most out of this chapter, you will need a recent copy (1.13+) of Go installed and your favorite IDE.

Full versions of all code examples and other related material can be found at **https:// github.com/corsc/Beyond-Effective-Go/tree/master/Chapter05**.

What is Code UX?

As programmers, we consider a good day as one spent staring at our preferred code editor, furiously mashing the keyboard. What if I told you that it's possible to make these days even more pleasant? This is where *code UX* comes in. *code user experience* (code UX) measures how usable or user-friendly the code is. Let's unpack this. Firstly, what is code?

Code is the language that we programmers use to communicate with the computer and each other. Like any language, it has syntax, semantics, and conventions. Like natural languages, while there are necessary parts, there is also a great degree of freedom in style and self-expression.

Excellent communication focuses on two integral aspects: the audience and the message. For code, our audience consists of two types: computers and other programmers. Computers as an audience are easy to satisfy; as long as the code compiles, they will listen, no matter what we tell them. Programmers, on the other hand, are much more challenging to satisfy. They will expect the code to work, but they also want to understand the author's intent or message. When code clearly expresses the author's intentions, it will convey what the code does and any significant decisions and tradeoffs the author has made.

It is important to remember that, as the author, your code is clear to you; the real question is, does it make sense to everyone else on the team? Even that intern that joined last week?

Adding to our problems is the fact that code is not static; it evolves over time. So being understood is the first step. Our code must also be easy to navigate. It must also be extendable, debuggable, and reliable.

We will examine three key aspects to code usability in this chapter: **clarity**, **consistency**, and **predictability**.

Clarity means the code is easy to read. Consistency makes the code easier to navigate and increases our comfort level. Predictability determines the level of trust in the code and, by extension, how much we can rely on the code.

Writing code with good UX is one of the most challenging aspects of coding, but, after this chapter, we will be well-equipped to communicate with programmers of all levels.

Achieving Clarity

Code clarity can be thought of as how easily a piece of code can be read and understood. But let's aim for better. We should aim to be understood quickly and intuitively.

While being easily understood is the goal of any communication, we are often pressed for time as programmers. So, when we enable our teammates to quickly understand our code, they can promptly return to value-adding activities like fixing bugs or adding new features.

This section will discuss a series of ideas that we can implement to achieve a minimum level of readability. My challenge to you is to use these ideas as a base and use your experience to achieve more.

While reading other people's code, notice how long it takes to understand a piece of code. Consider what they could have done differently to make it easier for you. If this code is under your control, consider making and submitting those changes so everyone can benefit. Sometimes, your team's perspective on clarity and readability differs from yours, but that debate is invariably beneficial.

Take a quick glance at the following code and see if it makes sense:

```go
func do(o O) error {
    if e := v(o); e == nil {
        if r, e := c(o); e == nil {
            ec := make(chan error, 2)
            wg := &sync.WaitGroup{}
            wg.Add(2)
            go s(o, r, ec)
            go i(o, ec)
            wg.Wait()
            for e := range ec {
                if e != nil {
                    return e
                }
            }
            return nil
        } else {
            return e
        }
    } else {
        return e
    }
}
```

This code compiles and performs the function it's supposed to, but it is also needlessly complicated. Additionally, it does not follow established Go standards and, as a result, takes way too long to wrap your head around. If you would like to see what this code should be like, you can find both versions for this chapter **https://github.com/corsc/Beyond-Effective-Go/tree/master/Chapter05/01_clarity/01_bad_example/**.

Now that we have seen how bad things can be, and before diving too deep into code on this one, we need to define idiomatic code and why it is vital for code clarity.

Why idiomatic code?

The term *idiomatic* describes communication that is natural to a native speaker. In our context, when an experienced Go programmer reads the code, it feels right. Please note that I said "experienced Go programmer" and not just "experienced programmer". In a later section, we will see how bringing experience from other languages is not always beneficial.

Idiomatic is not a term that should be thrown about to win style or formatting arguments, especially without further proof. I apologize for the rant on this. I have seen this tactic used too many times. As professionals, we should be exploring and debating the merits of different approaches, but calling something idiomatic is not the path to winning the debate; data and proof are. When looking for proof, I recommend looking for mature code written by experienced Gophers, such as the GitHub repositories for companies like HashiCorp, Ardan Labs, or the standard library.

With the rant out of the way, let's discuss my interpretation of some of the things that make for idiomatic Go code; please take this as one person's professional but singular opinion.

Formatting

Unsurprisingly, how code is formatted significantly impacts how easy or hard it is to read. The Go language developers have done us all a massive favor by preventing many hours from being wasted on unresolvable debates like those about bracket placement. As such, the single biggest win for Gophers is to run **gofmt** over the code.

If you vendor your dependencies or want an easy and consistent way to run the formatter, then an effective way to call **gofmt** is with a script. This is the script that I use:

```
#!/bin/bash

if [ -z "$1" ]; then
    echo "Please supply a destination directory"
    exit -1
fi

# Ensure the inputted directory is in a predictable format
DIR=${1%...}
PKG_DIR=${DIR%/}/
```

```
DIRS=$(find $PKG_DIR -type f -name '*.go' -not -path "*/vendor/*")

# Clean and simplify the code
gofmt -w -s -l $DIRS
```

We will discuss this script and more like it in *Chapter 7—Improving Your Development Productivity.*

Whitespace

Whitespace, also known as negative or blank space, is a concept from design where space is intentionally left between different elements. The goals of this space are to give the viewer's eyes a rest, to visually separate the different elements, and to draw attention to different locations.

The whitespace in code is the empty space between parts that we add to make it easier to read. It allows our eyes to scan the code and quickly identify the logical groupings, rather than having to read every single line.

Consider the following HTTP server handler:

```
func handler(resp http.ResponseWriter, req *http.Request){
    payload, err := io.ReadAll(req.Body)
    if err != nil {
        resp.WriteHeader(http.StatusBadRequest)
        return
    }
    createReq := &userCreationRequest{}
    err = json.Unmarshal(payload, createReq)
    if err != nil {
        resp.WriteHeader(http.StatusBadRequest)
        return
    }
    err = doCreateUser(createReq)
    if err != nil {
        resp.WriteHeader(http.StatusInternalServerError)
        return
    }
```

```
    _, _ = resp.Write([]byte("okay"))
}
```

If you took a quick glance at this code, all you saw was a wall of code. To fully understand this code, you must slow down and read it line by line.

The whitespace indentation for the errors makes them stand out a little, but otherwise, it's a pretty solid block. Now, look at what happens by adding just a few blank lines.

```
func handlerWhitespace(resp http.ResponseWriter, req *http.Request){
    payload, err := io.ReadAll(req.Body)
    if err != nil {
        resp.WriteHeader(http.StatusBadRequest)
        return
    }

    createReq := &userCreationRequest{}
    err = json.Unmarshal(payload, createReq)
    if err != nil {
        resp.WriteHeader(http.StatusBadRequest)
        return
    }

    err = doCreateUser(createReq)
    if err != nil {
        resp.WriteHeader(http.StatusInternalServerError)
        return
    }

    _, _ = resp.Write([]byte("okay"))
}
```

In the second version, we have introduced whitespace, essentially paragraph breaks, between the logical code groups. Now when we read just the first one or two lines of code from each block, we get:

- Read the request body.

- Unmarshal the request into an object.

- Call the create user function.

- Output the result.

These paragraph breaks have allowed us to understand the code without processing every line. Another common place where whitespace can significantly improve the readability of code is with **select** and **switch** statements. Compare the following example:

```
func speak(animal string) {
    switch string {
    case "dog":
        fmt.Print("Woof!")
        fmt.Print("Woof!")
    case "cat":
        fmt.Print("Meow")
    case "mouse":
        fmt.Print("Squeak")
        fmt.Print("Squeak")
    default:
        fmt.Print("???")
    }
}
```

For many readers, it is difficult to quickly identify where one **case** statement ends, and the next begins. Now compare that with this:

```
func speakWhitespace(animal string) {
    switch string {
    case "dog":
        fmt.Print("Woof!")
        fmt.Print("Woof!")

    case "cat":
        fmt.Print("Meow")

    case "mouse":
        fmt.Print("Squeak")
        fmt.Print("Squeak")

    default:
```

```
            fmt.Print("???")
      }
}
```

This is a simple and easy improvement that has long-term benefits. The most notable will be less fatigue caused by reading the code.

Before you add whitespace everywhere, I need to highlight that blank lines do not always improve readability. Consider the following example:

```
func doCreateUser(req *createUser) error {
    err := validate(req)

    if err != nil {
        return err
    }

    err = saveToDB(req)

    if err != nil {
        return err
    }

    return nil
}
```

In this example, we have incorrectly separated the code that throws an error from the code detecting and processing those errors. This separation breaks the code's logical grouping and forces us to perform this grouping in our heads. In both this and our original example with no whitespace, we burden the reader and force them to read and understand every line. This is a mental cost that they don't need to pay.

What's in a name?

Names are a critical factor in determining code's UX. A good name is informative, intuitive, meaningful, and obvious. On the other hand, bad names are misleading and distracting and cost readers more mental effort than necessary.

Many programmers instinctively know when a variable, method, or struct's name needs to be improved. This is when they start adding comments. The next time you feel the need to add a comment to explain something, try finding a name that would remove the need for the comment instead.

The essential aspects of good names are:

- They should be meaningful.
- They should be concise.
- They should be consistent.
- They should be context-aware.
- They don't need to be original.

Let's explore these points a little more.

Names should be meaningful

Variable and struct names should describe what they are. Method and function names should describe what they do. Let's look at some examples. First, some structs:

```
// Bad
type cur struct {
    // fields removed
}

// Better
type create struct {
    // fields removed
}

// Best
type userCreationRequest struct {
    // fields removed
}
```

The first example, **cur**, is terrible because it has been abbreviated to the point of being incomprehensible. Only programmers intimately familiar with the code will understand it without a slow, careful read.

The second example, **create**, is an improvement because it can be read more easily. However, it still needs more context. It does not tell us what it relates to, and *create* is a verb and not a noun, so it does not describe what it is.

The final example, **userCreationRequest**, is much better than the other two options as it can be read quickly and easily; it clearly describes what the struct is, and the reader can quickly understand how to use it.

Now let's look at some functions:

```
// Bad
_ = get()

// Better
_ = userDecision()

// Best
_ = getUserDecision()
```

The first example, **get()**, is terrible because it does not give the reader any context. We don't know what this function is getting or returning without being familiar with the rest of the code.

The second example, **userDecision()**, is better because we can infer what the function is doing. However, we need to know the function's implementation to know what kind of variable to expect. It is also a noun, so some readers might not expect the function to return anything.

The final example, **getUserDecision()**, is much better because it is quick and easy to read; we can quickly understand what the function does and, by extension, understand what kind of data it might return.

If we revisit our bad example from earlier, what are the contents of the variables **o, r**, and **ec** in this code snippet?

```
go s(o, r, ec)
```

There is no way to tell without reading the rest of the code. Similarly, what does **s()** do? Again, no idea without more effort.

Now contrast our example with a version with meaningful names:

```
go sendReceipt(order, receiptNo, errorCh)
```

Without any knowledge of the rest of the code, we can form a reasonable idea of what this function does and the contents of the variables.

Names should be concise

This point may seem at odds with the previous one, given that **o** is far more concise than **order**. A better way to express this is to say names should be as concise as possible without compromising readability. We could have named our **order** variable **customerOrder**. But this does not give us any more clarity and only results in many more characters to read and type.

This preference for conciseness should be extended to decisions related to adding type information to variable names. For example, having a variable called **userList** is acceptable, assuming it is a slice or an array, but **users** is better as it's more concise. On the other hand, if we had a map and a slice of users in the same area of the code, naming them **userMap** and **userList** ensures they are never confused.

Some Go literature recommends using single-letter variables; I'm afraid I have to disagree as they add too much mental burden on the code reader. Single-letter variables require you to have to remember what the variable contains rather than having the name make it obvious. I do have two very specific exceptions to this. The first exception is small loop indices like this:

```
for x := 0; x < len(items); x++ {
    // implementation removed
}
```

Assuming the loop body is relatively short, readability is not sufficiently improved by renaming **x** to **index**. Between the short loop body and the commonality of this pattern, this code is eminently readable.

The second exception is method receivers. Reserving single-letter variables for method receivers gives the following code a lot more context:

```
o.items = append(o.items, item)
```

At a glance and without reading the peripheral code, we can quickly tell that we are modifying member data of the current struct and not modifying a local variable. When applied consistently, this small optimization significantly reduces both the mental burden and variable-scope mistakes.

Names should be consistent

While we will talk more deeply about consistency later in this chapter, consistent naming is so important that it deserves a separate mention.

When naming is consistent, code inherently feels a lot more natural. Consider the function names **Get()**, **Fetch()**, and **Retrieve()**: the result of each of these functions may be identical. Choosing a consistent name will ensure that other programmers can quickly discover, understand, and use the functions. Similarly, variable naming within a codebase, package, or struct should be strongly consistent. This is especially important when passing a variable through multiple layers of functions; if the variable does not change purpose or significantly change its scope then changing a variable name within the callstack significantly adds to the mental burden of the code.

Okay, so consistency is important, but consistent with what? There are three aspects to this. In order of importance, they are:

- Team style
- Industry norms
- Programming norms

Firstly, team style. When a piece of code is inconsistent with team norms, it will create a jarring experience for the reader, perhaps even to the point at which team members are reluctant to work on it. A typical example of this is legacy code. Legacy code is often considered as such because it was developed by a different set of programmers using different norms. Frequently programmers want to avoid this kind of code, and the uncomfortable reading experience is part of why. For this reason, we should strive to write code that feels natural to our team. This doesn't mean we should never make changes to our team norms; when improvements are possible, you will find that convincing the team tends to assuage the discomfort that comes with the new norm.

Secondly, we should be consistent with industry norms. When a new team member joins from another part of the company or from one of your direct competitors, they should be able to understand your code without having to learn the "local language". For example, if you work in the transport industry, having objects called passengers, drivers, and destinations is easily understood.

Lastly, we should be aware of programming norms. Programmers often have a solid software engineering, computer science, and even mathematics background. Terms like singleton, factory, vectors, tuples, and even abbreviations like DTO or DAO are widely understood and should be preferred over inventing new terms.

Names should be context-aware

Spend some time doing Go, and, before long, a linter or code review will complain that the name you have chosen stutters. Typically this means that the name of the struct or function contains the package's name. This may seem annoying or pedantic, but it really is an issue, and that issue is context-awareness.

Assuming we have a struct that manages users inside a user package, an instinctual name for such a struct would be **UserManager**. However, when this struct is used in other packages, this would then read as **user.UserManager**. As you can see, the user part has been repeated, stutters, and is unnecessary. We must remember that because types are written in this form, the package name provides additional context, enabling us to use a shorter name.

This context awareness should not be limited to public type names; this same concept can and should be used for private elements and even internal naming. Consider the member variable naming in the following struct:

```
type Address struct {
    AddressStreet string
    AddressTown string
    AddressState string
    AddressCountry string
}
```

Hopefully, this example looks ridiculous to you, but the point here is to realize that the longer names add burden and not clarity to the reader, and we can use context to optimize them. Even small changes like changing a field from **User.UserID** to **User.ID** can improve the code.

Names don't need to be original

Often you will find the same concepts and patterns being used across a codebase. Unoriginal and boring names like **Client**, **Storage**, and **Config** are great. If these names are accurate, their consistent usage ensures clarity and frees brain cycles to worry about other things.

Never is this more true than the naming of errors in Go. Let me be more direct about this because I care way too much about it; all errors should be called **err** whenever possible. This is concise, consistent, and completely unoriginal. It is also natural for Gophers to read and immediately understand. There is only one exception to this position: when doing so would cause variable shadowing. As we will see in an upcoming section, this introduces confusion and a high potential for errors.

Adopting early return

Early return is an often debated topic in other languages, and sometimes these debates spill over into Go teams. However, it is the default style for Go. In case you are unfamiliar, the early return or multiple returns approach aims to reduce indentation and simplify the flow of functions.

We should aim for simplicity at all code levels, starting with functions. Consider the following code:

```
func validateItems(items []item) error {
    if len(items) <= maxItems {
        return nil
    } else {
        return errors.New("too many items")
    }
}
```

This code is valid and works as intended, but what happens when we extend it to add more checks? We'd have a choice between adding more logic and indentation to the **if** block or performing a much larger refactor.

Conversely, we can use an early return strategy and invert the conditional logic so that we immediately return whenever we encounter an error. When applied to our example, we get the following:

```
func validateItemsUpdated(items []item) error {
    if len(items) > maxItems {
        return errors.New("too many items")
    }

    return nil
}
```

There are a couple of things to notice here; firstly, we have dropped one of the code blocks. Our code is less indented, and this will make it easier to read. Secondly, the error handling for a particular issue is beside the condition that caused it; this prevents the need to jump back and forwards when reading the code. Finally, if we need to add more conditions, we can add a new **if** block under the first one without any additional refactoring or indentation.

Consequently, reading functions becomes much more straightforward as the code reads "straight through". Issues are immediately dealt with and can be put out of mind when reading the rest of the function. The happy path execution of our function runs the entire length of the function. This further improves our ability to mentally map the different parts of the function.

After adopting this style, our functions often take on a validate, process, and return pattern. The commonality of this pattern only further improves our ability to scan through our functions.

Switching to extended switch

The early return pattern works great for validation and error handling but is not the best option for all situations. In cases where we have multiple valid return values, a series of **if** statements can be rather long and cumbersome to read. Similarly, a single **if/else** block with many **else if** blocks like the one below does not read well:

```go
func getCupSize(milliliters int) string {
    if milliliters <= 300 {
        return "small"
    } else if milliliters <= 500 {
        return "medium"
    } else if milliliters <= 650 {
        return "large"
    } else {
        return "bucket"
    }
}
```

We can improve the code's readability by changing to a **switch** statement like this:

```go
func getCupSizeImproved(milliliters int) string {
    switch {
    case milliliters <= 300:
        return "small"

    case milliliters <= 500:
        return "medium"

    case milliliters <= 650:
        return "large"

    default:
        return "bucket"
    }
```

```
        }
```

While the preceding two examples are functionally equivalent, the second is more readable. It clearly shows each condition as a logical block, thereby incurring less mental burden for the reader.

Avoiding shadowing

Variable shadowing is an easy mistake to make and an insidious one to find. Take a quick look at the following code:

```
func performTask() error {
    resultCh := make(chan error)

    err := doWork(resultCh)
    if err != nil {
        return err
    }

    for err := range resultCh {
        handleError(err)
    }

    return err
}
```

Do you see anything weird or wrong with it? After a quick glance, you may not have noticed that the variable we use in the **for/range** loop **err** is shadowing the variable defined earlier. It is shadowing because we are creating a new variable with the same name but a different scope. This raises the question: which value did we intend to return at the end of the function? If they are separate variables, then we need to find a new name for the **for/range err** and clarify to the reader that they are different and we didn't make a mistake. Or if the intention was to use the same **err** variable both times, then for **err :=range resultCh** should use a simple **=** (assignment) rather than **:=** (declaring a new variable).

Suppose you find yourself in this situation, and creating a new name for the variable feels strange. In that case, you should split the function into separate parts, allowing you to keep the variable names but have a clear separation and variable scope.

Better struct initialization

You might be seeing a pattern in the last few sections, from early return to extended switch to avoiding variable shadowing: these practices are minuscule investments with much larger dividends. This section on struct initialization is yet another. Take a quick look at the following code:

```
jane := &Person{
    "Jane",
    "jane@example.com",
    22,
    65,
}
```

While the first two fields are obvious, what do the values **22** and **65** indicate? Sure, we could look up the definition of the **Person** struct and learn its internals, but that takes time and effort. Similarly, what happens if the owner of the **Person** struct reorders the fields? That would likely not end well. We can quickly and easily bring clarity and safety to this code by always adding the field names during initialization. Depending on your development environment, this will take almost no extra time and bring us lasting value.

Avoiding foreign idioms

By far, the most common mistake Gophers make is to bring patterns that belong to other languages into Go. In many cases, they are great ideas, but either they are not supported well by the language, or there is a more idiomatic way to achieve the same thing. Some common examples of these mistakes include:

- A strict application of the singleton pattern
- Using too much formality
- Applying interfaces at the wrong place
- Overuse of the functional programming style

Let's dive a little deeper into these.

Firstly, the singleton pattern: the singleton pattern's goal is to ensure that there is only one instance of something. Typically, this is to avoid duplicate creation of resource-hungry objects or to introduce the predictability of a single source of truth. As we saw in the previous *Chapter 4—Exploring Software Design Principles & Patterns*, it is possible to implement the singleton pattern in Go, but the results are clunky and far from ideal. Instead of using the singleton pattern and enforcing a single instance of an object, we should switch to dependency injection. Consider the following code that uses a singleton object pool:

```
var pool = &ObjectPoolSingleton{}

type Encoder struct {}

func (e *Encoder) Encode() ([]byte, error) {
    object := pool.Get()
    result, resultErr := json.Marshal(object)
    pool.Put(object)

    return result, resultErr
}
```

Beyond the issues with the singleton pattern we have highlighted previously, the main issue is that this code is inconvenient to test, especially when considering concurrency. Switching this code to use dependency injection, we get:

```
type ObjectPool interface {
    Get() *myObject
    Put(object *myObject)
}

func NewEncoder(pool ObjectPool) *Encoder {
    return &Encoder{
        pool: pool,
    }
}

type Encoder struct {
    pool ObjectPool
}

func (e *Encoder) Encode() ([]byte, error) {
```

```
    object := e.pool.Get()
    result, resultErr := json.Marshal(object)
    e.pool.Put(object)

    return result, resultErr
}
```

With these changes, we have entirely decoupled our **EncoderDI** from the implementation and instantiation of **ObjectPool** and solved any concurrent testing issues. This decoupling will also make the code more flexible and reusable going forward.

With this change in place, we must ensure we create a single instance of the object pool. To do this, we should trust ourselves and develop a convention whereby all singleton object creation occurs in the **main()** function of the application and is then injected as needed.

I realize that this convention of trusting yourself has some risks. Still, the likelihood and cost of making this mistake are significantly lower than the complexity cost of enforcing the single instance using the singleton pattern.

Now, let's dive deeper into the idea of having too much formality in our code. When a team has been using an *object-oriented* (OO) language, like Java, for a while, it often develops a formality to how it structures objects and their relationships. When this occurs, it is common to see Go code that looks like this:

```
type FileBuilder struct {}

func (f *FileBuilder) Build(version int, encoder Encoder, decoder Decoder) (File, error) {
    switch version {
    case 1:
        return &fileV1{encoder: encoder, decoder: decoder}, nil

    default:
        return nil, errors.New("unknown version")
    }
}
```

There is a lot to unpack in this code. Firstly, we have a builder for an object with only one implementation. A cry of YAGNI (you ain't going to need it) comes to mind. Secondly, we inject encoders and decoders, which likely have their own builders. Beyond this, the encoder and decoder might be tied to a version, in which case injecting them is unnecessary and introduces a potential source of bugs.

My solution for this is simple: don't add any of it until it becomes absolutely necessary. If we only support one version and one set of encoders and decoders, then a constructor with the signature **NewFile() *File** will suffice. (Yes, I have dropped the **File** interface as well.)

The next mistake is defining interfaces in the wrong place. This is the most common and most challenging habit to break. We have been conditioned by other OO languages to provide interfaces and use those interfaces to explicitly state "I provide this functionality". With Go's support for implicit interfaces and the axiom "accept interfaces and return structs", the perspective is completely reversed. Instead of stating, "I provide this functionality", we should state "I require this functionality".

This change in perspective allows us to decouple the functionality provider from the caller. It also makes our packages' and objects' goals and dependencies more explicit and self-contained.

Our functions and objects can explicitly state what they need using interfaces without caring how the caller achieves that, and it makes no promises to fulfil anyone else's interface.

If this complete decoupling makes you uncomfortable, any "implements" relationship can be easily enforced using either of the following two options in a test file.

```
// Option 1: Creating a compile-time assertion
var _ File = &fileV1{}

func TestFileV1_implementsFile(t *testing.T) {
    // Option 2: using a test and the Testify assert library
    assert.Implements(t, (*File)(nil), new(fileV1))
}
```

The last mistake we will examine is the overuse of the functional programming approach. As you know, Go has first-class support for functions. This may tempt you to use functional programming ideas, like *function currying* or *accepting callback functions as parameters*. As we will see in *Chapter 8—Examining Unusual Patterns for Go*, it is possible to use these approaches, but we should use them either sparingly or not at all.

These approaches are not commonly used in Go, therefore, when a programmer encounters them, they will likely feel uncomfortable or confused. At the very least, these patterns will be more challenging to read than their common Go alternatives.

These are just some of the many mistakes caused by misapplying great ideas from other languages that don't fit into regular Go code. Please be on the lookout for others in your code.

Writing useful documentation

Some folks will offer concrete, extensive rules about documentation like "all methods must be documented" or "anytime you have to study to understand a piece of code, write a comment, so the next person doesn't have to", but I will not do that. Instead, I want to extend the idea that code is communication, and therefore comments should only be used to communicate what the code doesn't. Consider the following code:

```go
func ProcessOrder(o Order) error {
    // validate order
    err := v(o)
    if err != nil {
        return err
    }

    // charge customer
    r, err := c(o)
    if err != nil {
        return err
    }

    // send receipt
    err = s(o, r)
```

```
if err != nil {
    return err
}

// inform the warehouse
return i(o)
}
```

In this example, the comments are making up for lousy function names. If we remove the comments and change the function names to match the comments, then the code would be just as easily read. In fact, the code will be better over time, as function names are more likely to be read and maintained than comments. This brings us to out-of-date comments. Out-of-date comments are worse than no comments as they add to the burden of reading the code and introduce confusion.

Also, comments should focus on their audience, and the definition of the audience differs depending on the code's level. In our previous example, the audience was a programmer tasked with owning and/or maintaining the code in that function. Through refactoring, we could remove the need for comments, and the audience would still be able to understand the code. There will be times when this is not true—particularly when the code is shared with an external or unknown audience, like with libraries, or when the purpose of the code is so complex that the audience may not understand it, like in the case of complex mathematical or computer science implementations. In these cases, we should include comments but ensure to keep them accurate, concise, and easily understood by the intended audience. Another legitimate reason for adding comments for other maintainers will be because of unusual implementation decisions or explicit functional or business requirements that are not readily apparent.

Returning to the **ProcessOrder()** function from our example, we should also be aware that our comments are useless to users of the function. We cannot expect them to read the implementation to understand the purpose or functionality of our function. External users are a completely different audience and, as such, require a different kind of comment.

While these users will still appreciate concise comments, they want to know what to expect from the function without reading the implementation. For example, comments like the following provide no value:

```
// ProcessOrder processes an order.
func ProcessOrder(o Order) error
```

Let's improve this comment by adding more detail:

```
// ProcessOrder coordinates all processes related to the order including validation,
// charging the customer, issuing the receipt, and informing the warehouse.
func ProcessOrder(o Order) error
```

This might be a lot to read, but it sets clear expectations. Moreover, it intentionally does not detail *how* it will perform its task. This is very important. Users of a function seldom need to know how the function performs its job, only that it does. A quick and easy way to check your user-focused comments is to run the **godoc** tool using the command:

```
$ godoc -http 0.0.0.0:6060
```

Then, open that address in your preferred web browser. This way, you will see your code as your users will see it from the outside without implementation details.

Remember to write valuable documentation by focusing on concise communication and the intended audience. Don't add details that are known or not needed by the audience, and most of all, don't write comments unless the cost of writing and maintaining them is worth it.

Errors are not exceptional

When starting out with Go, errors were definitely something I got wrong, and it took me a long time to realize. Given my experiences with other languages, I thought of errors as something that only happened when things went wrong, i.e., in exceptional circumstances. But Go errors are not exceptions.

Exceptions are part of a program's control flow, typically used to quit, panic, or otherwise stop what you're doing and give up. On the other hand, errors are a return value indicating that we failed to perform the intended task. This may result from exceptional circumstances, programmer errors, or expected outcomes. Imagine a function that performs validation on user inputs; a user failing to enter a valid value is to be expected occasionally. Similarly, imagine failing to load a particular record from a database; this is unlikely to be a cause for panicking or quitting the entire program, but is very often normal behavior.

As Go errors are just return values, they don't necessarily control the flow of the program. Based on the error's type, content, and context, it is up to the caller of the function to decide whether the error will impact the program flow.

Another pattern that is found in other languages but should almost always be avoided in Go is returning a specific value to indicate an error has occurred, like in the following code:

```go
// Extract version from ID in the format xx-yyyy
func ExtractVersionFromID(id string) int {
    if id == "" {
        return -1 // bad input
    }

    chunks := strings.Split(id, "-")
    if len(chunks) < 1 {
        return -2 // invalid format
    }

    version, err := strconv.Atoi(chunks[1])
    if err != nil {
        return -3 // failed to parse version number
    }

    return version
}
```

The UX of this example is terrible; users of this function will need to be intimately aware of the function's implementation details or need to read some pretty comprehensive documentation as to exactly what the different return values mean. A more appropriate implementation of this feature in Go is:

```go
var (
    ErrBadInput      = errors.New("bad input")
    ErrInvalidFormat = errors.New("invalid format")
```

```
        ErrParseFailed    = errors.New("failed to parse version")
)

// Extract version from ID in the format xx-yyyy
func ExtractVersionFromIDImproved(id string) (int, error) {
    if id == "" {
        return 0, ErrBadInput
    }

    chunks := strings.Split(id, "-")
    if len(chunks) < 1 {
        return 0, ErrInvalidFormat
    }

    version, err := strconv.Atoi(chunks[1])
    if err != nil {
        return 0, ErrParseFailed
    }

    return version, nil
}
```

Now it is clear to callers of this function when it has errored, and they can then decide if they need to worry about the type of error. Additionally, the type of error is easily visible from the **godoc** for this package, and there is no need to dive into the code.

Named errors

In the previous example, we defined some named errors using exported global variables when we could have just used something like **errors.New()** or **fmt.Errorf()**. Why? When we use named errors, they become a part of the API contract for our function/package. Named errors are a way for the function's creator to highlight to users that a particular error could occur and that it is notable—so notable, in fact, that the caller may wish to take a different action in response to each of the different errors.

In the previous example, it is not likely the caller would do anything different for each type of error. In all cases, the reaction will likely be to quit processing and return an error to the end user. The only advantage named errors gave us in that example is highlighting to the caller that these errors were both possible and likely. However, consider the following example:

```
var (
    ErrBadID        = errors.New("ID supplied is empty or invalid")
    ErrNotFound     = errors.New("user not found")
    ErrNotAuthorized = errors.New("permission denied")
)

func loadUser(ID string) (*User, error) {
    // implementation removed
    return nil, errors.New("not implemented")
}
```

Our **loadUser()** function has at least three different errors, and each error will likely provoke a different response by the caller. For example, if **loadUser()** was used as part of an HTTP handler, the responses may look like this:

```
func Handler(resp http.ResponseWriter, req *http.Request) {
    userID := req.Form.Get("userID")

    user, err := loadUser(userID)
    if err != nil {
        switch err {
        case ErrBadID:
            resp.WriteHeader(http.StatusUnprocessableEntity)

        case ErrNotAuthorized:
            resp.WriteHeader(http.StatusUnauthorized)

        case ErrNotFound:
            resp.WriteHeader(http.StatusNotFound)

        default:
            resp.WriteHeader(http.StatusInternalServerError)
        }

        return
    }

    encoder := json.NewEncoder(resp)
```

```
        _ = encoder.Encode(user)
    }
```

If we didn't use named errors in our example, then either the caller would have to return **http.StatusInternalServerError** for all errors, which would be infuriating and uninformative to the end users, or the caller would have to perform some string parsing on the error message. Such parsing will likely break if we refactor **loadUser()** or any functions it calls.

In the previous example, we should also note that the **switch** we use to differentiate the errors has a **default** block. This is there not only because it is good **switch** block hygiene but also because not all errors returned will be named errors. While it is possible to add named errors for every possible error response from **loadUser()**, this would incur a non-trivial amount of effort and for no gain. Instead, we highlighted the notable errors that the caller may want to react differently to and then left the rest to become "system errors". Such errors are hard to predict, occur infrequently, and do not require special processing by the caller.

At this point, you may think that named errors are fantastic, and you want to switch everything to named errors. Some folks take that style, but it is solely a stylistic choice.

In our example, we used public named variables and discussed how this made those errors part of the API contract and its costs. We did not talk about private named errors. As a stylistic choice, using private named errors can bring the following benefits:

- The code's readability may improve, since the variable name is shorter than the equivalent **errors.New()** call.

- It may improve the performance of the code, given that we are creating fewer objects.

- There is no increase in maintenance cost, like there is for public named errors, as they are not part of the API contract.

A common argument against the use of named errors is that they are fixed and therefore cannot provide any additional or contextual information regarding the current situation to the caller. This is where wrapped errors come in.

Wrapped errors

Before Go 1.13, if we wished to have a function return known, identifiable errors, we had two options: we could use named errors or define custom error types. The handling of these custom error types was then the following somewhat clunky code:

```
type BadRequestError struct {
    field string
}

func (b *BadRequestError) Error() string {
    return b.field + " was missing or invalid"
}

func Usage(err error) {
    if err != nil {
        if _, ok := err.(*BadRequestError); ok {
            // bad request
            return
        }

        // other errors
    }
}
```

As you can see in this example, while the error type is a prominent part of the API contract, detecting and handling the error type is more demanding than with a named error. The advantage of this approach over named errors is the ability to provide additional context in the error itself: in our example's case, which field had a problem. However, with wrapped errors, we can do better. Wrapped errors give us the ease of use of named errors and allow us to decorate the error with additional context.

Let's revisit our named error example and upgrade it to wrapped errors. First, we define our named errors as we did before:

```
var (
    ErrBadID    = errors.New("ID supplied is empty or the wrong format")
    ErrNotFound = errors.New("user not found")
)
```

Then we implement our **loadUser()** function:

```
func loadUser(ID string) (*User, error) {
    userID, err := strconv.Atoi(ID)
    if err != nil {
        return nil, fmt.Errorf("%w - %s", ErrBadID, err)
    }

    user, err := loadFromDB(userID)
    if err != nil {
        return nil, fmt.Errorf("%w - userID: %d", ErrNotFound, userID)
    }

    return user, err
}
```

In this example, you will notice that we are using **fmt.Errorf("%w")**; this is how to wrap errors. The **%w** directive identifies the error that we are wrapping. By wrapping the named error, we can easily identify which named error was returned and the rest of the **fmt.Errorf()** message will give us additional, request-specific context.

After adopting wrapped errors for our **loadUser()** example, we can detect if the returned error was one of the named errors using the function **errors.Is()**. This function enables a clean comparison between the current error value and the known wrapped errors, as we can see in our updated **Handler()** example below:

```
func Handler(resp http.ResponseWriter, req *http.Request) {
    userID := req.Form.Get("userID")

    user, err := loadUser(userID)
    if err != nil {
        switch {
        case errors.Is(err, ErrBadID):
            resp.WriteHeader(http.StatusUnprocessableEntity)

        case errors.Is(err, ErrNotFound):
            resp.WriteHeader(http.StatusNotFound)

        default:
```

```
                resp.WriteHeader(http.StatusInternalServerError)
        }

        return
    }

    encoder := json.NewEncoder(resp)
    _ = encoder.Encode(user)
}
```

So far, in our wrapped error examples, we have wrapped named errors to add additional information. There are other ways wrapped errors can be used. We can also wrap errors at different levels in the error-handling chain. This can be extremely useful for adding business-logic context to errors generated by lower-level code, like Go's standard library. Consider the following error message:

```
sql: transaction has already been committed or rolled back
```

Assuming we use the **sql** package in several places in our system, we may need help to quickly identify the source of this error message. After wrapping any errors returned by the **sql** package, our error becomes:

```
failed to update password with error: sql: transaction has already been committed or rolled
back
```

After wrapping, our error contains both the cause of the problem and sufficient context to know exactly where the error was thrown in the code.

The use of globals and init()

If you find yourself thinking of using global variables, like the **init()** function, or monkey patching using named function variables, don't. In almost all cases, they are the wrong solution, and here is why. Take a look at the following function signature:

```
func LoadUser(ctx context.Context, ID int) (*User, error)
```

This function looks okay at a quick glance, but ask yourself this: where are we loading the user from? Let's say this function is loading users from a database. Which database? How was the database pool initialized? How can we be sure that it has been initialized before we call this function?

All of these problems revolve around the same fundamental issue: our function depends on global state, and this dependency is not readily apparent to the user of this function. Because this relationship is opaque, users must break the encapsulation of the function and be aware of and satisfy any pre-conditions before using the function. In our example, the resolution is simple: once we recognize that our function has state, we can convert our function to a struct method that includes the database connection pool as member data. Doing so ensures the relationship between the pool and the function is obvious and predictable. Please note that I do not mean to suggest that every method that accesses the database must be added to one giant struct or that every struct that accesses the database must have its own database pool. We should still initialize one pool for the application and inject it into these objects.

Opaque dependencies are not the only problems caused by using global state like this; it is also a common source of data races. Never is this more obvious than when we attempt to write unit tests for these functions. If we revisit our earlier example, this time considering the complete implementation:

```
var db *sql.DB

func LoadUser(ctx context.Context, ID int) (*User, error) {
    row := db.QueryRowContext(ctx, "SELECT name FROM users WHERE id = ?", ID)

    out := &User{}
    err := row.Scan(out.Name)
    if err != nil {
        return nil, err
    }

    return out, nil
}
```

To test this function, we would need to swap out the database pool for every test; consequently, we cannot run these tests concurrently. When this code runs in production, the data race can occur between the initialization of the database pool and its use. We often address this by adding initialization calls (e.g., **sync.Once()**) to all functions that access the pool. However, this should be thought of as a code smell; we should be able to initialize the pool once during the app start, and then all code that uses it will be simplified and sure the pool is initialized and usable.

Hopefully, by now, I have convinced you to stop using globals and **init()**. Before you go and remove all your globals, we should quickly note there are some exceptions. We looked at named errors earlier. They are globals and are extremely valuable. Another notable exception is enums.

Enums

An enum or enumerated type is a fixed set of variables that outline all possible values for a particular type. A classic use of enums is for compass directions, as you can see below:

```
const (
    North  Direction = "north"
    East   Direction = "east"
    South Direction = "south"
    West  Direction = "west"
)
```

```
type Direction string
```

Our implementation uses constants instead of global variables, so we haven't broken any rules yet, but look what happens when we add JSON unmarshalling to our **Direction** type:

```
var allDirections = map[Direction]struct{}{
    North: {}, East: {}, South: {}, West: {},
}
```

```
func (d *Direction) UnmarshalJSON(bytes []byte) error {
    var directionString string

    err := json.Unmarshal(bytes, &directionString)
    if err != nil {
        return err
    }

    direction := Direction(directionString)

    _, found := allDirections[direction]
    if !found {
        return fmt.Errorf("invalid direction: '%s'", direction)
    }
```

```
    *d = direction

    return nil
}
```

To achieve efficient parsing we've defined a map containing all of the Directions and compared the input value with the map's keys. Even though the map of Directions is effectively a constant because of Go's language design, we cannot define it as such. We can allow this exception to our no-globals rule because we have made the global value private and ensured that it never changes once initialized. Thus we have avoided any issues with magic state or data races.

Don't panic()!

The **panic()** function is another language feature I strongly recommend avoiding. Like globals and **init()**, **panic()**'s main issue is that its use is opaque, somewhat magic, and not the right kind of magic.

If you have a background in languages that use exceptions for program flow control, you may see panic as the Go equivalent; if you squint hard enough, it is close to unchecked exceptions from Java. While Java cannot deprecate unchecked exceptions, the widespread adoption of Optional types and assertion annotations are doing their best to prevent them from being thrown. We should aim for the same outcomes in Go and avoid using **panic()** unless we intend to make the application crash.

When we write a function or method that either calls **panic()** or causes a panic due to nil-pointer issues or data races, we introduce behavior that has an impact beyond our function's scope. The program will crash if the code caller is unaware of the panic and does not provide a **recover()** function. Let's look at an example that uses panic in an attempt to avoid the error-handling code:

```
func LoadUser(idAsString string) (out *User, err error) {
    defer func() {
        if r := recover(); r != nil {
            err = fmt.Errorf("failed to load user with err :%s", r)
        }
```

```
        }()

        id := parseID(idAsString)
        out = loadByID(id)

        return
    }

    func parseID(idAsString string) int {
        out, err := strconv.Atoi(idAsString)
        if err != nil {
            panic(err)
        }

        return out
    }
```

As you can see, by removing the error-handling logic from our top-level function **LoadUser()**, it is much shorter than it would have been if we had used errors. Instead of errors, the lower-level functions call **panic()** when an error occurs and then rely on the top-level **defer/recover** function to clean up and prevent the application from crashing. In a vacuum, this seems like a win. However, what happens if we reuse our **parseID()** somewhere else and forget to include a **recover**?

Beyond that issue, this is not normal Go code. Go developers expect functions that could cause errors to return them and then allow the caller to decide if the error is fatal. When **panic()** is involved, the fact that an error is possible is not readily apparent.

As with everything, I have exceptions to offer you. There are only two places where it is appropriate and efficient to use **panic()**: in the **main()** function and inside tests. Inside **main()**, there is no magic. Issues in the **main()** function typically cause the application to be terminated, and as the maintainer of that function, we are entirely responsible for this decision. For **main()** code, I recommend going one step further and replacing **panic()** with **log.Fatalf()** like so:

```
    func main() {
        cfg, err := config.Load("my-config.json")
```

```
    if err != nil {
        log.Fatalf("failed to load config with err: %s", err)
    }

    server := server.New(cfg)
    server.Start()
}
```

By switching to **log.Fatal()**, the application still exits as it would with **panic()**, but can provide a helpful error message to go along with the error.

This is the same pattern that we should use during tests, as you can see in this example:

```
func TestGenerateHash(t *testing.T) {
    result, err := GenerateHash(time.Now().UnixNano())
    if err != nil {
        t.Fatalf("unexpected error: %s", err)
    }

    if result == "" {
        t.Fatal("result should not be empty")
    }
}
```

As you can see, tests, like **main()** functions, are limited in scope, and the execution flow of both is entirely controlled by the author. As such, the author can decide whether the application can proceed or stop if a failure occurs.

Striving for Consistency

The consistency in our codebase impacts how easy it is to read and our general comfort level when reading. It also impacts other ways we interact with our code. It determines how easy it is for us to navigate the code, making it easier to find the relevant parts and skip over the unimportant or low-level implementation details. Also, consistency in API design and implementation decisions can determine how easy it is to use the various functions and modules.

The best argument about consistency I can offer you is this. Consider a garden filled with 1000 different plants. If the gardener planted whatever they felt like all over the place, then to anyone visiting the garden, it would take a while to find any specific plant. Now consider the same garden, but the gardener grouped the plants by type and then sorted the plants in the groups alphabetically. Now, it would always be easy to find a particular plant. However, the garden would likely not be appealing, and the gardener would feel like their self-expression was ignored. My ideal garden, like my ideal codebase, is an appropriate balance of consistency and expression. There is a high level of consistency, a certain level of predictability, and, as a result, a high level of usability—but it's not so restrictive that it prohibits any self-expression.

Achieving a consistent style

The first and perhaps most important aspect of consistency is code style. Sadly, it's also the aspect of the code that programmers identify with as their self-expression or generally who they are as a programmer. A lot of the long-running debates from other languages, like tabs vs. spaces, the placement of curly brackets, or snake-case vs. camel-case don't exist because we have clearly defined conventions for these in Go. On top of this we should layer team conventions; not following these just adds tension and cognitive complexity to the team. But even with all these conventions to follow there is still plenty of room for personal expression. Take Go's error handling format: which one of the following examples is correct?

```
// example 1
if err := doTask(); err != nil {
    return err
}
```

```
// example 2
err := doTask()
if err != nil {
    return err
}
```

There is no definitive right answer to that question. If the team hasn't explicitly decided on a style, then you should feel free to use whichever suits you.

The first and easiest step on the road to style consistency is the use of **gofmt**. We should be running **gofmt -s** on all code before submitting it for review. By doing so, all code will have a predictable base level of style consistency.

The next step is to study the recognized industry standards; for the Go community, this is the following two pages:

- **Effective Go—https://go.dev/doc/effective_go**

- **Go Code Review Comments—https://go.dev/wiki/CodeReviewComments**

Like many things relating to Go, there is an absolute treasure trove of information, knowledge, and experience crammed into these documents—so much so that I recommend re-reading these documents every six months. As your experience with Go progresses, the knowledge and rationale outlined in these documents will become more apparent.

The last step in resolving style issues is acknowledging that different teams have different styles. There is nothing wrong with this; this is part of the team's self-expression. That said, these decisions should be identified, discussed, and documented so that new members have something to quickly onboard with. This documentation and discussions are essential as they improve the team members' ability to discuss and produce better code.

It is perfectly acceptable and normal for a team's stylistic choices to run counter to the two web pages mentioned above. Common examples include:

- Using a test assertion library instead of an **if** block.

- Naming channels with a **Ch** suffix.

- Using a single character for variable names.

- Using **if err := doSomething; err != nil** instead of breaking it over two lines.

You can find comparative examples of these decisions in the source code for this chapter

https://github.com/corsc/Beyond-Effective-Go/tree/master/Chapter05/02_consistency/ 01_style/

Good arguments can be made for either side of these issues, but the key is consistency. A consistent style ensures that reading the code feels intuitive and natural. Consistency does not mean we never change our style or experiment with different approaches. This is definitely something that I strongly encourage. If you find a new and better approach, the next task is to convince and help your team to adopt this new style.

Once you and your team have decided on a style, you should look for tools to support it. Adopting **gofmt** and **goimports** should be standard, as they are from the Go project. But we can go further. Tools like golangci-lint **https://golangci-lint.run/** are highly configurable and can be used to identify and sometimes automatically fix style issues, lessening programmer and reviewer effort.

Building consistent packages

Go packages are yet another part of Go that looks simple and familiar but is, in fact, very different from what most people expect. However, like with style, the key to packages is consistency. With consistent packages, we will be able to quickly find the right package and know where to find things inside the package.

The size and scope of packages

Packages should be organized by feature or module rather than programming purpose. As such, we should not have any packages with names like **util**, **dto**, **errors**, or **constants**—but we will get back to that.

There is no maximum or minimum size for a Go package, but they should be only just big enough to achieve their task. A simple litmus test for determining the size of the package is to write the package documentation. In case you are unfamiliar, package-level documentation is written at the top of one of the files in the package, often in a file called **doc.go**, in the form **"Package xxx ...."**. If you can write a single sentence that adequately conveys the package's purpose and scope, then the package is the right size. If you need to write multiple sentences or have a sentence with multiple ands, then the package is likely too big. Also, if you find you are writing similar sentences in multiple packages, you may have split the packages prematurely.

Let's look at some examples from the standard library. The **http** package comment is:

```
// Package http provides HTTP client and server implementations.
```

As you can see, this is a single, simple sentence and a very clear scope. You could argue that the authors could have split the package into a client and a server, but then the main types for those packages would have been **httpserver.Server** and **httpclient.Client**. However, there would have been a bunch of code shared between them. This likely gives us a **httpcommon** package. Hopefully, you can see that this is creating quite a mess.

Conversely, the standard library also includes a **httptest** package, whose comment is:

```
// Package httptest provides utilities for HTTP testing.
```

Again, a single, clear sentence that gives us purpose and scope. So why wasn't this included in the **http** package? Firstly, think about what the package comment for the combined package would be. Probably something like "**client and server implementations and utilities for testing**". The multiple *ands* here indicate that such a package provides multiple features.

Packages should be self-contained

Usually, when we talk about decoupling, we mean object-level decoupling. However, package-level decoupling is just as essential as object-level decoupling. A great barometer of the level of coupling your package has is the number of packages from the same project being imported; a small number of imports—three or fewer—indicates low coupling.

This chapter's code includes a script called **depgraph.sh**, which you can use to generate a dependency graph and quickly identify excessive coupling between packages. Let's look at an example. The following diagram shows a traditional object-oriented structure for a fictitious transfer module:

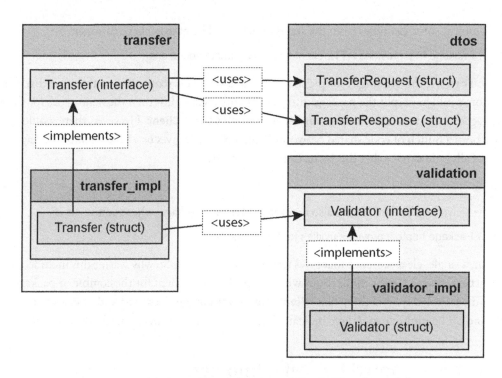

Figure 5.1—Traditional dependency graph for the Transfer module

As you can see, we have separated the structs and their implementation. All data transfer objects (request and response objects) are in a separate package. As a result, there is a link (coupling) between our transfer implementation and the validation package. Now, there are many things wrong with this from a Go perspective.

For starters, too many packages are involved in our **transfer** module. The first and easiest package to drop is the **transfer_impl** package. We achieve this by deleting the **Transfer** interface and moving the **Transfer** struct into the **transfer** package. Because of Go's support for implicit interfaces, the **transfer** package does not need to define "this is what I provide" with an interface. If another package wishes to use and mock our **Transfer** struct, it can define its own interface and mocks.

Additionally, any such interfaces should follow the interface segregation principle and specify only the methods they need. In this way, interfaces change perspective from "this is what I provide" to "this is what I need".

The next thing we should address is the **dto** package. This is not a pattern we should be using here. There are many reasons for this, but I will offer the most important two. Firstly, clarity. Because we refer to types using the form **dto.TransferRequest** the generic name **dto** does not tell us anything. We have missed our chance for the code to express which package this struct belongs in and how and when to use it. After moving this struct into the **transfer** package, ownership becomes evident, and we can even shorten the name to just **transfer.Request,** giving us less typing and mental burden.

The second reason to avoid the use of common, shared packages is decoupling. When we have a shared package, very quickly, most of our application comes to depend on that package. Not only does this turn our dependency graph into one big pile of wet spaghetti, but it becomes impossible to clearly tell when packages are coupled due to their use of a shared type.

The last two changes we can introduce together as they have the same intention. In the traditional style, we have a **Request** struct and a dependency link between our **Transfer** implementation struct and the **Validator** interface. We can replace both of these with local interfaces—again, changing the interfaces to a "this is what I need" perspective. Our **transfer.Request** interface defines the data access methods (getters) that outline what data we need; this is better as an interface than as a struct, because it allows users to reuse their objects rather than forcing them to construct new ones to call us. Finally, we redefine the **Validator** interface, reducing it to only include methods used in this **transfer** package.

After all of these changes, our updated dependency graph looks like this:

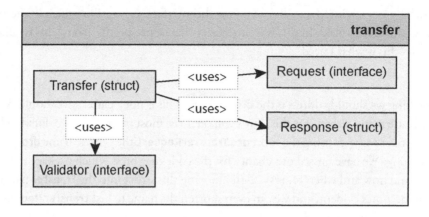

Figure 5.2—Improved dependency graph for the Transfer module

Initially, we had four packages and six objects involved in our "simple" **transfer** module. To fully understand this feature, we would have had to jump around between all these packages. With this new structure, everything related to our **transfer** module is in one place; it could even be in one file. Our package is now wholly decoupled and self-contained.

It's all in the package name

When it comes to choosing a name for your package, there are three things we should do:

- Read Effective Go—**https://go.dev/doc/effective_go#package-names**

- Read this excellent article from the Go blog—**https://go.dev/blog/package-names**

- Remember how the package name will be used in the code.

It's probably strange for a book to ask you to read a webpage, but these articles are fantastic and something we should be reading and re-reading until it becomes second nature. To expand on the *"remember how the package name will be used"* point, consider this. It is easy to quickly choose a package name with little or no effort and write the following:

    package utils

After writing this line, we get on and start filling up the file with the features. After all, they are what we are being paid for. In our haste, we have forgotten that any use of this package will be in the form of **utils.DoSomething()**. By choosing a generic name, we have missed a golden opportunity to make our package name informative and useful. Also, because we didn't put enough effort into choosing our package name, we missed the chance to use the package's name to define the package's scope and intention.

The final point to remember regarding how package names are used concerns name collisions. Let's say you had a package called **errors**. Setting aside the issues we have already highlighted regarding generically-named packages, the issue here is that the package name is the same as one from the standard library. Because of this, when you write **errors.New("something failed")** the Go tooling will not be able to automatically resolve the imports for you. This may seem like a minor issue, but it will slow down you and everyone else working on this project—something that can be easily avoided by finding a unique package name.

File organization

How code in Go files should be organized is surprisingly undocumented for something that tremendously impacts a codebase's usability. This section aims to remedy that deficiency. As with everything in this section, consistency is paramount. Organizing code consistently helps everyone know where and how to find things with minimal effort. The best way to think about the ordering of code in a file is like a newspaper. The important and attention-grabbing items should be at the top, followed by the details, with the least significant details coming last. Readers should be able to quickly understand the purpose of the file by reading the start of the file and then only have to read to the bottom if they need more details. This translates into the following order:

1. Constants

2. Global variables (like named errors)

3. The constructor

4. The struct definition

5. Public struct methods and functions

6. Private struct methods and private functions

7. Input interfaces and private types

Let's examine and explain why this order is both important and valuable. Constants, global variables, and the constructor all form part of the API; as such, they are the most commonly sought out and used by users. This is particularly true for public constants and named errors. Additionally, when constants are used as configuration or to replace magic numbers, being at the top of the file makes programmers more likely to see them. As such, they are more likely to reuse and maintain them.

Similarly, moving private globals to the top of the file is essential as it increases the visibility of these variables to code maintainers. These variables cause the package to have state, which is a very significant and impactful decision. Therefore, it should be introduced to new maintainers early and remain in front of mind at all times.

As for the rest, the underlying idea is to start with macro concerns and work our way to micro. A public struct definition is often the most significant thing in a file; it is frequently the reason the file was created.

The next level down from the struct is the public methods. Again, we are putting the most frequently accessed and significant parts as high as possible.

For the private methods and functions, these are implementation details that only need to be read if we need to refactor them. And finally, the input interfaces: while they are part of the public API, they have been placed at the bottom and treated more like implementation details. There are two ideas here. For users, the input interfaces are only significant once the user decides to use the public methods or functions, at which time they can easily find the interfaces because these are in a predictable location. For code maintainers, they are implementation details, and their exact details don't need to be kept front of mind when working on the rest of the code.

The final point to consider here is that we are often time-constrained as programmers. So reading every last line of code is somewhere between impossible and inefficient. Hopefully, our top-level public functions are relatively short—say, less than 40 lines—and, if need be, somewhat abstract. Consider the following method:

```go
func (o *OrderManager) Process(order Order) error {
    err := o.validateOrder(order)
    if err != nil {
        return err
    }

    receiptNo := o.chargeCustomer(order)

    o.sendReceipt(order, receiptNo)

    o.informWarehouse(order)

    return nil
}
```

After reading the above code, do you understand what this method does without reading the other methods? If all you had time for is a general understanding, then reading this method is sufficient. The sub-methods are "implementation details" that we can find lower in the file if we need to.

Please do not fret if your code's ordering does not precisely match the one outlined here. There are two key takeaways. Firstly, when the arrangement is consistent, you can find what you need faster and easier. Secondly, favor putting the more significant pieces towards the top and the nitty-gritty implementation underneath. Both of these actions will give you the same benefits: predictability and ease of use.

How many files should be in a package?

There is no correct answer to how many files should be in a package or, by extension, the appropriate length of those files. It's determined by the scope of the package and the complexity of the tasks it is performing.

As we've discussed, a package is a logical grouping of related features. Therefore, the most straightforward organization would be having one file per feature. Please note the use of the word *feature* and not *function*. Using one file for a feature minimizes the number of files we interact with when adding or maintaining features.

One file per feature is a guiding ideal, not a rule. We should avoid adding new files unnecessarily, especially "other files" like a file just for constants or errors. Constants and errors should be defined close to where they're used, unless they're used throughout the package.

The one notable exception is the **doc.go** file: if we're writing package documentation—and we should be for most packages—then, by convention, this documentation should be in **doc.go**.

Do I need a function or a method?

This may seem like a strange question, but, surprisingly, many programmers struggle with this aspect of Go. Depending on their previous programming languages, programmers will tend towards one or the other. As Go does not force us into a particular solution, we must adopt a style that keeps us out of trouble.

My first style convention is: *functions should be stateless*. Yes, combining a function with a global variable is possible, but that's a recipe for trouble. If a function needs to have state, we should convert it to a method. This ensures the method and the state it relies upon are logically grouped together in the struct.

My second style convention is: *grouped methods are not required to be stateful*. No, this does not contradict the first convention. Adding methods to a struct also serves to logically group methods together. This grouping allows the author to express that these methods are related and should be dealt with as a group.

My last style convention is: *always consider the user*. If the feature you provide is likely to be dependency injected or mocked for testing, then it's better to provide it as a struct and method. While it is possible to mock/substitute functions, it's somewhat clumsy and foreign to programmers from an object-oriented background. Consider the function **time.Now()** from the standard library. The easiest way to provide this feature is as a function, but sometimes we want to mock or stub this function to have predictable timing in our tests. This could have been provided as a method, but then to get the time, everyone would have to write **time.Time{}.Now()**, which is clumsy. By considering the users, we have to conclude that, nearly always, users want to access the time and don't care about mocking. We then optimize for the most common use case.

How long should our functions and methods be?

If you're looking for a concrete number to set your linter, then 30 lines. How did I come up with this number? I opened my IDE and looked at how many lines of code fit on one screen of my laptop. (Actually, it fits 35; I rounded it down). Similar to files, functions and methods should only be as long as they have to be; generally speaking, the shorter, the better. The shorter a function is, the easier it is to understand and, therefore, to work with. When all of the code for a function fits on the screen, we don't need to scroll or remember the rest of the function.

The last motivation I offer you about keeping functions small is that it encourages us to organize our code in line with the singles principle, i.e., a single purpose, a single responsibility, and a single abstraction level.

When our functions and methods get too long, then it's time to refactor: to split the function into separate functions based on purpose, or extract the different parts and introduce a level of abstraction as we did in the *Writing useful documentation* section earlier in this chapter.

Consider parameters and return values

Beyond naming, the number and organization of parameters and return values is the most significant factor determining the UX of our functions and methods. It is, therefore, surprising that it is so consistently overlooked.

As Go does not restrict the number of return values, the considerations presented in this section apply equally to parameters and return values, but as two separate groups. For brevity going forward, I will use the term *arguments* to refer to the parameter list or the return values list.

Often, arguments are added as the need arises without consideration; this is completely wrong. Before adding any arguments, we should consider the following:

- The number of arguments

- The scope of the arguments

- The grouping of the arguments

- The ordering of the arguments

Let's dive a little deeper.

The number of arguments

From a UX perspective, the ideal number of arguments is zero. When there are no parameters, passing in the wrong parameters is impossible. Assuming the function is well-named, it should be easy to understand how to use it and what it does without knowing its implementation details. Similarly, if there are no return values, we can't misuse them either.

Clearly, an application with no parameters and no return variables will not be able to achieve much, so the question becomes: how many arguments should we aim for? Given that the usability of our functions is inversely proportional to the number of parameters and return values, the fewer, the better; but if you were to push me for a number, three of each.

Consider what parameters are. They are data passed into the function that we then use to perform some action. Therefore, the more parameters we pass in, the more complex the action we perform. This same logic holds true for return values. This complexity creates a mental burden for both the maintainers and the users of the function. It is often also an indication that we have a singles-principle issue.

The last and easiest consideration regarding the number of arguments is how easy it is to read the code. The more arguments a function has, the more likely the function signature is to extend off the screen or beyond any line length limit set by the team and be wrapped. Both of these cases make the function significantly harder to quickly scan.

The scope of the arguments

When attempting to reduce the number of arguments, moving them elsewhere is one of the first things that come to mind, like moving parameters from a method to the constructor. This can be the right option, but it depends heavily on the argument's scope or lifecycle. Consider the following function for sending emails:

```
func SendEmail(server string, auth smtp.Auth, from string, to string, subject string, message
string, attachments []os.File) error {
    // implementation removed
}
```

As you can see, the argument list is rather long, and even as long as it is, it doesn't cover all of the options and email features that might be needed in the future. In other words, it could get even worse later.

When considering an argument's scope, the questions we should be asking ourselves are:

- **Is the data known at the time the object is initiated?** If yes, this is init-scoped data.

- **Is the data set once and then never or seldom changed?** If yes, this is init-scoped data.

- **Do we need to pass in this argument every time we call this method?** If no, this is init-scoped data.

- **Is the data likely different for every request?** If yes, this is request-scoped data.

- **Is the data related to or influenced by the request?** If yes, this is request-scoped data.

Init-scoped data should be supplied as public member data or constructor parameters during object construction. If the data needs to change but is not request-scoped, it can be changed by accessing the public member data or via a setter function. Just be wary of data races.

On the other hand, request-scoped data should be arguments of the individual methods.

In our example, the **server** and **auth** parameters are init-scoped and, as such, are perfect candidates for promotion to a constructor or public member data, like so:

```
type Sender struct {
    Server string
    Auth    smtp.Auth
}


func (s Sender) Send(from string, to string, subject string, message string, attachments
[]os.File) error {
    // implementation removed
    return nil
}
```

The UX of our function has definitely improved with the shorter list of arguments; it's easier to read the function signature, and users of this function will have to juggle fewer parameters. However, our function is still long and unwieldy. Don't worry, there are more improvements ahead.

The grouping of the arguments

As we strive to improve the UX of our function, the next thing we should consider is argument grouping. Argument grouping can take two forms in Go. The first form is the traditional object-oriented approach of grouping parameters by their logical purpose.

If we re-examine our email sending example, we can quickly see that the subject, message, and attachments form a logical group that comprises the email we are trying to send. We can therefore promote these parameters into a group by moving them into either a separate struct or an input interface, like so:

```
func (s Sender) Send(from string, to string, email Email) error {
    // implementation removed
    return nil
}


type Email struct {
    Subject      string
    Message      string
    Attachments []os.File
```

```
}
```

This change has also given us additional benefits. We have future-proofed ourselves against changes to the **Email** struct. Should the business requirements change and we have to add more attributes to the **Email** struct, we can do so without detracting from the usability of our **Send()** function. Additionally, any such changes would not necessitate updating all existing usages of the function.

After grouping these arguments, we have also reduced the likelihood of bugs caused by users supplying the arguments in the wrong order. Our new approach makes that close to impossible.

And the last benefit we should highlight is that by grouping the parameters together, we have ensured that the data now lives as a group with a single lifecycle. This encourages us to relate to the **Email** object as a single entity and perform actions on or with that entity rather than the individual pieces. The assertion that this object is a single entity becomes even more significant when we pass our grouped objects to others.

The second form of grouping available to us in Go is less structural and more stylistic, but it is by no means less significant when it comes to improving the UX of the function. This grouping is achieved by removing types when two or more consecutive arguments of the same type exist. After applying this grouping to our example, we get the following:

```
func (s Sender) Send(from, to string, email Email) error
```

As you can see, we have removed the **string** between the **from** and **to** parameters. This is a small thing, but it has shortened our function signature and reduced the mental effort required to read and understand it.

The ordering of the arguments

Have you ever wondered why, when **Context** is used, it is always the first parameter? How about why, when a function returns an error, it is always the last return value? These are conventions, yes, but the motivation for these conventions is UX. Conventions bring consistency and predictability and, from this, ease of use.

The advantages of consistent ordering apply not only to commonplace conventions like these but to all levels of our code. Let's re-examine our simple email sender again and, this time, add a private method called **validateAddresses()**; this method will validate the email addresses and have the following signature:

```
func (s Sender) validateAddresses(to, from string) error
```

This seems reasonable, but when we compare it with the function signature for **Send()**, we notice that ordering of the parameters is inconsistent. You might be thinking, *it's a private method, it doesn't matter*, but it does. With this inconsistency, we have made it harder for ourselves to use this method. Also, because the parameter types are the same, we have an increased chance of making mistakes. The improvements here may be minor, but so is the cost of consistently ordering the arguments.

Boolean arguments are evil

Boolean input parameters are insidious because adding them is simple but comes with a very high cost. Consider the following code fragment:

```
result := user.CheckGender(true)
```

What does **true** represent? It is only possible to know by reading the documentation or implementation of this method.

Let's assume for a moment that a boolean is the ideal internal representation of this variable; then, how can we improve the UX? For this example, the best option is to replace this method with two methods **IsMale()** and **IsFemale()**; in this way, users do not need the documentation and are unlikely to make a mistake. There is nothing wrong with retaining the original function as a private method to reduce duplication. As the maintainers of this object and methods, we should be familiar with the implementation and how to use it. We could even add private constants and make the code read slightly nicer.

There are other ways boolean parameters could trip us up. Consider what happens if the requirements change, and now we need to allow users not to specify a gender. We'd then need to change both our internal representation and the input parameters.

Sadly, boolean return values also suffer from issues. A function that returns a single boolean value is terse but okay. However, like with input parameters, if requirements change and we need to change the type, this could lead to much refactoring. As a result, it is worth pausing and considering the likelihood of extensions before adoption. The main issue with boolean return values surfaces when we move beyond a single return value. Consider the following code fragment:

```
newQty, exists, err := addToOrderQuantity(orderID, productCode, additionalQty)
if err != nil {
    return err
}

if !exists {
    return fmt.Errorf("failed to load order with id %s", orderID)
}
```

In this code, our **addToOrderQuantity()** method returns a boolean to indicate if the supplied order was found and an error to indicate that something technical went wrong. This is a common mistake caused by thinking of errors as exceptions. As you can see from the code fragment, the function's caller doesn't care if there was a technical failure or if the order was not found in both cases, it's a failure. As such, we can reduce the effort required by the users by replacing the boolean with a named error. Then users can decide if they wish to react differently between the different possible outcomes.

Reducing constructor arguments

We talked earlier about reducing the parameter count of functions and methods and proposed to move init-scoped parameters from the methods to constructors. But it's not hard to see how this can quickly make the UX of our constructors downright disgusting. So this raises the question: is there anything we can do about that?

To address this problem, I offer you two strategies:

- Employing private constructors
- Adopting config injection

Let's examine each of these in a little more detail.

Employing private constructors

When employing private constructors, we're not reducing the number of arguments being used during construction but rather removing as many as we can from the public constructor to improve the UX for external users.

Consider the following function:

```
NewUserManager(minNameLen, maxNameLen int, pwdEncoder PasswordEncoder, storage
Storage, now func() time.Time, risk RiskManager) *UserManager
```

For our example, we have two parameters (**minNameLen** and **maxNameLen**) that configure the settings for user names, we have three interface dependencies (**pwdEncoder**, **storage**, and **risk**) being dependency injected, and we're also injecting a closure called **now**.

The first question we should ask ourselves is "are any of these dependencies passed in purely for the purposes of testing?"

In this example, the **now** closure fits this description as it is being passed in to allow us to replace calls to **time.Now()** and have predictable tests.

Mocking and stubbing during testing are powerful tools for creating high-quality tests; however, in this case, it is negatively impacting the user. Users are expected to pass in a parameter for a purpose that is not theirs. Additionally, asking them to do so is leaking implementation details.

To address this problem we introduce a private constructor and remove the test-only concerns from the public function. The resulting code is:

```
func NewUserManager(minNameLen, maxNameLen int, pwdEncoder PasswordEncoder,
storage Storage, risk RiskManager) *UserManager {
```

```
        return newUserManager(minNameLen, maxNameLen, pwdEncoder, storage, time.Now,
    risk)
    }

    func newUserManager(minNameLen, maxNameLen int, pwdEncoder PasswordEncoder,
    storage Storage, now func() time.Time, risk RiskManager) *UserManager {
        return &UserManager{
        // implementation removed
        }
    }
```

With our updated structure, we're still injecting the **now** closure and have predictable tests, but we've improved the UX for external users.

The second question we should ask ourselves is "are there parameters for which all users will pass in the same value?"

Let's assume for our example that the **PasswordEncoder** is defined and implemented by us in the same package as our **UserManager**. There is only one implementation, and probably there will only ever be one implementation. I know it's a little controversial, but why require all users to inject the same value? We can inject it for them using the private constructor.

If you ask folks why they chose to separate concerns into separate objects, their answer will often include a desire to decouple the objects and allow any future extension. Decoupling is a great goal; however, allowing for potential future extension can be a waste of effort. With this approach, you can have the good parts of dependency injection, like decoupling and mocking, but not detract from the UX.

Adopting config injection

Even after applying the private constructor approach, our example still has four parameters, two of which are not dependencies but configuration. Our contrived example is relatively simple, and it's not uncommon for a constructor to require significantly more config parameters. To address this problem, let me introduce you to *config injection*.

Config injection acknowledges the fact that configuration often comes from a single place, generally a file or config management system, and is often loaded and managed by a single object. Because this configuration object is expensive to create, we will frequently use a singleton pattern on this config instance. Because of this, the config instance is a great place to store other singletons like database connection pools. To better illustrate this point, let's zoom out and look at how our constructor is used. Let's assume the **minNameLen** and **maxNameLen** config values are part of a more extensive set of configuration for the application and are stored in a JSON file. We must load this config from the file and then pass it to our constructor. A simple implementation would look like this:

```
// load the config
rawJSON, err := os.ReadFile("testdata/config.json")
if err != nil {
    return fmt.Errorf("failed to load config with err: %w", err)
}

config := &AppConfig{}
err = json.Unmarshal(rawJSON, config)
if err != nil {
    return fmt.Errorf("failed to parse config with err: %w", err)
}

// Call our constructor
example.NewUserManager(config.MinNameLen, config.MaxNameLen, storage, risk)
```

By applying config injection, we will collect all of the configuration and any other singletons, like database pools or instrumentation clients, into an interface like this:

```
type Config interface {
    GetDBPool() *sql.DB

    GetMinNameLen() int
    GetMaxNameLen() int
}
```

I've included a database pool for illustration purposes only in this example. With our interface in place, we can now update our constructors by merging all of the configuration into one variable like this:

```
func NewUserManager(cfg Config, storage Storage, risk RiskManager) *UserManager {
    return newUserManager(cfg, &myPasswordEncoder{}, storage, time.Now, risk)
```

```go
}

func newUserManager(cfg Config, pwdEncoder PasswordEncoder, storage Storage, now
func() time.Time, risk RiskManager) *UserManager {
    return &UserManager{
        cfg:        cfg,
        pwdEncoder: pwdEncoder,
        storage:    storage,
        now:        now,
        risk:       risk,
    }
}
```

In this example, we've only reduced two variables into one, which is a minor win. However, most applications will have much more configuration than this. Additionally, configuration has a habit of increasing throughout an application's lifetime, making the adoption of config injection more valuable over time. When additional configuration is added, we no longer need to add constructor parameters but only more methods to our **Config** interface.

One compelling benefit of this approach is that we have no direct coupling between our code and the source of the config. This improves our code's reusability across other projects.

Finally, let's return to the earlier point about using the config injection pattern to manage config and singletons. Suppose you're like me and favor a style heavy on dependency injection and averse to using globals. In that case, you'll find that many of your constructors become burdened with the injection of cross-functional concerns. Before long, most constructors have the logger and the instrumentation clients as parameters. Given the underlying idea that fewer parameters are better, these two or more parameters become a drag on the UX. Therefore, I recommend moving these cross-functional concerns like the logger and instrumentation client instances inside the same struct as the configuration. This keeps these clients out of the parameter list and gives me a proxy singleton implementation of the logger and instrumentation instances. I know this violates the name of config injection, and I should probably come up with a better name, but from a UX perspective, I find it highly compelling.

Becoming Predictable

Earlier in this chapter, we characterized predictable code as reliable, logical, and containing no surprises or gotchas. And, so far, we've talked about many things, like naming and avoiding global state, that contribute to code being logical and reliable. This section will take it up a notch and examine how users interact with our structs and packages from an external perspective.

APIs: export only what you must

There is a simple rule when deciding whether to make struct methods, member data, or functions private or public. Make everything private ... until you have no other choice. Any time we export something, someone else can use it. The moment they use it, then we are expected to maintain it. This means we cannot remove, refactor, or rename it without dealing with existing usage.

This resistance to change can encourage us to make other mistakes, like avoiding maintenance, creating an overly complicated UX to account for all use cases, and sometimes duplicating or deprecating code to avoid dealing with existing usage. This is a significant source of technical debt.

Because of this, we should consider all exported code as having an ongoing cost: a small one, perhaps, but as the amount of code in a project increases, so does this cost. This cost is the main reason it's so tricky to refactor legacy code.

This approach is another strong argument for favoring the KISS principle over the DRY principle we examined in the previous chapter. A rigorous application of DRY inevitably results in many tiny functions or packages. However, they must be exported to ensure high reusability across the application. This is when the costs we mentioned start creeping in. Sometimes, this is a cost we must bear—but it can be mitigated. When the package is supposed to be used only by a few others and not the entire application, we can employ an **internal** directory under the user's package and make it into a module, enforcing the relationship and limiting the scope and cost. More on this concept in the next section.

APIs: good fences make good neighbors

To explain how to separate our code into modules, we first need to define what we mean by a module and then take a quick refresher on the **internal** package and its usage. We're not talking about modules from a **go mod** sense; we're talking about modules in traditional software design. A module is a logical grouping of one or more Go packages to achieve a single goal.

Depending on how you structure your codebase, these goals could be feature-based (like a user module or an order module) or software layer-based (like an API or a storage layer). Here's a quick refresher on the **internal** package. Packages under an **internal** package can only be imported by the following:

- Other packages under that **internal** package

- The package immediately above the **internal** package

- Packages at the same level as the **internal** package

Let's use an example to demonstrate how to use **internal** to create modules. Consider the following structure:

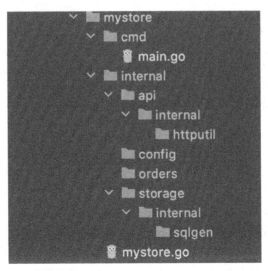

Figure 5.3—Sample application structure

This structure shows a fictitious online store called MyStore. This project is an HTTP REST service with the **main** function under the **cmd** package.

The **api**, **config**, **orders**, and **storage** packages are under an **internal** package. The **cmd** package can import the **api**, **config**, **orders**, and **storage** packages because they're children of the **internal** package that has the same parent as **cmd**. However, the **cmd** package cannot import the **httputil** package. We've created an API module by adding another **internal** package under the **api** package and placing our **httputil** package under that **internal** package. The same goes for the **sqlgen** package; this is part of a **storage** module.

By separating our code into modules this way, we can have clean boundaries or fences between our modules and simultaneously allow ourselves to extract functionality into concise, logical containers, thereby avoiding the cost that we would incur by making these features public.

Additionally, using modules offers additional encapsulation of the implementation decisions within the modules, which forces looser coupling between the modules.

Predictability with encapsulation

Many programmers are first introduced to encapsulation while learning an object-oriented language. It is frequently represented as a combination of an object, its state, and some methods that mutate that state. But this perspective doesn't accurately explain the goals of encapsulation. Encapsulation is really about information hiding.

But what are we hiding, and why is hiding it desirable?

At the *struct* level, we're hiding the object's internal state and private methods. At the *package* level, we're hiding the functions, private objects, and interfaces used to achieve our goal. And at the *module* level, we're hiding the sub-packages. In all cases, we're hiding the implementation details. We are doing so to future-proof our code: to protect ourselves from our current implementation decisions and any future change in requirements. When the implementation decisions are hidden, we can refactor without impacting our users. Consider the following function:

```go
func Authenticate(username, password string) (*storage.User, error) {
    err := performBusinessLogic(username, password)
    if err != nil {
        return nil, err
    }

    return storage.LoadByUsernamePassword(username, password)
}
```

On the surface, this function looks fine. However, it is not correctly encapsulated and leaks dependency details as it returns the **User** type from the **storage** package. Thus, any changes to the **storage** package may unintentionally impact this function's users. To fully encapsulate our choice of dependency, we change the output parameter to a type defined inside this package. It may seem extreme or wasteful to marshal and unmarshal data through layers like this, and in many cases, it is. My goal here is to highlight a potential problem and allow you to decide which trade-off you want to make, complete encapsulation versus marshaling and unmarshalling.

There is another common way that encapsulation can leak unnoticed, leaking implementation details. Consider the following code:

```go
type OrderManager struct {
    storage Storage
}

type Storage interface {
    DoQuery(q string, args ...interface{}) ([]interface{}, error)
}
```

The issue here is pretty hard to spot. The **Storage** interface we inject maps too closely to the underlying choice of storage, an implementation detail. From the definition, **Storage**'s implementation likely wraps around an SQL database, but what happens when we want to change it to something else? Even if we never change this decision, why should the users of **OrderManager** need to be aware of the SQL queries, the implementation details, of another object? To rectify the encapsulation, we need to use an interface that doesn't leak the implementation choices, like this:

```
type OrderManager struct {
    storage Storage
}

type Storage interface {
    LoadByID(int) (*Order, error)
    Save(*Order) error
}
```

In this new approach, the relationship defined by the interface is abstract and does not leak any implementation details. As such, **Storage**'s implementation could be refactored without impacting this code, and any test for this code needs no knowledge of how **Storage** works.

By applying encapsulation in these ways, we also decrease the coupling of our objects, packages, and modules. This has additional benefits. Firstly, it drives each piece of our code to be more self-contained and therefore easier to understand. Secondly, because each piece is more self-contained, it is simpler to test. And finally, because of the first two points, debugging is simpler. When there's a problem, we can verify each piece easily and in isolation until we find the piece behaving unexpectedly.

Constructors

As I am sure you know, constructors are not a required or even an official part of Go, but we can still benefit from this pattern. As they're not an official part of the language, constructors can be or do anything, which leads to some mistakes. Let's examine what constructors are and what they should and shouldn't do.

Constructors are just regular functions that return a newly created object.

Constructors can be named anything, but a consistent naming style will make them easier to find and use. Typically, just the word **New** or **New** followed by the name of the struct is entirely predictable.

We should only bother to create constructors when we need them to do more than create the object. The following constructor, while it does construct a new instance of a struct, doesn't provide us with any additional value:

```
func NewStorage() *Storage {
    return &Storage{}
}
```

Constructors should ensure that an object is ready for use, but they should not open connections or initialize. This is where many people go wrong; we must separate construction from initialization. Consider this: we're writing a struct representing a gRPC client that talks to some third-party system. There are many reasons this remote system might be inaccessible when our constructor is called. Therefore, if our constructor attempts to initialize a connection pool and fails because we cannot call this remote system, our application initialization also fails. By coupling our application startup with the availability of that external system, we've forfeited the chance to be resilient and auto-recover from this failure, and, perhaps more damning, we've created a situation where the external service must be started before ours. The code smell to look out for here is a constructor that returns an error. If your constructor returns an error, it's probably doing more than just initialization.

Returning to the idea that the object is ready to use, constructors should take care of ensuring the internal state of the object is appropriately configured, as the following code does:

```
func NewStorage() *Storage {
    return &Storage{
        cache:  map[string]interface{}{},
        stopCh: make(chan struct{}),
    }
}
```

After calling this constructor, our **Storage** object is ready to use and has a predictable internal state. The internal resources, like maps, channels, and wait groups, are initialized and usable.

Finally, constructors should be as usable as you can make them. We talked earlier about reducing constructor arguments through private constructors and config injection, but often there's even more we can do to improve their usability. In cases where we have optional arguments, we can employ the *functional options* approach to differentiate between the required and optional arguments. Consider the following constructor:

```
func NewStatsDClient(host string, port int, sampleRate int, sendBuffer int, validateKeys bool,
tags []string) *StatsClient
```

By replacing all optional parameters with functional arguments, we make it very clear which arguments are required and which are optional, and significantly reduce the likelihood of usage mistakes. The resulting constructor signature is improved to:

```
func NewStatsDClient(host string, options ...Option) *StatsClient
```

If you're unfamiliar with the functional options pattern, it is discussed in more detail, including the full details of this transformation, in the *Functional Options* section in *Chapter 8*.

A little copying vs. a little dependency

You may not realize it, but every dependency a piece of code has comes at a price. Not only does importing code increase the build time, but we add complexity and coupling for each additional dependency. The added complexity comes from being unable to fully understand the code without knowledge of the imported code. Typically, we attempt to lessen this complexity cost with informative abstractions and excellent naming.

As to the coupling, there are two forms. The first is the obvious and intended. For our code to work, the imported code must perform correctly. Of course, there is nothing wrong here; that's why we're importing code in the first place. Assuming that the imported code is reliable, the cost of this coupling is far less than the gains of the import.

The second form of coupling is far less apparent and can be a lot more costly. When we import a piece of code, we become a blocker for that code to change and evolve. We depend on the import having the arguments and behavior that it had when we adopted it. If other users of this code need to change the parameters or behavior, they have to do so in a manner that doesn't break our code.

I do not offer these arguments as a reason for implementing everything ourselves or avoiding dependencies "at all costs". As with everything, there is a balance. These costs are small, but they do exist. Next time you think, "I have a function in that other package that does this", I would ask you to stop and consider a moment. Consider the costs of making that function public. Consider the costs in build time, complexity, and coupling. Please do not fall into the trap of moving this "shared" code into a **util** or **common** package without consideration. This only compounds the costs we're trying to avoid. For small amounts of code, like a single function, you will find that copying the implementation instead of adding a dependency will leave the code in a better, simpler place.

Dealing with Conflicting Goals

The types of people drawn to programming are also drawn to situations with a single correct answer. This is one reason we spend so much time and energy debating which tools/languages/ methodologies are "the right ones". My experience has led me to believe that programming is all about context, and as such, the "correct" answer differs based on the context.

Instead of offering you a "right way" for every situation, I would offer you a guiding principle. By default, we should always focus on code UX. Code with a good UX is optimized for the primary users, programmers.

It ensures the code is easy to read, maintain, and extend. There will be times when we need to intentionally write code with poor UX—for example, in cases where we need extreme performance—but these cases are rare, and this trade-off should be consciously made.

Tradeoffs between code UX and performance

In those rare cases where our application is guaranteed to have very high use or be deployed into a resource-constrained environment, then favoring performant code makes sense. As you may have seen in the first book in this series, high-performance code is often the most challenging implementation style to create, read, and maintain. If you find yourself in need of faster code, I have an 80/20 rule for code performance:

> 80% of the application's CPU time is typically spent
> in 20% of the code.

Yes, I am being tongue-in-cheek here, but it is surprising how often only a tiny portion of the code is being run most of the time. Any time spent measuring to identify this hot code path and then optimizing it, even just a little, will give significant returns. To give this a more concrete example, imagine you have two endpoints: one allows users to upload the end-of-day report, and the other performs the login. Improving the upload from 10 to 7 seconds sounds like a big win compared to improving the login from 100 to 80 milliseconds. However, the end-of-day reports API is seldom used, and the login is used all day. So, by reducing its cost, we are reducing the load on the system as a whole, which will increase the overall system capacity.

Tradeoffs between code UX and code UX

As you have undoubtedly noticed throughout this chapter and the previous one, code UX ideals and design patterns often conflict. Take the *don't repeat yourself* (DRY) principle. The DRY principle conflicts with ideals like "a little copying vs. a little dependency" or "self-contained packages". This doesn't make any of these ideas wrong or less important; it just highlights that we must make a trade-off. For this conflict, we need to ask ourselves: does our current situation prefer less but more complicated code or looser coupling and more thorough encapsulation?

There is no correct answer here, but I would reiterate my earlier point that coding is communication. While telling the computer what we want it to do for us is necessary, conveying our intentions and explaining our decisions to other programmers is vital. Just as different regions of the world speak English with different slang, idioms, and style, programmers should be aware of their team, company, and industry norms and embrace them.

Summary

The fundamental goal of code UX is usability. When code has good usability, it feels right; it feels natural, and it feels comfortable. It is important to remember that code is a form of communication with two different audiences, computers and humans. Computers are easy to satisfy—the code either compiles or doesn't—but humans are not easy to satisfy.

In this chapter, we've examined various concepts that, when selectively applied to our code, will improve its usability. We can then leverage the time savings from this improved usability and spend more time maintaining and extending the code than learning and understanding it. To wrap all of these ideas up, I would offer you one of my personal favorite mantras:

> Make it work, make it clean, then (maybe) make it fast.

We often spend too much time on the "make it work" and not enough on the "make it clean"; hopefully, this chapter has equipped you to see and address this imbalance. In the next chapter, we'll look at testing, which will help us ensure our code works and continues to do so while we're making the code clean.

Questions

1. What is code UX?

2. Why is code UX important?

3. Why is code clarity important?

4. Why is code consistency important?

5. Why is code predictability important?

6. What is the trade-off between performance and UX?

7. How do we decide between two conflicting code UX principles?

Chapter 6

Advanced Unit Testing Techniques

Introduction

Being able to write and maintain high-quality unit tests is an integral part of being an efficient and effective programmer. Yet, often, minimal effort is spent teaching people how to produce and maintain great tests. This chapter aims to remedy this.

This chapter will discuss the motivations and approaches we should use when writing unit tests, what we should and shouldn't be testing, and how much effort we should allocate to testing.

First, we will examine the theoretical aspects of unit testing. Then, we will examine Go's *table-driven test* format and leverage it to quickly produce a comprehensive and maintainable test suite. We will then expand on this and discuss test scenario construction.

We will discuss improving our tests' quality, UX, and resilience and how and when to best leverage test stubs, mocks, and recorders.

We will introduce a catalog of tricks we can use to make our tests more efficient, effective, or reliable. We will then round out the chapter and examine how testing can sometimes be detrimental and how to avoid this test-induced damage.

The following topics will be covered in this chapter:

- The What, When, Why, and How of Testing
- Table-Driven Tests
- Test Scenario Construction
- Mocks, Stubs, and Test Recorders
- Test UX and Quality
- Achieving Test Resilience
- Test Tricks That You Might Not Know

- Identifying Test-Induced Damage
- Make it Work, Make it Clean, and then, Maybe, Make it Fast

Code

To get the most out of this chapter, you will need a recent copy (1.13+) of Go installed and your favorite IDE.

Full versions of all code examples and other related material can be found at **https://github.com/corsc/Beyond-Effective-Go/tree/master/Chapter06**.

The What, When, Why, and How of Testing

When it comes to testing, the most common mistake is misunderstanding the motivations of testing itself. Some folks see testing as a burden imposed from on high. Some folks see testing, specifically test coverage, as a metric determining how well they did their job. Sorry, but neither of these is true. Writing automated tests is something programmers do to make their work life more enjoyable.

Why do we test?

We write tests to enable us to work faster and more effectively. It seems backward to claim that writing more code can make us go faster, but bear with me. We write code to add behavior to a system; to prove that behavior has been added, we must test. We could run a quick manual test; this wouldn't cost us much, and doing so would be immediately valuable. However, this value is short-lived. Once we make additional changes to the code, we can only be 100% sure that our desired behavior exists with more manual testing.

Contrast this with automated tests. It may initially cost a little more to write than manually testing, but they continue to provide value for as long as they exist. We can and should run these tests constantly as they provide a little value every time we do. Because these tests continuously ensure that the system has the desired behavior, we don't need to waste time going back and manually re-testing, nor do we run the risk of regression without noticing.

Automated tests become a safety net that reduces the risk of any additions or refactoring that we may make. Consequently, they also reduce any fear we might have relating to unknown or complex code.

With sufficient tests, our confidence in the code increases so we can make more frequent, faster, and even more adventurous changes without fear of introducing bugs.

Finally, automated tests document the author's intent for the code and are an efficient way for newcomers to learn why a piece of code exists and its expected behavior. This, in turn, improves the time newcomers take to onboard to the project and reduces the cost to existing developers to explain the code to them.

When do we test?

Many in our industry have spent a great deal of energy debating this point; I won't provide you any dogma to add to this issue. However, I will say that as long as you are testing, it doesn't matter if you write the tests before the code or after. That said, I recommend grabbing a copy of *Test Driven Development: By Example* by Kent Beck. The book's ideas are relevant to all forms of testing, and mastering them will make your tests more efficient and effective. While I often don't do test-driven development (TDD), many of the intentions, approaches, and tricks I present in this chapter are compatible with Kent's ideas.

How much should we test?

We should test just enough and no more. While we want to write tests to work faster, writing and maintaining tests has a cost. If we have too many tests, then their costs can outweigh the value they bring.

Managers often push me to give them a minimum test coverage number; when pushed, I tell them 70% per package for non-generated code. There are two reasons for this:

First, test coverage is measured by lines of code. But it doesn't matter how many lines of code we have or how many of those lines are run during our tests, what matters is behavior coverage. For each of our code's behaviors, we should have one or more tests that confirm it.

Second, there are often times when we have code that cannot reasonably be tested, and any attempt to do so would be detrimental to the quality of the code and result in test-induced damage. Consider the following code:

```
func GetUserAPI(resp http.ResponseWriter, req *http.Request) {
    ID := getID(req)

    user := loadUser(ID)
```

```
    payload, err := json.Marshal(user)
    if err != nil {
        resp.WriteHeader(http.StatusInternalServerError)
        return
    }

    _, err = resp.Write(payload)
    if err != nil {
        resp.WriteHeader(http.StatusInternalServerError)
        return
    }
}
```

Testing every single line of this code is somewhere between extremely hard and impossible. The **json.Marshal()** and **http.ResponseWriter.Write()** can both return errors, but these errors should never happen. We could pass in a mock implementation of **http.ResponseWriter** that returns an error, but what would we be testing? We'd be testing the mock and the fact that we handled the error. Neither of these are features, but somewhat insignificant implementation details. Additionally, we would end up with a test that returns little value, a mock, and a test that we now have to maintain. This is a form of test-induced damage that we will examine more at the end of this chapter.

The final reason I offer 70% is experience. It has been my experience that 70% is easy to achieve and maintain, and the more we push beyond this number, the more time and effort it takes. We can achieve higher coverage, but often the costs outweigh the benefits.

Returning to our question of how much we should test, we should also acknowledge that tests come in many forms and consider how much time we should devote to each form. The three most common forms of tests that I use are unit tests, user acceptance tests (UAT), and end-to-end (E2E) tests. Each type of test has differing goals, strengths, and weaknesses that we must be mindful of when using them.

Unit tests

Unit tests aim to confirm the existence of a particular behavior in the unit being tested. Please note that I am choosing my words very carefully here. A unit is not necessarily a single function; it is not necessarily a single struct. A unit can be these things, but it can also be a collection of structs and functions that collaborate to add a behavior to a package.

Let's explore an example. Assume we have a **bank** package responsible for interaction with an API provided by an external company. Inside our **bank** package is a struct called **Account** with the following method:

```
func (a *Account) Transfer(amount int, recipient string) error
```

Without looking at the implementation, we can define our expected behaviors as follows:

- When we try to transfer a negative amount, we should receive an error.

- When we try to transfer to a non-existent account, we should receive an error.

- When the API is down, we should receive an error.

- When the API returns an unexpected or garbled response, we should receive an error.

- When we make a valid request, and the API works, we should not receive an error.

We should have at least one unit test for each of these behaviors. By doing so, we ensure that all our intended behaviors are present and document these behaviors for posterity.

Returning to our definition of "units", if all of the code required for interacting with our external API existed within a single struct, our unit tests would only involve this single struct, but what happens if our implementation looks like this?

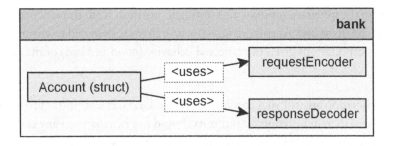

Figure 6.1—Sample Bank package structure

If we defined our units as structs, we would have to test **Account**, **requestEncoder**, and **requestDecoder** separately. This is unnecessary and wastes time and effort. Look at our previously listed desired behaviors; request encoding or decoding is not mentioned. This is not because they're not essential; it's because they're a small part of the broader behavior. Having acknowledged that our three structs would not exist without each other and they must collaborate to achieve our goal, we should treat them as a single unit.

With this definition of *unit*, we can see both the strengths and weaknesses of unit tests. The main strength and weakness of unit tests is their small scope. Because the scope is small, the tests are easy to write and understand. These unit tests will document and enforce the author's intentions on a small scale. Also, these tests are fast to execute, so we can run them constantly. Conversely, the test's small scope is also a weakness as it only confirms a unit's behavior rather than the system's behavior (or features). For this, we need to take a system-level perspective.

User acceptance tests

User acceptance tests focus on confirming that the system behaves as the user expects it to, independently and in isolation from its external dependencies. The main difference between unit tests and UATs is the scope of the tests. In our unit tests, we focused on an individual unit of the code, perhaps introducing mocks or stubs to isolate that unit from the others. For UATs, we are testing most (or all) of the codebase.

It is possible that my definition of UATs differs from yours. I apologize for any confusion. The nature and goal of these tests don't fit into the definitions of component tests because the scope is too broad and the testing is done from outside the system (i.e. from the user's perspective). Nor do these tests qualify as integration tests, because we are intentionally decoupling from the integration points and testing in isolation from those dependencies. I have chosen to call them user acceptance tests because they are designed to ensure the system meets the user's expectations given the expected behavior (good and bad) of the dependencies.

Test scope and isolation are still vital considerations for UATs. It's important to remember that we're testing our system in isolation, so our tests should not be reliant on any external systems. I should note I do not mean that these tests must mock databases, filesystems, caches, or any resources that can reasonably be expected to exist in a development environment or CI build slave, but rather any third-party systems. You can mock the database and caches, but it often has a terrible cost-to-value ratio.

UAT scenarios should be constructed from the perspective of the system's users with minimal awareness of the implementation details. For example, if we had a login API, the scenarios might be:

- When the database is running correctly, and the username and password are correct, we should receive success.

- When the database is down, then we should receive an error.

- When the database is running correctly and the username or password is missing, we should receive an error.

- When the database is running correctly, and the username or password is wrong, we should receive an error.

As you can see, the only implementation detail in these scenarios is the existence of the database. We could refactor these scenarios to remove this awareness, but it doesn't give us any value.

As written, our scenarios are somewhat generic. We could tighten them up to match our API contract and include aspects like expected response codes. Doing this would enforce and document our API contract more thoroughly. However, please don't take this too far and enforce responses to the minute detail; doing this would make the tests brittle and more troublesome to maintain. Balancing scenario strictness and brittleness will vary from project to project and personal preference. Try to find the minimum strictness you can get away with and then be more strict when bugs or deficiencies are discovered or when the risk and cost of mistakes become significant.

When considering the coverage for UATs, we cannot measure it from a lines-of-code perspective but rather from a feature perspective. Some features are more important than others and, as such, should be tested more comprehensively. Some features are more complicated or prone to bugs than others and, as such, will require more scenarios to ensure that they work as expected. Some features will involve more dependencies than others and, consequently, will have more ways to fail and therefore need more scenarios.

Moving on to the strengths and weaknesses of UATs: the key strength of UATs is that they confirm that the system does what the user expects. By extension, UATs demonstrate that the application delivers the value intended.

UATs function independently of external systems, which is both a strength and a weakness. It's a strength because the tests are entirely under our control and highly dependable. However, it's a weakness because we're testing against mocks, not external dependencies. There is, therefore, a risk that our mocks and the external dependency have different behavior. We can address this weakness with end-to-end tests, as we will see in a moment.

However, the main weakness of UATs is the scope of the tests. Because the scope is broad, it can be time-consuming to locate the underlying cause when there are problems. There is no real counter to this weakness. Often, all we can do is write a failing UAT, fire up the debugger, and then step through the code to find the bug or the area where the bug might be and throw some unit tests at the problem area.

End-to-end tests

End-to-end (E2E) tests are essentially UATs performed with all external dependencies. These tests aim to build on the behavior confirmed by the UATs and verify that the system has the desired behaviors when involving all external dependencies.

When constructing our E2E scenarios, we only need to look as far as our UAT scenarios. They already define our system's features and how our application should react when our dependencies work as expected.

Unless we also control the external dependencies or have a great collaboration with the teams that do, we will generally only be able to test the happy path scenarios involving these external dependencies. This is fine; we've already used UATs to confirm that our system works as intended. We only need E2Es to confirm that the external systems behave how we think they do (the same as our mocks).

The strength of E2E tests is also their weakness: they involve external dependencies. They will confirm our system performs as expected in a production-like environment; however, because our tests rely on these external resources, they will only be as reliable as these resources and the test environment. Therefore, we may see test failures not caused by our code.

The test pyramid

Now that we've defined the different types of tests and examined their strengths and weaknesses, we can return to our original question: *how much should we test*? As an industry, we are always time-constrained, so we must spend our time as efficiently as possible. The *test pyramid* is a handy visual mnemonic first introduced by Mike Cohn and often discussed by Martin Fowler and others, whose goal is to remind us where and how we should spend our testing effort. Here is my version of the test pyramid:

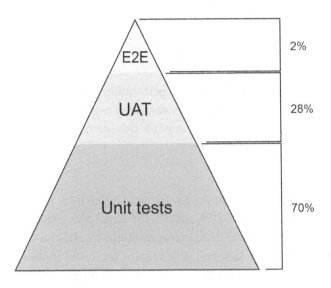

Figure 6.2—Test Pyramid

As you can see in this diagram, I recommend spending most (70%) of our testing effort on unit testing. This is because we spend most of our programming effort adding behaviors to our units of code. Unit tests, therefore, support our primary task. The fact that these tests are also the easiest to understand and the cheapest to write and run are pleasant additional benefits.

I recommend spending most of the remaining effort (28%) verifying that the system has the behaviors our users expect by adding UATs. At the end of the day, adding user-focused behavior is what we are being paid for. But, compared to unit tests, UATs tend to have higher construction costs, debugging, and maintenance costs. This is why, despite the fact they are aligned with user value, we should be spending less effort on UATs than on unit tests.

Allocating only the remaining 2% of our effort to E2E tests may be shocking, but these tests have very high construction and maintenance costs. Additionally, they have a poor signal-to-noise ratio, given that they can fail for reasons unrelated to our code. In my experience, when a system has sufficient unit tests and UATs, most of the remaining issues are configuration, which is not addressed well by E2E tests. Testing how our system responds to missing or inappropriate configuration should be done at the unit or UAT level; I prefer to test with unit tests and then have the rest of the codebase assume that the config is sane. This will result in less code and a faster system overall.

When issues are caused by external systems not performing as expected, this is not a reason to add more E2E tests. Instead, we should add these failures as mocked responses in our UATs. This way, we ensure that our system can account for this unexpected behavior and respond predictably.

The primary thing to remember about the test pyramid is that it is a mnemonic. While I have given you concrete numbers of 70%, 28%, and 2%, the actual percentage of effort depends on your application, your team, and the deployment environment. It is possible to have a successful application without E2E tests; I've seen many successful applications like this. If you have no tests and want to start, start with unit tests. After you are comfortable with testing, adding some UATs will be significantly easier and further improve your confidence in your application.

What should we be testing?

After choosing whether or not to test, choosing what to test is the most impactful decision. I am not talking about a choice between unit tests and UATs but rather the tests' entry points. Consider the following struct:

OrderManager
Process(order Order) error validate(order Order) error chargeCustomer(order Order) error sendReceipt(order Order, receiptNo int) error

Figure 6.3—OrderManager struct

You will notice that this struct has four methods, one public and three private. The public method forms the API or entry point from which other parts of the system interact, and the three private methods are implementation details. If our goals were test isolation and writing the smallest, simplest possible tests, we could test all four of these methods individually. With the exception of the tests for **Process()**, all of our tests would have a small scope and be easy to understand. This sounds great, right?

Consider what happens when we want to make changes. What happens when we decide to have multiple payment options? At a minimum, the tests for **chargeCustomer()** (which is specific to the card payment option) need to be drastically changed, perhaps even discarded. However, if we've written all our tests against the **Process()** method, only a few (preferably none) of the existing tests would break when we make these changes. When tests break, there are two causes. The first is regression. Highlighting and preventing this regression is one of the primary purposes of the tests. The second occurs when the test implementation is too tightly coupled with the implementation of the code under test. This form of test breakage indicates an issue with the tests rather than the code. In this case, the problem is our choice of "unit" for our unit tests. The existence of **chargeCustomer()** is an implementation detail, not a behavior. Because it is an implementation detail, it has a high potential to change. Any tests relying on the current implementation are likely to break during refactoring and, therefore, introduce resistance to this change. As a result, we may become reluctant to refactor our code, which leads to technical debt. Or if we do perform the refactoring, the fact that these tests are tightly coupled to the implementation has cost us additional work to maintain the tests.

To avoid these problems, we take our unit as the object or objects that process an order and then test the unit from its entry point. With this approach, our tests are more stable and less a reflection of the current implementation. In this example, the unit is the entire **OrderManager** struct, and the entry point is the **Process()** method. Additionally, as **Process()** is the API contract between this unit and our other units, it is naturally resistant to change.

If you are familiar with the TDD or BDD ideologies, you will notice some parallels here; we are attempting to verify the behavior of our code without any coupling to the implementation details. This focus on behavior and avoidance of implementation details will ensure that our tests are resilient to refactoring and, therefore, low cost. This is best demonstrated with some examples. Let's assume the **validate()** method of our **OrderManager** looks like this:

```
func (o *OrderManager) validate(order Order) error {
    if order.CustomerName == "" {
        return errors.New("customer name cannot be empty")
    }
```

```go
    if order.ShippingAddress == "" {
        return errors.New("shipping address cannot be empty")
    }

    return nil
}
```

Now, consider the following test scenario for name validation:

```go
func TestOrderManager_Process_sadPath_nameValidation(t *testing.T) {
    // inputs
    order := Order{
        CustomerName: "",
    }
    expectedErr := errors.New("customer name cannot be empty")

    // call object under test
    orderManager := &OrderManager{}
    resultErr := orderManager.Process(order)

    // validation
    require.Equal(t, expectedErr, resultErr, "expected error: %s. was: %s", expectedErr,
resultErr)
}
```

At first glance, this looks fine, but there are two issues. Firstly, this test only passes due to its intimate knowledge of the implementation details. If we were to change the validation sequence, this test would break and need to be changed. The second issue is that the test validates the exact error thrown. This is a prevalent mistake; if the error changes for any reason, this test will break. This is a simple example, but hopefully you can see that these tests will likely break when we refactor our **OrderManager** implementation. Tests suffering from this problem should be considered brittle tests because they will break easily and require continued attention. Maintaining brittle tests upsets the cost/benefit ratio of our testing and refactoring efforts, which, in turn, discourages us from testing and refactoring. Fortunately, the fix for these issues is simple. Compare the following code with the previous implementation:

```go
func TestOrderManager_Process_sadPath_nameValidationImproved(t *testing.T) {
    // inputs
    order := Order{
        CustomerName:  "",
```

```
        ShippingAddress: "123 Sesame Street",
    }
    expectAnErr := true

    // call object under test
    orderManager := &OrderManager{}
    resultErr := orderManager.Process(order)

    // validation
    require.Equal(t, expectAnErr, resultErr != nil, "expect an error: %s. err was: %s",
expectAnErr, resultErr)
}
```

You can see that our **order** input is now completely valid, except for the condition we are testing, and instead of testing for a specific error, we are testing that an error was returned. Additionally, our test only focuses on the behavior described as: "When the customer name is missing from the order, we should throw an error." I would also like to draw your attention to the boolean variable **expectAnError**. This is perhaps not what you might have expected. This choice is intentional and it allows us to test behavior and not implementation details. This change brings us looser coupling between the implementation and the tests and will give the test greater durability against future changes. When writing a single test like this we can just use **require.NoError()** instead of **require.Equal()**, but I have written it this way because most of the time we should be using the table-driven tests pattern, which we will be looking more at in an upcoming section, and in that structure some scenarios will return an error and some won't.

This same approach can and should be applied to the configuration of mocks. The following are some tips relating to the use of mocks:

1. We should configure mocks even if we know they will not be called by the current implementation. The goal is to be resilient to refactoring.

2. We should only verify whether a mock was called or not called when the call is significant. For example, suppose our **OrderManager** had a mock for charging the customer. In that case, we should verify that it was not called when validation failed, to ensure we were not charging customers inappropriately.

3. In most cases, we should only verify that the mock was called and not check every individual parameter sent to the mock. Again, the yardstick is the significance of the parameter and the likelihood of mistakes. If you feel the need to verify a parameter's

value, try not to do so for all the test scenarios, as this increases the maintenance costs of your tests. For example, if our **OrderManager** had a mock for emailing the receipt, we might decide to verify that the email address was passed. However, we should avoid validating the complete content of the email body, as this is likely to change frequently.

The line between behavior and implementation detail can be tough to determine, but I offer three additional tips to address this:

1. It is more efficient to default to loosely coupled tests and only add specificity when necessary—with "necessary" to be determined by experience, business requirements, or bug reports.

2. When in doubt, remember that our goal is to write tests that confirm behavior but are reasonably resilient to refactoring.

3. It does get more comfortable with experience.

When we focus on testing behavior and construct our tests to be as ignorant of the implementation as possible, the result will be cheap, resilient, and valuable tests.

What should we not be testing?

After reading the previous section, you may have thought, "If we are testing behaviors, then why don't we skip unit tests and only write UATs?". This is not an irrational thought. However, as we have discussed, the weakness of UATs is their broad scope, which makes for larger, more complicated tests and slower debugging. Additionally, code reuse would be risky without unit tests to ensure our units' behaviors.

Given that I have spent most of this chapter trying to convince you to test and discussing the best options for writing your tests, it might seem strange to assert that there are things we should not be writing tests for. But here goes. The following is a list of aspects of our system we should not test or not test directly:

1. **Non-API methods and functions**—Any methods or functions not directly called by other parts of the code should not be tested directly. They are implementation

details and likely to change. We will indirectly test this code via tests of our code unit's entry points. However, there is no need to be too dogmatic about this point. If you have a particularly complex function that you want to test in isolation, applying tests directly to this function can be efficient.

2. **Anything too simple for us to get wrong**—Writing tests for code that we cannot possibly get wrong is a waste of effort. Once in a while, we might have to write a test to appease some arbitrary unit-test coverage requirements, but if we can, we should save time.

3. **Other people's code**—Similarly to the previous point, writing and maintaining tests for code we do not own wastes time. We should trust the libraries and modules provided by others. If there is ever a case when we don't trust and need to test, it is better for everyone to open a pull request with tests for the external party. There is an exception to this point. When dealing with unknown or undocumented code, writing tests to explore and confirm the behavior can be helpful. That said, these are tests we want to either not check into our project or skip running most of the time.

4. **Generated code**—Extending from the previous point, when we use third-party tools to generate code, we should consider the result "other people's code". The owner of the code generation tool is responsible for ensuring that the code they generate works as expected; we're not. Yes, it is possible to also generate tests to test generated code, but most of the time, this wastes time and effort.

Hopefully, throughout this section, you have seen the underlying threads of productivity and value. The what, why, when, and how of testing presented here is all about engineering a situation where we spend the minimum possible effort writing and maintaining tests but still extract maximum value from this effort.

Table-Driven Tests

As experienced Gophers, you are familiar with table-driven tests (TDT); they are the most efficient way to write Go tests and should be used most of the time. The reasons for this include:

- They result in a significant reduction in the duplication between different tests of the same unit.

- They make adding more test scenarios to existing unit tests very easy.

- They are very cleanly organized.

- The resulting test output is cleanly and usefully grouped.

This section will explore how to get the most out of TDTs by working through an example. First, let's introduce the code we're going to test:

```go
type OrderManager struct {
    bank   Bank
    sender ReceiptSender
}

func (o *OrderManager) Process(ctx context.Context, order Order) (receiptNo string, err error)
{
    // implementation details removed
}

type Bank interface {
    Charge(ctx context.Context, customerName string, amount int64) (string, error)
}

type ReceiptSender interface {
    SendReceipt(ctx context.Context, customerEmail string, amount int64, receiptNo string)
error
}
```

I have intentionally removed all the implementation details and left only the publicly visible parts: the API and the injected dependencies. The object under test is reasonably straightforward. It has one public method, **Process()**, which serves the API for users; it has two injected and abstracted dependencies, **Bank** and **ReceiptSender**, for which we've defined local interfaces. We're using local interfaces so that we're entirely decoupled from where these interfaces are implemented and so that we are very explicitly stating our requirements. This approach follows the interface segregation principle and the dependency inversion principle. If you want to see the full implementation, it is here: **https://github.com/corsc/Beyond-Effective-Go/tree/master/Chapter06/02_table_driven_tests/example.go**.

Now, let's introduce the test:

```
func TestOrderManager_Process(t *testing.T) {
    scenarios := []struct {
        scenarioDesc       string
        inputOrder         Order
        configureMockBank  func(bank *MockBank)
        configureMockSender func(sender *MockReceiptSender)
        expectedReceiptNo  string
        expectAnErr        bool
    }{
        // scenarios removed
    }

    // test implementation removed
}
```

In this first part, we've defined the test name using the godoc format. This is not required, but it's a good practice. We've also defined a slice of inline structs that hold our test scenarios. An inline struct is not required but rather an optimization that removes the need to formally define a struct that we wouldn't use outside of this test. In this format, the struct type is inside the test and, therefore, very easy to find and change as needed.

The first struct field **scenarioDesc** is a string used to describe the test. We will use this to differentiate the different test scenarios in the results. We can enter anything as a description, but every description should be unique and informative within a single test.

The next field **inputOrder** will contain the value used when calling **Process()**. If our test had multiple inputs, then we would add more fields alongside **inputOrder**. Typically, it's best to prefix them consistently, like **inputOrder**, **inputItem**, etc., as this will improve our ability to quickly scan the code. It is also important to note that our test inputs are sometimes insignificant—for example, if we're not validating the input values, or if different inputs do not result in fundamentally different outputs. In these cases, we can save some work and hardcode the inputs.

Next, we have **configureMockBank** and **configureMockSender**; these are closures we will use to configure our mocks. We use closures instead of listing the mock responses as a series of variables (input and outputs) because it makes the tests more comfortable to read. Also, depending on the mock library, it also gives us greater flexibility using the mocks. Using closures can result in long scenarios and significant duplication, but we have some tricks later in the chapter to reduce that cost.

The next field, **expectedReceiptNo**, holds the expected result of the **Process()** call. In cases where our method under test has multiple outputs, we would need to come up with a better name, but **expectedReceiptNo** is just fine when there is only one. This consistency also allows us to use code generation or copy/paste and be usefully consistent across tests.

The final field, **expectAnErr**, is another example of testing behavior and not implementation details, as we discussed in the previous section. If we were to check for the exact error, our tests would become very tightly coupled with the implementation, and any refactoring or any change in the error description would break the tests and cause us extra work.

There are cases when testing for the exact error or checking for a wrapped error is necessary, as the error itself is a significant part of the API contract. But, generally, we should refrain from validating the exact error returned.

Moving on, I'll skip over the test scenarios for a moment as we'll dive deeper into this in the next section. Instead, let's look at the rest of the test:

```go
func TestOrderManager_Process(t *testing.T) {
    scenarios := []struct {
        scenarioDesc        string
        inputOrder          Order
        configureMockBank   func(bank *MockBank)
        configureMockSender func(sender *MockReceiptSender)
        expectedReceiptNo   string
        expectAnErr         bool
    }{
        // scenarios removed
    }
}
```

```go
for _, s := range scenarios {
    scenario := s
    t.Run(scenario.scenarioDesc, func(t *testing.T) {
        // inputs
        ctx, cancel := context.WithTimeout(context.Background(), 1*time.Second)
        defer cancel()

        // mocks
        mockBank := &MockBank{}
        scenario.configureMockBank(mockBank)

        mockReceiptSender := &MockReceiptSender{}
        scenario.configureMockSender(mockReceiptSender)

        // call object under test
        orderManager := NewOrderManager(mockBank, mockReceiptSender)
        result, resultErr := orderManager.Process(ctx, scenario.inputOrder)

        // validation
        require.Equal(t, scenario.expectAnErr, resultErr != nil, "expected error: %t err
was: %s", scenario.expectAnErr, resultErr)
        assert.Equal(t, scenario.expectedReceiptNo, result, "expected receipt no")
    })
}
```

As you can see, we are completing the TDT style by iterating over our scenarios with a **for** loop. On the line after the **for** statement, we create a copy of the test scenario, so we don't have any data race/concurrency issues when using the scenario object. On the next line, we are using **t.Run()** to run all of the scenarios as separate sub-tests. When using sub-tests, we must be mindful of concurrency and object reuse. Any variable declared outside of the sub-test scope will be used by all sub-tests, which can impact the tests. Similarly, if we use **t.Parallel()** and run the sub-tests concurrently, all the tests can potentially run at the same time, which may also have an impact if we are not careful. You will also notice that we use the **scenarioDesc** field in our scenario to give the sub-tests useful names.

The use of **t.Run()** to create sub-tests is also significant because now each test scenario is run in a separate function, which allows us to use **defer** to clean up our tests, which we could not do with a naked **for** loop that didn't call out to separate functions.

As for the sub-test, we are using a fairly standard structure with four steps:

1. Define and build the inputs.
2. Build and configure the mocks by calling the appropriate closures on our test scenario.
3. Build and call the object under test, including injecting our mocks.
4. Validate the results against our expectations.

There are two notable tricks here that I would highlight. Firstly, when using a context, we are explicitly setting a timeout instead of using **context.Background()**, ensuring that our tests will end, either as they are supposed to or by context timeout. This will save us some time if our code has dependency or concurrency issues.

The second trick is how we are validating the results. We are checking **resultErr** before the **result**. This likely feels backward; however, the ordering is significant. When our tests fail, they will often return an error we were not expecting. When this happens, the other output values are likely less meaningful, and the comparison between the **expectedReceiptNo** value and the **result** value (which will not match) adds a lot of noise to the test output.

We are also using **require.Equal()**, which calls **t.FailNow()** when the assertion fails. This immediately stops the test's execution, ensuring the test output is concise and easier to use.

Test Scenario Construction

The secret to test scenario construction is to remember that our goal is to verify the expected behavior of the unit we are testing. Our goal is not to test every possible input or even every line of code in our unit but to test just enough to be comfortable that the unit behaves as expected. The difference here is like the difference between an opinion poll and an election. A poll attempts to record sufficient samples to get an accurate prediction of the outcome without going through the immense time, expense, and complexity of running a full election. There may be times when testing every possible input is worth the expense, e.g. when someone's life is on the line, but in most cases, there is just not enough return on investment.

When constructing test scenarios, there are three main aspects to consider:

1. What are the intended features and behaviors?
2. What's the impact of different input types?
3. How could things go wrong?

Let's dig deeper into these aspects using the **OrderManager** example from the previous section as a reference.

What are the intended features and behaviors?

The intended features and behaviors tend to be obvious; after all, they are the reason for the unit's existence. These scenarios are often our *happy path* scenarios. Happy path scenario tests ensure we observe the expected outcome when all the inputs are correct and complete and all dependencies work correctly. Please note that by "observe the expected outcome" we are not always talking about output values. Sometimes units have an impact beyond their returned values, like, for example, writing data to a file or database. In such cases, our tests should verify these outcomes and the returned values. Returning to our example from the previous section, the happy path test looks like this:

```
scenarios := []struct {
    scenarioDesc        string
    inputOrder          Order
    configureMockBank   func(bank *MockBank)
    configureMockSender func(sender *MockReceiptSender)
    expectedReceiptNo   string
    expectAnErr         bool
}{
    {
        scenarioDesc: "Happy path",
        inputOrder: Order{
            CustomerName: "Oscar",
```

```
            CustomerEmail:  "me@example.com",
            Amount:            123,
        },
        configureMockBank: func(bank *MockBank) {
            bank.On("Charge", mock.Anything, mock.Anything,
    mock.Anything).Return("ABC-123", nil)
        },
        configureMockSender: func(sender *MockReceiptSender) {
            sender.On("SendReceipt", mock.Anything, mock.Anything, mock.Anything,
    mock.Anything).Return(nil)
        },
        expectedReceiptNo: "ABC-123",
        expectAnErr:        false,
    },
}
```

Hopefully, nothing is too surprising in the above example, but I would draw your attention to a few aspects. We are populating all of the fields by name. This ensures that our scenarios are always easy to read and that if we add more fields, it will continue to work without changes.

You will also notice that we are not validating our mocks' inputs and how often the mocks are called. This might seem weird or even wrong to you, but it is an intentional, strongly recommended choice. If we were to validate these things, our tests would become strongly coupled with the current implementation and, as such, would be more likely to break due to refactoring. This risk of breakage would then incentivize us to avoid refactoring and would make the tests cost more to maintain. None of these are beneficial. There will be times when it is imperative to test the exact parameters passed to the mocks—for example, when they are the observable side effect of the unit we are testing. There are also times when it is vital to validate the number of times a mock is called—for example, when calling a mock related to charging a customer's account. But, in most cases, the coupling and maintenance costs outweigh any benefits of verification. This is another instance of the idea from earlier to test just enough to be confident of the code and then only go further later if/when it is proven necessary.

What's the impact of different input types?

There are three possible situations when considering the impact of different input values on our unit under test:

1. **Different input values do not impact the observable outcomes**—In these cases, we don't need to include inputs in our test scenarios. Defining and reusing a single set of request parameters is sufficient.

2. **Different input values change how the unit behaves**—In these cases, we should add additional happy path tests for each behavior type.

3. **Some input values can cause errors**—These error inputs are user errors. The volume of possible mistakes a user might make is often significant, and adding one scenario for each would be a lot of work. To reduce this burden, it's best to only add scenarios for mistakes that users are likely to make and, wherever possible, to categorize error types and create additional scenarios accordingly.

In our example, incomplete inputs will result in an error, and therefore we will need to add a *sad path* scenario like this:

```
scenarios := []struct {
    scenarioDesc        string
    inputOrder          Order
    configureMockBank   func(bank *MockBank)
    configureMockSender func(sender *MockReceiptSender)
    expectedReceiptNo   string
    expectAnErr         bool
}{
    {
        scenarioDesc: "Sad path - customer name is missing",
        inputOrder: Order{
            CustomerName: "", // name missing
            CustomerEmail: "me@example.com",
            Amount:          123,
        },
        configureMockBank: func(bank *MockBank) {
            bank.On("Charge", mock.Anything, mock.Anything,
mock.Anything).Return("ABC-123", nil)
```

```
        },
        configureMockSender: func(sender *MockReceiptSender) {
            sender.On("SendReceipt", mock.Anything, mock.Anything, mock.Anything,
    mock.Anything).Return(nil)
        },
        expectedReceiptNo: "",
        expectAnErr:         true,
    },
}
```

Contrasting this scenario with the happy path, you will notice that we've changed the input and then specified that we expect an empty string result and an error. You will also notice that the configuration of the mocks is exactly the same as the happy path, even though, if we were to look at the implementation, the dependencies are not called in the case of a validation error. This may seem strange, but this choice reduces the scope of the behavior we verify to only the input validation. If our validation logic was not implemented correctly, this scenario would fail, and the outputs would not be the expected values. Such an error is more evident than one resulting from the mocks not being configured.

How could things go wrong?

We have discussed that incorrect input values can cause errors and that we should construct sad path scenarios for them, but this is not the only way our unit can result in errors. It is also possible for our dependencies to fail. When constructing test scenarios for dependency issues, it is essential to remember that there are often many possible return values from the dependencies, and we don't need to test them all.

We should also remember that it is not the dependency or its implementation we are testing but how we react to the different types of responses from the dependency. For example, our **Bank** dependency's **Charge()** function might return errors for an invalid credit card number, insufficient funds, or a timeout. However, if we don't handle these errors differently, the additional scenarios are a waste of effort. As a general rule of thumb, we should have at least one sad path scenario for each dependency. In our example, we have two dependencies and two matching scenarios. Below is one of these scenarios:

```
scenarios := []struct {
    scenarioDesc        string
```

```
        inputOrder          Order
        configureMockBank    func(bank *MockBank)
        configureMockSender func(sender *MockReceiptSender)
        expectedReceiptNo    string
        expectAnErr          bool
    }{
        {
            scenarioDesc: "Sad path - charge failed",
            inputOrder: Order{
                CustomerName: "Oscar",
                CustomerEmail: "me@example.com",
                Amount:        123,
            },
            configureMockBank: func(bank *MockBank) {
                bank.On("Charge", mock.Anything, mock.Anything, mock.Anything).Return("",
errors.New("failed"))
            },
            configureMockSender: func(sender *MockReceiptSender) {},
            expectedReceiptNo:    "",
            expectAnErr:          true,
        },
    }
```

In the above code, you will notice that we have configured our **MockBank** to fail and not configured the **MockReceiptSender** at all. In the previous example, we configured the mocks to return successfully, even though we expected them not to be called. This is the most durable approach, but in this case, there are other considerations. From a behavior perspective, it is wrong for us to send a receipt if we fail to charge the customer. To ensure this, we do not configure the **MockReceiptSender** and ensure the test fails noisily if this expectation fails.

If you are interested in the other dependency failure scenario or seeing the testing in its entirety, you can find it here:

**https://github.com/corsc/Beyond-Effective-Go/tree/master/
Chapter06/02_table_driven_tests/example_test.go.**

Mocks, Stubs, and Test Recorders

Mocks, stubs, and test recorders are different tools we can inject into our units during testing. We use them to replace our dependencies with objects that perform predictably. In the case of mocks and test recorders, they also record how our code interacts with our dependencies and enable us to verify our usage of the dependencies.

This section will examine each of these testing tools, discuss some tips for using them more effectively, and mention some pitfalls to avoid. Firstly, let's start with some tips that apply to mocks, stubs, and test recorders:

Tip #1: We are testing units of code and not necessarily individual objects. Therefore, we do not need to mock every dependency, only those that do not form part of the unit under test. A typical unit boundary is the package or the module (e.g., sub-packages). We should seldom mock objects from within the same package.

Tip #2: Tests should be isolated from each other. Tests must be constructed so that they cannot impact each other. Otherwise, they will not be reliable. If we have code that utilizes global or external state, replacing this state with an injected mock will ensure the tests are independent. This tip should not be taken to mean that we must mock every external dependency. For example, databases can be mocked, but this can be a lot of trouble, so you might find it more efficient to let the tests write to the database but write them so that they do not impact each other.

Tip #3: Mocks are test code and should always reside in a **_test.go** file. Folks who hold the DRY principle dear often publish mocks from one module for use in others. I appreciate the intent, but this introduces risk and coupling where there does not need to be. These mocks could accidentally be used during production execution, which could be disastrous.

This mistake is sometimes triggered by the incorrect placement of the interfaces. When programmers take a Java-style approach and define the interfaces beside the implementation, rather than the Go approach of defining interfaces where the implementation is used, the natural instinct is to define the mock in a central location and share it. As we will see later in this section, generating mocks and keeping them up to date can be automated, so the duplication cost is negligible.

Tip #4: When using mocks, we must remember that we are not testing our dependencies but rather how our code interacts and reacts to the dependency. We can save some effort by not testing every possible response from the dependencies but instead designing our tests to only include the significant cases and the different outcomes. Similarly, while we can configure our mocks to test the parameters we are sending to the mocks, this is often unnecessary as these are mistakes we are unlikely to make. This is especially true in cases where our unit under test is not modifying the inputs provided by the user before passing them to the dependency.

Now, let's look at tips and pitfalls relating to the specific tools.

Mocks and the Mockery tool

While writing your own mock implementations is possible, I do not recommend it. The most effective way to use mocks is to adopt a mock library that includes the ability to generate mocks. Personally, I use **https://vektra.github.io/mockery/**. Mockery is a command-line tool that generates mocks based on interfaces. To use Mockery, we can either create a config file or decorate our interfaces with go generate configuration like this:

```
//go:generate mockery --name=Bank
type Bank interface {
    Charge(ctx context.Context, customerName string, amount int64) (string, error)
}
```

With the configuration in place, we can use the call **go generate** on our file, package, or project. This command will find the interface **Bank** and generate a mock implementation for us. This gives us a very efficient way to generate our mocks and keep them up to date. Now that we have generated our mock, let's examine the three most common ways to use it.

The first and most common approach involves simple parameters and return values. We have actually mentioned this already:

```
bank.On("Charge", mock.Anything, mock.Anything, mock.Anything).Return("ABC-123", nil)
```

This command tells our mock: "when the **Charge()** method is called with three arguments of any value, return a **receiptNo** of **ABC-123** and a **nil** error".

This approach is excellent for most situations, but it has a weakness in that it will return the same outcome no matter how many times the mock is called; this leads us to the second approach. We can configure the mocks to react differently based on when or how they are called. Consider the following code:

```
bank.On("Charge", mock.Anything, "John", mock.Anything).Return("", errors.New("insufficient
funds"))

bank.On("Charge", mock.Anything, "May", mock.Anything).Return("ABC-123", nil)
```

In this example, we use the inputs to differentiate which response we get. When the customer is "**John**", the mock returns insufficient funds, but it passes when the user is "**May**".

Similarly, you can have the mocks react differently based on the execution order, like so:

```
bank.On("Charge", mock.Anything, mock.Anything, mock.Anything).Return("",
errors.New("timeout")).Once()

bank.On("Charge", mock.Anything, mock.Anything, mock.Anything).Return("ABC-123", nil)
```

In this example, the mock returns an error the first time but succeeds on the second attempt. This can be very useful for simulating transient errors. This same approach can also return different successful values for the different calls.

This final and least common usage of Mockery is the **Run(func())** method. This version is helpful for methods that mutate the input variables, when we need to validate parts of the input without specifying the entire object or to control the mock's output value based on a function instead of a static result. For this example, we are using a different interface and mock, as you can see below:

```
// The interface we are mocking
type ReceiptDecorator interface {
    Decorate(receipt *Receipt) error
}
```

```
// configuring the mock of the ReceiptDecorator using the Run(func()) style
decorator.On("Decorate", mock.Anything).
    Run(func(args mock.Arguments) {
        receipt, ok := args.Get(0).(*Receipt)
        assert.True(t, ok)

        receipt.ID = "ABC-123"
    }).Return(nil)
```

In the example, we defined an anonymous function and supplied it to the **Run()** method. Inside this function, we are accessing the argument used to call the mock and then mutating that object, presumably for a similar outcome to how the actual dependency would have done. As discussed earlier, this approach offers many different test options; it can even be used to add signals (i.e., writes to a channel) for testing concurrent code or for introducing panics to test panic recovery. Despite its flexibility, I recommend using it sparingly, as the resulting tests are a little more complicated and more work to create and maintain.

Stubs

Stubs differ from mocks in that they are simpler and focus solely on returning either a fixed or simple value. If we revisit our previous example and, this time, create a stub implementation of our **Bank** interface, it would look like this:

```
type StubErrorBank struct {}

func (s *StubErrorBank) Charge(ctx context.Context, customerName string, amount int64)
(string, error) {
    return "", errors.New("charge failed")
}
```

The example above is the most straightforward possible stub implementation, as the outcome is fixed. Sometimes, more is needed. For those cases, we can extend this further and use member variables to provide simple values like this:

```
type StubErrorBank struct {
    receiptNo string
    err       error
}
```

```
func (s *StubErrorBank) Charge(ctx context.Context, customerName string, amount int64)
(string, error) {
    return s.receiptNo, s.err
}
```

This second approach is more flexible but requires us to configure the outputs for every test case.

When working with stubs, I will typically use the fixed response style first, and only if needed will I upgrade the stub to a combination of these two styles. In this way, the stub returns a default value if it is not configured but allows configuration when necessary. As always, the underlying goal is to achieve my goals with the least amount of hassle.

Quick mocks and stubs

There is another quick way to generate mocks and stubs using a little-known language feature: embedding an interface into a struct. Let's say you have an interface like the following:

```
type Crud interface {
    Save(u *User) error
    Update(u *User) error
    Delete(u *User) error
}
```

Let's assume that while our interface has three methods, we only need one for our tests, as is often true when we use interfaces from other packages. We can quickly create a struct that satisfies our interface like this:

```
type MockSave struct {
    Crud
}

func (m *MockSave) Save(u *User) error {
    // mock or stub implementation
}
```

This approach works fine for stubs where we only want a simple or hardcoded response, but we can take it a step further and make a simple mock using delegation. First, we add a closure as a member variable to our struct and then have the method under test delegate all calls to it. Here is the result:

```go
type MockSave struct {
    Crud

    OnSave func(u *User) error
}

func (m *MockSave) Save(u *User) error {
    return m.OnSave(u)
}
```

With the above implementation, for every instance of **MockSave**, we must supply a closure for **OnSave** to do whatever we need.

Test recorders

The last test tool we are going to examine is test recorders. Where stubs focus on only returning simple values, test recorders focus solely on observing or recording the inputs provided to the dependency. Test recorders are ideal for mocking dependencies like loggers and instrumentation clients: cases where the data we send to the dependency is significant and there are no outputs. Suppose we have a **Logger** interface that looks like this:

```go
type Logger interface {
    Error(message string, args ...interface{})
}
```

As you can see, there are no return values; any tests regarding this interface would focus on our dependency usage. We could use a mock for such tests, but it is reasonable to expect that we call **Logger** many times in a piece of code. As such, mock-based tests would require a lot of configuration, not to mention that it would also make our tests very tightly coupled with the current implementation. Instead, we can build a test recorder like this:

```go
type LogRecorder struct {
    Usage []string
}

func (r *LogRecorder) Error(message string, args ...interface{}) {
    r.Usage = append(r.Usage, fmt.Sprintf(message, args...))
```

```
    }

func (r *LogRecorder) AssertContains(t *testing.T, contains interface{},
msgAndArgs ...interface{}) {
        assert.Contains(t, r.Usage, contains, msgAndArgs...)
    }
```

As you can see, our implementation of the **Logger** interface records all usage to a slice. Once we have done this, we can apply any validation we would like. In this example, we used an **AssertContains()** method to scan all recorded log lines for the supplied value. This permissive assertion is another example of decoupling the tests from the implementation to make less brittle tests.

Test UX and Quality

The code quality and code UX for test code should be as good as, if not better than, for production code. This may seem counterintuitive to some, but codebases with good code coverage will have the same amount of test code as production code. It follows then that we will spend a significant amount of time reading and maintaining test code. As such, we should use all the tricks and techniques we discussed in the previous two chapters, and more, on our test code.

Tests are one of the tools we use to ensure our production code has the behavior we require. They are also the code that programmers new to a project often use to learn the code. Poor code UX and low code quality will interfere with these use cases. This section examines some test-specific improvements we can make to our test UX and quality.

The predictability of a pattern

When code has a consistent layout and formatting, readers can navigate it efficiently. This ease of navigation enables the reader to find what they are looking for quickly and gloss over details (until they are required). Fortunately for us, it is very easy to write consistent tests. Almost all tests can be broken down into the following five-step flow:

1. Define the inputs

2. Configure the dependencies (e.g., mocks, populating the DB, etc.)

3. Build and call the unit under test

4. Define the expectations

5. Validate the outputs

Not all tests will require all five of these steps, and the ordering of the steps does not need to follow this exact sequence, but all tests should be broken down this way. We can even take this a step further and develop a team style where the ordering of the steps is consistent. Such consistency will bring the team comfort and speed when reading the tests and improve the speed at which tests are written by allowing the use of code templates, AI code generators, copy/pasting, or even just muscle memory. If we revisit our earlier example, you can see the different steps defined and organized using the TDT format:

```go
scenarios := []struct {
    scenarioDesc       string
    inputOrder         Order
    configureMockBank  func(bank *MockBank)
    configureMockSender func(sender *MockReceiptSender)
    expectedReceiptNo  string
    expectAnErr        bool
}{
    // scenarios removed
}

for _, s := range scenarios {
    scenario := s
    t.Run(scenario.scenarioDesc, func(t *testing.T) {
        // inputs
        ctx, cancel := context.WithTimeout(context.Background(), 1*time.Second)
        defer cancel()

        // mocks
        mockBank := &MockBank{}
        scenario.configureMockBank(mockBank)

        mockReceiptSender := &MockReceiptSender{}
        scenario.configureMockSender(mockReceiptSender)
```

```
                // call object under test
                orderManager := NewOrderManager(mockBank, mockReceiptSender)
                result, resultErr := orderManager.Process(ctx, scenario.inputOrder)

                // validation
                require.Equal(t, scenario.expectAnErr, resultErr != nil)
                assert.Equal(t, scenario.expectedReceiptNo, result)
        })
    }
```

The above format mostly follows the ordering we have outlined, with only the "Define the expectations" step not being readily apparent. In this example, the expectations are defined inside the scenario rather than the test scenario closure.

Improving test readability

The readability of tests is, perhaps, their second most important feature beyond the fact that they are correct. As such, after achieving consistency, we should aim to reduce the mental burden required by the reader. For me, this boils down to three main things: simplicity, using an assertion library, and avoiding the ambiguity of magic constants.

Using assertion libraries

This point is controversial and perhaps a feature of my background in languages like Java. Still, I find using an assertion library more concise and more comfortable to read than vanilla Go tests. Contrast a simple vanilla Go example:

```
if resultErr != expectedErr {
    t.Fatalf("resultErr '%v' did not match expectedErr '%v'", resultErr, expectedErr)
}
```

with the assertion library equivalent:

```
require.Equal(t, expectedErr, resultErr, "resultErr '%v' did not match expectedErr '%v'",
    expectedErr, resultErr)
```

or the even more efficient:

```
require.Equal(t, expectedErr, resultErr)
```

Not only is the assertion library less code, but it is automatically handling the creation of useful debugging messages. This second point cannot be overstated; useful debug messages allow us to quickly identify the difference between the expected and actual outcomes and save significant debugging time.

Avoiding the ambiguity of magic constants

As we are using tests to verify and document our code's behavior, the tests themselves must be abundantly clear. Consider the following code:

```
result := NewPerson("Shah", 35, true)
```

Now ask yourself, what do these input parameters represent? We would likely guess that **Shah** is a name; **35** is probably an age, but what does **true** represent? Without knowledge of the implementation, we have no idea what the boolean means, and the rest of the parameters are equally just guesses. This test would read far more clearly if it were:

```
name := "Shah"
age := 35
isRightHanded := true

result := NewPerson(name, age, isRightHanded)
```

After making the above change, our tests are less ambiguous and more durable. This durability comes from us being able to reuse these inputs in our assertions like this:

```
assert.Equal(t, name, result.Name)
```

Now, I don't mean to imply that inputs must always be extracted and named in this fashion; this extra effort does not always benefit us. Applying this approach is a judgment call. When the inputs are significant and/or ambiguous, it is worth the extra effort.

Reducing duplication

Tests, by their nature, contain a lot of duplication. Switching to TDT tests reduces the duplication that comes from the five testing steps that we outlined earlier. However, this still leaves three prevalent causes of duplication: dependencies, mocks, and test inputs.

Duplication caused by dependencies

Let's assume we have some code that uses Redis in its implementation, and we have decided that we do not want to mock Redis in our tests. Therefore, every test for this code will require a connection to Redis.

We should extract this common logic into a convenience function, just as we would in production code. Such a convenience function could look like this:

```
func getRedisConn(t *testing.T, ctx context.Context, host string) redis.Conn {
    client, err := redis.DialContext(ctx, "tcp", host)
    if err != nil {
        t.Skipf("skipped due to failure to init Redis. err: %s", err)
    }

    return client
}
```

With this, we have reduced the duplication caused by the dependency and improved the readability of the test code. Additionally, by using **t.Skipf()** we have also improved the test output's usability, as our tests will not fail when Redis is unavailable but rather be skipped. This is a trick we will explore more later in the chapter.

Duplication caused by mocks

When using TDT tests and mocks, we will inevitably have a lot of duplication in the configuration of our mocks across different scenarios. This is particularly true for the happy path execution of our mocks.

In the example we've been using throughout this chapter, our happy path scenario looked like this:

```
{
    scenarioDesc: "Happy path (long version)",
    inputOrder: Order{
        CustomerName:  "Oscar",
        CustomerEmail: "me@example.com",
        Amount:        123,
```

```
		},
		configureMockBank: func(bank *MockBank) {
			bank.On("Charge", mock.Anything, mock.Anything,
mock.Anything).Return(testReceiptNo, nil)
		},
		configureMockSender: func(sender *MockReceiptSender) {
			sender.On("SendReceipt", mock.Anything, mock.Anything, mock.Anything,
mock.Anything).Return(nil)
		},
		expectedReceiptNo: "ABC-123",
		expectAnErr:       false,
	},
```

The **configureMockBank** and **configureMockSender** closures are configured to return happy path results from our mocks. This happy path configuration will be duplicated across many of the other scenarios. We can, therefore, put a severe dent in this duplication by extracting these closures into helper functions like this:

```
func happyPathBankCharge(bank *MockBank) {
	bank.On("Charge", mock.Anything, mock.Anything, mock.Anything).Return(testReceiptNo,
nil)
}

func happyPathReceiptSend(sender *MockReceiptSender) {
	sender.On("SendReceipt", mock.Anything, mock.Anything, mock.Anything,
mock.Anything).Return(nil)
}
```

After this extraction, our scenario is reduced to this:

```
	{
		scenarioDesc: "Happy path (concise mocks)",
		inputOrder: Order{
			CustomerName:  "Oscar",
			CustomerEmail: "me@example.com",
			Amount:        123,
		},
		configureMockBank:   happyPathBankCharge,
		configureMockSender: happyPathReceiptSend,
		expectedReceiptNo:   "ABC-123",
		expectAnErr:         false,
```

```
    },
```

You will also notice that replacing the mock configuration closures with well-named functions makes the test scenario much easier to scan. While replacing all of the closures with named functions would similarly improve the readability of the test scenarios, it is not worth the extra effort. On the other hand, the value of the reduced duplication is well worth the cost.

Duplication caused by test inputs

The final common cause of duplication is test inputs. Test inputs, particularly objects, can add many lines to our tests and test scenarios. The solution to this is, not surprisingly, to extract the creation of these objects in the same way we did with the mock configuration.

When considering where to extract the input creation, we need to consider if the input value impacts the test's outcome. For example, could the variable's content cause the unit under test to return an error?

Scenario 1: The input value influences the outcome

When our unit under test validates the inputs or uses the input to calculate the result, the input must be part of the test scenario to test this behavior. In this situation, the test scenarios for the happy and sad paths related to dependency failures will require a valid set of inputs. We can reduce this duplication like we did with duplication caused by mocks, extracting to a test global. If we extract our input and expected values to globals like this:

```
    var (
        validTestOrder = Order{
            CustomerName:  "Oscar",
            CustomerEmail: "me@example.com",
            Amount:        123,
        }

        testReceiptNo = "ABC-123"
    )
```

we can then reduce our scenarios to look like this:

```
    {
        scenarioDesc:      "Happy path (concise)",
```

```
    inputOrder:            validTestOrder,
    configureMockBank:     happyPathBankCharge,
    configureMockSender:   happyPathReceiptSend,
    expectedReceiptNo:     testReceiptNo,
    expectAnErr:           false,
},
```

This also has the added benefit of giving us a single place to update our **Order** should we need to add or remove fields or change what we consider a valid order.

It is important to note that if the unit under test modifies the input, then we will need to replace our global variable with a function that creates a new object for each test scenario, thereby ensuring that the test scenarios cannot impact each other. In both cases, I recommend putting the variable or the convenient method at the bottom of the test file so that it can be ignored unless needed. This leaves the tests at the top of the file, and then our code scans like a newspaper, i.e., the important things at the top and the details towards the bottom. Readers can then find what they want quickly and only get into the details if they want to.

Scenario 2: The input has no influence on the outcome

When the value of the input has no influence on the outcome, then the input does not need to be part of the test scenario. As such, we can define the variable in a single location.

Typical locations include:

- **At the start of the test before the scenarios**—This is useful if the mock configuration or the expectations are based on the input value, and the value is only needed for this single test.

- **As a global variable**—This is the best approach if the variable is used across multiple TDT tests.

- **At the start of the t.Run() closure**—Use this approach when the tests modify the input variable.

As you can see, there are many options here. Outside of the requirements dictated by how the unit under test interacts with the variable, the choice of method is mainly personal or team preference. Whenever possible, consistency is imperative.

Achieving Test Resilience

We should avoid constructing our tests to only work because of the current implementation. We must remember we are validating our code's behavior, regardless of the implementation. When tests break due to refactoring or adding new features, we should stop and ask ourselves, *Were the tests too specific? Can we restructure the test to make it more resilient to changes?* Let's consider an example. Assume our unit under test has three dependencies that we have mocked: **DepA**, **DepB**, and **DepC**. Our current implementation looks like this:

```go
func (u *Unit) Do() error {
    err := u.DepA.Do()
    if err != nil {
        return err
    }

    err = u.DepB.Do()
    if err != nil {
        return err
    }

    return u.DepC.Do()
}
```

The behavior we are trying to confirm is that when dependency **DepB** fails, our code returns an error. A typical test for this behavior might look like this:

```go
func TestTypicalImplementation(t *testing.T) {
    mockA := &MockDepA{}
    mockA.On("Do").Return(nil)

    mockB := &MockDepB{}
    mockB.On("Do").Return(errors.New("failed"))

    // not configured because we expect it not to be called
    mockC := &MockDepC{}
```

```
unit := &Unit{
    a: mockA,
    b: mockB,
    c: mockC,
}
resultErr := unit.Do()

assert.Error(t, resultErr)
}
```

This test confirms the behavior that we described. However, it only works because it mirrors the implementation. Consider what happens if we change the implementation by reordering the calls to the dependencies. Or what happens if the implementation calls the dependencies concurrently? In both cases, the tests will break, not because we have changed the behavior but the implementation, and we are forced to spend time refactoring them. To address this and make our tests less brittle in the face of refactoring, we should start with the happy path configuration and only change the minimum to construct the scenario we are testing.

If we combine this approach with the duplication reduction in the previous section, the result is concise, readable, and durable tests; essentially, we are maximizing the value of the tests while minimizing the cost of maintaining them.

As with many of the topics we have discussed, there are cases where this approach is inappropriate. Take, for example, our **OrderManager** example; we want to ensure we don't issue a receipt when we fail to charge the customer. As such, we need to construct the scenario like this:

```
{
    scenarioDesc: "Sad path - ensure no receipt is sent without a successful charge",
    inputOrder: Order{
        CustomerName: "Oscar",
        CustomerEmail: "me@example.com",
        Amount:        123,
    },
    configureMockBank: func(bank *MockBank) {
```

```
        bank.On("Charge", mock.Anything, mock.Anything, mock.Anything).Return("",
    errors.New("failed"))
    },
    configureMockSender: func(sender *MockReceiptSender) {
        sender.On("SendReceipt", mock.Anything, mock.Anything, mock.Anything,
    mock.Anything).Run(func(args mock.Arguments) {
            assert.FailNow(t, "receipt should not be sent as charge failed")
        }).Return(errors.New("failed"))
    },
    expectedReceiptNo: "",
    expectAnErr:        true,
},
```

In this example, we ensure the test noisily fails when we attempt to send a receipt when the **Charge()** fails. While this seems like an exception to our goal of making the tests durable in the face of refactoring, it is not, as this configuration ensures the behavior we require.

Test Tricks That You Might Not Know

This section will examine a series of tricks—including language features, standard library tooling, and some test construction patterns—that you might not know.

The lesser-known Go test features

For many of us, running tests is simply a matter of running **go test ./...**, but this is by no means the only way to run tests. Go test has several flags that you could find helpful.

The run flag

The **run** flag allows us to filter tests by name using a regular expression. This feature can be used to run a single test like this:

```
$ go test -run=TestOrderManager_Process ./...
```

Or we can use a regular expression and the godoc test naming convention to run all tests for our **OrderManager** with the command:

```
$ go test -run=TestOrderManager.* ./...
```

If you are unfamiliar with the godoc test naming convention, it is: **Test[ObjectName]_[Method or use case]**. This naming style is recommended but only enforced when writing godoc examples.

The short flag

The **short** flag allows us to skip any tests expected to take a long time to execute. This is subjective, as **go test** has no idea how long the tests will take. It is up to us to mark tests as long. To mark a test as a "long test", we need to add the following code to the start of the test.

```
func TestShortExample(t *testing.T) {
    if testing.Short() {
        t.Skip("test skipped due to short mode")
    }

    // normal test implementation
}
```

As you can see, using this flag requires some pre-planning and using the flag when testing, which can be irritating when running tests automatically or via an IDE. I prefer to ensure my unit tests run quickly and then protect the likely longer-running tests, like UATs, with specific environment flags, as we will see in the *Skipping tests* section later in this chapter.

The timeout flag

The **timeout** flag causes tests to panic if they take longer than the configured time. The usage of this flag looks like this:

```
$ go test -timeout=3s ./...
```

The above command will run all the tests, and if any individual test takes longer than three seconds, it will be forced to stop with a panic. This flag is most useful for running tests in continuous integration servers, as it will ensure that the tests will always return or end and never become livelocked.

The count flag

The **count** flag causes **go test** to execute the tests the supplied number of times. The basic format for this command is:

```
$ go test -count=3 ./...
```

The above command will cause all the tests to be run three times.

This flag is most useful when combined with other flags, particularly the **race** and **run** flags. Combining **count** and **run** allows us to re-run a selection of tests repeatedly. Combining **count** and **race** is helpful in running the race detector multiple times, which increases the chances of detecting or triggering race issues.

Tests with context

When writing tests that use **context.Context** as an input variable, it is very tempting to take the shortest route and write:

```
func TestTempting(t *testing.T) {
    resultErr := do(context.Background())

    require.NoError(t, resultErr)
}
```

This approach is undoubtedly the fastest to write, but it is not the most durable. It is better to set a timeout on the context like this:

```
func TestImproved(t *testing.T) {
    ctx, cancel := context.WithTimeout(context.Background(), 1 * time.Second)
    defer cancel()

    resultErr := do(ctx)

    require.NoError(t, resultErr)
}
```

Setting a timeout on the context ensures that the tests will fail by timeout when the test runs longer than expected. This method of setting test timeouts is more flexible and context-aware than the **timeout** flag, especially as we don't have to remember to use the **go test** flag, and the setting can be appropriately configured at the per-test level.

Test data

When tests are run, the current or executable directory is set to the directory that contains the **_test.go** file. We can leverage this fact to interact with the filesystem in a predictable manner. For example, if we wanted to load config from a JSON file in a test, we can use:

```go
func TestLoadConfig(t *testing.T) {
    config, err := os.ReadFile("testdata/test-config.json")
    require.NoError(t, err)

    expected := `{"address": "0.0.0.0:8080"}`
    assert.Equal(t, expected, string(config))
}
```

In our example, the **test-config.json** file is in a directory called **testdata**, which sits under the directory containing the **_test.go** file. The use of a directory called **testdata** is significant. This is not only a convention, but the Go tooling treats this directory as special and skips any directory named **testdata** when compiling, testing, or validating the code.

We can also use the **testdata** directory to test functions that generate binary data. Let's assume we have a function whose signature looks like this:

```go
func generateReceiptFile(filename string) error {
    // implementation removed
}
```

With a signature like that, our first instinct might be to mock the filesystem, but this is unnecessary. It is far simpler to create a file with the expected result and store it in the **testdata** directory. Then our test becomes:

```go
func TestGenerateJSON(t *testing.T) {
    destination := "testdata/result.json"
    testFixture := "testdata/expected.json"

    // call function under test
    resultErr := generateReceiptFile(destination)
    require.NoError(t, resultErr)

    // clean up the created file after the test completes
    defer os.Remove(destination)
```

```
        // compare the generated file with the expected file
        resultContents, err := os.ReadFile(destination)
        require.NoError(t, err)

        expectedContents, err := os.ReadFile(testFixture)
        require.NoError(t, err)

        assert.Equal(t, string(expectedContents), string(resultContents))
    }
```

As you can see, this test is very straightforward. We can call the function that generates a file and then compare the generated contents with another file with the expected result.

Tests like our example are great, not only for verifying behavior but also for preventing regression. However, we can make this test more efficient by making the test capable of generating the test fixture. This approach is handy when the test fixtures are files that are hard to generate manually. To do this, we will use an environment variable as a flag to switch the tests between running the tests and generating the test fixture. After adding this functionality, our example becomes:

```
func TestGenerateJSONWithGenerator(t *testing.T) {
        destination := "testdata/result.json"
        testFixture := "testdata/expected.json"

        if os.Getenv("UPDATE_FIXTURES") == "true" {
            generateReceiptFile(testFixture)
            return
        }

        // call function under test
        resultErr := generateReceiptFile(destination)
        require.NoError(t, resultErr)

        // clean up the created file after the test completes
        defer os.Remove(destination)

        // compare the generated file with the expected file
        resultContents, err := os.ReadFile(destination)
```

```
    require.NoError(t, err)

    expectedContents, err := os.ReadFile(testFixture)
    require.NoError(t, err)

    assert.Equal(t, string(expectedContents), string(resultContents))
}
```

With the above changes, we now regenerate our **testFixture** using the command:

```
$ UPDATE_FIXTURES=true go test ./...
```

Testing and private constructors

As we have seen in *Chapter 5—Optimizing for Code UX*, injecting lots of dependencies can seriously detract from the UX of our objects. In that chapter, we introduced private constructors to remove the need to inject test-only dependencies and prevent them from detracting from the code UX of our constructors. This approach should be taken further to address test-only config, internal initialization, function-based dependencies, and testing with globals.

Test-only config

Timeouts, latency budgets, and retry attempts are types of configuration that we often want to change during testing to trigger a particular error condition and generally improve the test speed. Of course, we can promote this configuration to parameters in our constructor, but this is unnecessary; instead, moving this configuration to a private constructor allows our tests to inject this configuration, but the external UX remains clean. Here is a simple example:

```
const defaultEmailTimeout = 3 * time.Second

func New() *OrderManager {
    return newOrderManager(defaultEmailTimeout)
}

func newOrderManager(timeout time.Duration) *OrderManager {
    return &OrderManager{
        emailTimeout: timeout,
    }
```

```
        }
```

This example may seem like overkill, especially as we can initialize the **OrderManager** directly and set the **emailTimeout** member variable. However, as we will see next, this approach becomes far more relevant when our object has internal initialization.

Internal initialization

Our structs will frequently contain member data fields that need initialization, such as channels, maps, or WaitGroups. This should be done in a constructor to ensure the fields are correctly and efficiently initialized for all users. However, it is common to see tests that look like this:

```
func TestOrderManager(t *testing.T) {
    mockSender := &MockReceiptSender{}

    orderManager := &OrderManager{
        sendTimeout:    1 * time.Millisecond,
        emailTemplates: map[string]string{},
        sender:         mockSender,
    }

    // rest of the test was removed
}
```

By adding a private constructor that initializes the object's internals, we can decouple the tests from the current internal implementation, reduce duplication between tests, and make the tests cleaner. As an added bonus, if refactoring leads to adding or removing member data, then we will only need to do this in one place.

Function-based dependencies

Many examples in this chapter use interfaces and interface-based dependency injection for decoupling; however, it is also possible to achieve the same result for functions. This approach can help mock code that we do not control, like the standard library, or do not want to refactor, like legacy code. Consider the following method:

```
func (r *ReceiptSender) Send(to string, order Order) error {
    payload, err := r.buildReceipt(order)
    if err != nil {
```

```
        return err
    }

    err = smtp.SendMail(r.server, nil, r.from, []string{to}, payload)
    if err != nil {
        return fmt.Errorf("failed to send receipt with err: %w", err)
    }

    return nil
}
```

As you can see, we are using the **smtp.SendMail()** function from the standard library. With the code as is, if we wanted to write a test to verify our handling of an error from the **SendMail()** function, we would have to dig into its implementation and figure out how to make it throw an error. However, a more straightforward approach is to mock this dependency using a private constructor. The first step is to define a custom type with a signature that matches the **SendMail()** function like so:

```
type sendMail func(addr string, a smtp.Auth, from string, to []string, msg []byte) error
```

This step is unnecessary, but it does clean up the code quite a bit, as we will see in a moment. The second step is to add a member variable with this type and replace the direct call to **SendMail()** to use this member variable instead like this:

```
type ReceiptSender struct {
    server      string
    from        string
    sendFunc sendMail
}

func (r *ReceiptSender) Send(to string, order Order) error {
    payload, err := r.buildReceipt(order)
    if err != nil {
        return err
    }

    err = r.sendFunc(r.server, nil, r.from, []string{to}, payload)
    if err != nil {
        return fmt.Errorf("failed to send receipt with err: %w", err)
    }
```

```
        return nil
    }
```

After the above changes, we can mock calls to **SendMail()**, but we need one final step. We need to use a private constructor to initialize the member variable for external users while leaving us a clean injection point, like so:

```
func New(server, from string) *ReceiptSender {
    return newReceiptSender(server, from, smtp.SendMail)
}

func newReceiptSender(server, from string, sendFunc sendMail) *ReceiptSender {
    return &ReceiptSender{
        server:   server,
        from:     from,
        sendFunc: sendFunc,
    }
}
```

With these changes in place, we have decoupled ourselves from functional dependency and allowed ourselves to be completely ignorant of its implementation details. These factors allow us to create tests focused purely on our code.

Finally, a special note to those using monkey patching to replace functions during tests. This approach achieves the same result without introducing data races or the need to restore the functions after each test.

Testing with globals

We can apply the same approach as we did with function-based dependencies when using global variables: namely, removing direct access to the global and replacing it with a member variable. Then, initialize the contents of the member variable using a private constructor in the same way:

```
var dbPool *sql.DB

func New() *Repository {
    return newRepository(dbPool)
}
```

```go
func newRepository(db *sql.DB) *Repository {
    return &Repository{
        db: db,
    }
}
```

As you can see from the above example, our code has the same UX and works in the same manner as it does without the private constructor, but now we can write independent and data-race-free tests.

Testing fluent APIs

Fluent APIs can be a valuable pattern for dealing with APIs with a high degree of complexity and flexibility. However, they cannot be mocked or stubbed in the usual way. This leaves us with a dilemma: how do we test code that uses a fluent API? The first thing to remember is that we are not testing the fluent API but rather how our code reacts to the fluent API's various possible responses.

Let's take a look at an example. Let's assume that we have loaded all of the orders made in our system into an ElasticSearch server to make them searchable. Now, we want to search our order history for orders relating to a particular customer by name. The code for this might look like this:

```go
func (s *Search) Do(ctx context.Context, customerName string) ([]*Order, error) {
    termQuery := elastic.NewTermQuery("customer", customerName)
    results, err := s.esClient.Search().
        Index("orderHistory").
        Query(termQuery).
        Do(ctx)
    if err != nil {
        return nil, err
    }

    if results.Hits.TotalHits == 0 {
        return nil, errors.New("no results")
    }
```

```
        return s.unmarshalResults(results)
    }
```

If we tried to use our standard tools of mocks and stubs to test this method, we would end up writing a large and complicated mock. This assumes that mocking is even possible; but if our fluent API returns a struct instead of an interface, we will not be able to mock. In our example, the ElasticSearch client API looks like this:

```
func (c *Client) Search(indices ...string) *SearchService
```

As you can see, it returns a pointer to a struct, meaning it cannot be mocked as is. Our first step to addressing this problem is to define a custom type that has the same parameters and return types as the entire usage of the fluent API like this:

```
type historySearchFunc func(ctx context.Context, esClient *elastic.Client, termQuery
*elastic.TermQuery) (*elastic.SearchResult, error)
```

If you compare the **historySearchFunc** type with the usage of **esClient** above, you will notice that the parameters **termQuery** and **ctx** are the same. Similarly, the return types of **historySearchFunc** are identical to those of the **esClient.Do()** method. With our custom type **historySearchFunc** defined, we extract the usage of the fluent API to a private function like this:

```
func historySearch(ctx context.Context, esClient *elastic.Client, termQuery *elastic.TermQuery)
(*elastic.SearchResult, error) {
    return esClient.Search().
        Index("orderHistory").
        Query(termQuery).
        Do(ctx)
}
```

You will notice that the fluent API usage has not been altered, and the signature of our extracted function matches our custom type **historySearchFunc**. Now we define a member variable of type **historySearchFunc** and replace our call to the fluent API with the usage of this member variable like so:

```
type Search struct {
    esClient *elastic.Client

    historySearch historySearchFunc
}
```

```go
func (s *Search) Do(ctx context.Context, customerName string) ([]*Order, error) {
    termQuery := elastic.NewTermQuery("customer", customerName)
    results, err := s.historySearch(ctx, s.esClient, termQuery)
    if err != nil {
        return nil, err
    }

    if results.Hits.TotalHits == 0 {
        return nil, errors.New("no results")
    }

    return s.unmarshalResults(results)
}
```

With the refactoring of the production code complete, we can now test by stubbing the member variable. To do this, we define implementations of the **historySearchFunc** that return the values we need to exercise the rest of our **Do()** method. The full implementation of this test is available in the source code for this chapter here: **https://github.com/corsc/Beyond-Effective-Go/blob/master/Chapter06/07_patterns_tricks/05_fluent_api/ 02_second_iteration/example_test.go**.

Please note that you cannot verify the exact usage by removing the fluent API usage during testing. This introduces a risk that there is a mistake in this code that tests cannot help you with. You should minimize this risk by only extracting the single line that is the fluent API call. You should also ensure that the extracted code is closely scrutinized by you, the author, and by the code review.

Also, in our example, we have replaced the fluent API usage with a call to a closure. If this pattern makes you uncomfortable, we can replace it with an interface and then mock or stub using our standard tools. This results in a bit more code, but it is functionally equivalent as long as we remember to minimize the risks, as mentioned above.

Testing concurrent code

Testing concurrent code is challenging and can be rather annoying. Additionally, tests of concurrent code are a frequent cause of test flakiness. Often, tests of concurrent code look like this:

```go
func TestTypicalMistake(t *testing.T) {
    objectUnderTest := &ConcurrentObject{}

    go objectUnderTest.DoWork()

    <-time.After(1 * time.Second)

    expected := 1234
    assert.Equal(t, expected, objectUnderTest.GetResult())
}
```

Often, these tests will work fine, albeit unnecessarily slowly, on the author's development machine, but when they get shipped to the CI server, the different CPU resources and system load can make this test fail. The typical response is to extend the delay in the middle of the test, but this is not a good idea as it wastes more of your valuable time. Instead of using delays, let's examine some strategies for testing concurrent code, including:

- Avoidance

- Switching outputs to channels

- Using a test latch

Avoidance

Perhaps the easiest option for testing concurrent code is not to test it or rather to test the business logic independently from the concurrency. If we were to refactor our **DoWork()** function and extract the business logic into a separate private method, we could then write tests for the business logic against this method. Then, if and only if we felt it necessary, we could test the concurrency separately.

Switching outputs to channels

If you take a closer look at our previous test, you will notice that our main problem is that we don't know when the result will be available via our **GetResult()** method. But if we refactor our **DoWork()** method to accept a channel for the result, we can remove the delay from our test and ensure that our test always passes or fails predictably. Here is the updated test:

```go
func TestServer_Shutdown(t *testing.T) {
    objectUnderTest := &ConcurrentObject{}

    resultCh := make(chan int, 1)

    go objectUnderTest.DoWork(resultCh)

    select {
    case result := <-resultCh:
        expected := 1234

        assert.Equal(t, expected, result)


    case <-time.After(1 * time.Second):
        assert.Fail(t, "test timed out")
    }
}
```

After applying this pattern and ensuring that our tests will always return a result, they will also only take the minimum amount of time to execute; no more time wasted sleeping. This same approach can also be successfully applied to remove polling from tests. In both cases, no more time is wasted with **time.Sleep()**.

Using a test latch

Test latches are the most involved and perhaps the weirdest strategy for testing concurrent code, but they are incredibly effective and don't require changing the inputs or outputs of our code. Let's imagine we have a long-running process that consumes data from a channel. When the data consumed is invalid, it is silently dropped. The implementation looks like this:

```go
func (c *Consumer) Consume(ordersCh chan *Order) {
    for order := range ordersCh {
```

```
            if !c.isValid(order) {
                continue
            }

            c.process(order)
        }
    }
```

In this form, we can't write a test that confirms the behavior of dropping invalid data as there is no side-effect that we can measure. Even if we changed this code to output the valid orders to another channel, we still can't construct a reliable and timely test to test for "a negative". This pattern frequently occurs with concurrent code: did our function not return an answer because we haven't finished processing it or because the data was dropped or filtered out? To address this, we can introduce a test latch. A test latch is a function that is a NOOP during production usage but can have an implementation during testing. The first change we should make is to add a closure as a member variable and add a NOOP implementation in the constructor like this:

```
func NewConsumer() *Consumer {
    return &Consumer{
        orderDropped: func(order *Order) {},
    }
}
```

With this in place, we can refactor our **Consume()** method to call the test latch like so:

```
func (c *Consumer) Consume(ordersCh chan *Order) {
    for order := range ordersCh {
        if !c.isValid(order) {
            c.orderDropped(order)

            continue
        }

        c.process(order)
    }
}
```

Our code now has an observable side-effect that we can use in our tests with the above changes. To do this, we will initialize our **Consumer** and provide a custom implementation of the test latch like this:

```
resultCh := make(chan *Order, 1)

consumer := &Consumer{
    orderDropped: func(order *Order) {
        resultCh <- order
    },
}
```

It is important to note that we are using a channel to gather the result. While unnecessary, this allows us to use the same test timeout pattern we used in the previous section. With the consumer and test latch set up, we can now call the **Consume()** method we are testing:

```
ordersCh := make(chan *Order, 1)
ordersCh <- newInvalidOrder()

go consumer.Consume(ordersCh)
```

The only other thing of note in this code is that we call **Consume()** in a goroutine, which allows us to have the tests time out. This means we can do the following:

```
select {
case <-resultCh:
    assert.True(t, true, "happy path")

case <-time.After(1 * time.Second):
    assert.Fail(t, "test timed out")
}
```

This pattern, perhaps, feels like test-induced damage, and I will begrudgingly admit that it is. However, the cost of this damage is confined entirely to the object under test and does not impact production performance. It is also the only method to add observable behaviors that enable us to test without impacting the end user's UX.

One last point about test latches is that they are extremely good at adding predictability to code that depends on the system's environment or current state. For example, you likely have code that calls **time.Now()**, and writing tests for this code is often troublesome because **time.Now()** always returns a different result. However, if we replace all calls to **time.Now()** with a latch that calls **time.Now()** in the production code but can be swapped out during testing, we now have highly predictable tests.

Ensuring tests always complete

We've already indirectly discussed this, but as a goal, it is imperative and bears repeating. Our tests must be written so that they will always complete, even if the result is a failure or a panic. Tests that fail to finish result in confusion, wasted time, and even jammed build servers. We can employ many strategies to ensure our tests finish, but in this section, we will highlight only four.

Strategy 1: go test -timeout

The first and simplest is to use the **go test -timeout** flag, as discussed earlier in this chapter. This option will force any test that takes longer than the timeout setting to throw a panic. Given that it is part of the tooling, it is 100% reliable. However, it does have downsides. Firstly, we must remember to use it (and type it) every time, which is annoying during local development. Secondly, we must find a setting that will work for all tests. A few seconds would be sufficient for most unit tests. Still, it might need to be longer for UATs or even some unit tests validating computationally intensive calculations. Whatever we set this value to determines the maximum amount of time a test can take and how long we have to wait before we can be sure a test has failed.

Strategy 2: Use channel results

As we have seen in the previous section on test latches, refactoring our outputs to channels allows us to use **select** to either receive a result on the channel or time out. When using this strategy, we can explicitly state the maximum amount of time we are willing to wait for this individual test to complete. This minimizes the amount of time that our test suite as a whole takes. We can also trigger a clean and informative error message when a timeout occurs, unlike with the **timeout** flag.

Strategy 3: Set context timeouts

It can be pretty common to see tests that use context like this:

```
func TestBadExample(t *testing.T) {
    resultErr := DoSomething(context.Background(), "ABC-123")
    assert.NoError(t, resultErr)
}
```

As you can see, we got lazy, and instead of creating a new context for this test, we used the default background one. In a vacuum, this seems reasonable considering that **go test** runs each test individually, and as such, the background context only lasts for the test's lifecycle. However, this ignores the most common reason for including context as a parameter: the fact that we are performing an indeterminate and/or concurrent operation over which we don't have total control. Every time we supply a context as a parameter in tests, we should set a timeout. This ensures our tests will finish, either correctly or due to the context timing out. This approach also allows us to explicitly state the timeout for this individual test, ensuring that our test suite can fail as fast as possible.

Strategy 4: Use give-ups

Let's assume you have a test that looks like this:

```go
func TestServer(t *testing.T) {
    server := &Server{}
    go server.Do()

    for {
        if server.IsDone() {
            assert.True(t, true, "test passed")
            return
        }

        time.Sleep(10 * time.Millisecond)
    }
}
```

Ideally, we would refactor the code under test to use a channel output, but sometimes this is impossible. As you can see above, our test is written so that if **IsDone()** never returns true, our test will never finish. We can avoid this issue and ensure the test will always finish by adding an attempt counter and a give-up clause like this:

```go
func TestServerImproved(t *testing.T) {
    server := &Server{}
    go server.Do()

    for attempt := 0; attempt < 5; attempt++ {
        if server.IsDone() {
            assert.True(t, true, "test passed")
```

```
            return
        }

        time.Sleep(10 * time.Millisecond)
    }

    assert.Fail(t, "test failed after maximum attempts")
}
```

With our give-up clause in place, our test is now guaranteed to finish. Please note that this test could still be flaky due to insufficient attempts or the **time.Sleep()** setting being too short. It could also take longer than necessary due to too long a **time.Sleep()** setting. It is generally a good idea to avoid using **time.Sleep()** in tests whenever possible.

Benchmarking concurrent code

Often, when we are writing benchmark tests, they look like this:

```
func BenchmarkDoSomething(b *testing.B) {
    for i := 0; i < b.N; i++ {
        DoSomething()
    }
}
```

As you likely know, the **DoSomething()** calls are executed sequentially, and the benchmark result is the total time taken divided by the number of iterations. You may not, however, be familiar with benchmark tests that look like this:

```
func BenchmarkDoSomethingParallel(b *testing.B) {
    b.RunParallel(func(pb *testing.PB) {
        for pb.Next() {
            DoSomething()
        }
    })
}
```

If you carefully compare this example with the previous one, you will notice the use of **b.RunParallel()**. It might seem nuts to run benchmarks in parallel, especially since we are usually trying to measure performance in isolation. However, when testing code that uses shared resources, like mutexes or atomic variables, we want to measure the performance of the code both in isolation and when the shared resources are under contention.

A regular benchmark test allows us to measure the performance of **DoSomething()** by itself and in isolation. The use of **RunParallel()** allows us to test the impact of any resource contention. **RunParallel()** divides the total iterations across the available number of threads, as determined by the **GOMAXPROCS** setting, and then returns the average time taken across all of the threads.

Asserting that an object implements an interface

There are two simple options when we want to ensure that an object implements a particular interface. The first is to define a global variable like this:

```
var _ AnInterface = &AnObject{}
```

This can be done anywhere, in production or test code; but, given that it functions like an assertion, putting this is in a **_test.go** file seems more appropriate.

This approach is not a test per se, but we are using the compiler to enforce the required relationship. The second and my recommended option is to achieve the same thing with a test, like this:

```
func TestMyObject_implements(t *testing.T) {
    assert.Implements(t, (*AnInterface)(nil), &AnObject{})
}
```

I prefer that approach because the resulting error message is cleaner. Also, as it is a test and not a compiler issue, it is possible to momentarily ignore it, wch can be helpful when performing larger refactorings.

Fixing bugs

When it comes to bugs, the only thing more annoying than having a bug is having to fix it more than once. Thankfully, the solution to this is simple and easy. When faced with a bug report, you should first write a test that fails because the bug exists. This test will confirm the bug's existence and will also verify that the bug has been fixed. It will also ensure that the bug never needs fixing again.

Suppose the bug report is inaccurate or not specific enough to write a test. In that case, the second-best option is to examine the code where we expect the issue to be and then hypothesize potential failures that could cause the reported issue. These hypotheses can then be proved or disproved via tests.

There is one more valuable feature to this approach to fixing bugs. After the bug has been fixed, we should examine what the existence of the bug tells us regarding both how we code and how we test. For example, the bug may highlight a particular scenario that we should have had a test for. Similarly, the bug might highlight a particular usage mistake or assumption we should have accounted for in the unit under test. These insights can and should then be rolled into our approach for the future.

Skipping tests

As a guiding principle, **go test ./...** should work immediately after an SCM clone without any future configuration or installation of tools or resources. However, there are times when tests require external resources that may not be available in every developer's environment; for these reasons, we should adopt the **testing.T.Skip()** feature. Let's assume we have a unit test that requires a MySQL server to be installed on the local host; clearly, such a test will fail if this is not the case. We could protect these tests with a build flag. However, this creates a situation where developers who do not use this flag can accidentally break those tests without noticing. Instead, let's examine three approaches that don't have this weakness.

Approach 1: use init()

For this first approach, we will leverage the fact that **init()** runs before everything else and have **init()** attempt to connect to our MySQL server. Here is the code:

```
var mysqlAvailable bool
```

```
func init() {
    db, err := sql.Open("mysql", "root@0.0.0.0/test")
```

```
    if err != nil {
        mysqlAvailable = false
        return
    }

    ctx, cancel := context.WithTimeout(context.Background(), 1*time.Second)
    defer cancel()

    err = db.PingContext(ctx)
    if err != nil {
        mysqlAvailable = false
        return
    }

    mysqlAvailable = true
}
```

The actual check we perform in **init()** depends on the required resource and how we want to validate its existence or accessibility. In this example, we attempt to create a pool of database connections and ping the server. With **init()** setting a global variable, we can now skip tests when MySQL is not available, using:

```
func TestSkipWithInit(t *testing.T) {
    if !mysqlAvailable {
        t.Skip("test skipped as MySQL is not available")
    }

    // rest of the test
}
```

Even though we are using a global variable here, we do not have to worry about data races as **init()** is guaranteed to run before the tests.

Approach 2: use an environment variable

In this approach, we use an environment variable's existence (or lack thereof) to determine if the tests should be run. Here is the code:

```
func TestSkipWithEnvVar(t *testing.T) {
    if os.Getenv("MYSQL_HOST") == "" {
```

```
            t.Skip("test skipped as MYSQL_HOST is not set")
        }

        // rest of the test
    }
```

In this example, we are using the existence of an environment variable **MYSQL_HOST** to determine whether the test runs. This approach fits our ideal that all tests should pass immediately after an SCM clone, as it is likely that the environment variable does not exist at that time.

This also enables individual developers to opt in to running these tests. We can also use this approach to categorize tests; for example, we can do the following:

```
func TestExampleUAT(t *testing.T) {
    if os.Getenv("RUN_UAT") == "" {
        t.Skip("UAT skipped")
    }

    // rest of the test
}
```

With this code, we can turn off all potentially slow-running UATs by default. I find this approach particularly useful. It allows me to run all the unit tests during active development and then run the UATs only when I am specifically working on them, just before I submit a merge request, and on the CI server.

Approach 3: check for installed applications

In this final approach, we check the local system for an installed application and then skip tests that will fail if that application is not present. First, let's look at the helper function that performs the check:

```
func mySQLIsInstalled() bool {
    if _, err := exec.LookPath("mysql"); err == nil {
        return true
    }

    return false
```

```
    }
```

In this example, we perform the check and return a boolean; we could also apply this same checking in an **init()** function as we did in the first approach. With our helper function in place, we skip the test in a similar way as the others:

```
func TestSkipWithHelper(t *testing.T) {
    if !mySQLIsInstalled() {
        t.Skip("test skipped as MySQL is not installed")
    }

    // rest of the test
}
```

Given that we are likely to call this method more than once, we probably should cache the result with a **sync.Once** block and slightly improve the test suite's speed.

The choice between our three approaches is purely personal preference; you may even want to use more than one approach in the same project. However, I implore you to only use the build flag approach when tests are based on a particular operating system or architecture. The likelihood that code gets broken because of the flags is very high.

Global variables

Hopefully, I have dissuaded you from using global variables in most circumstances by this point. However, if you still have code that uses globals, you need a way to avoid the issues arising from this shared state in your tests. The solution is simple: remove the test's global variable use. Assume our code looks like this:

```
var db *sql.DB

type OrderRepository struct{}

func (o *OrderRepository) LoadByID(ctx context.Context, id int) (Order, error) {
    _ = db.QueryRowContext(ctx, "SELECT * FROM order WHERE ID = ?", id)

    // implementation removed
    return Order{}, errors.New("not implemented")
}
```

As you can see, our **OrderRepository** uses a global database pool. To remove the test's dependence on this global variable without removing the global variable itself, we should replace all direct access to the global **db** with a member variable. We can then inject the global via a constructor and achieve our goals with minimal UX change to the caller of this code like so:

```go
var db *sql.DB

func NewOrderRepository() *OrderRepository {
    return &OrderRepository{
        db: db,
    }
}

type OrderRepository struct{
    db *sql.DB
}

func (o *OrderRepository) LoadByID(ctx context.Context, id int) (Order, error) {
    _ = o.db.QueryRowContext(ctx, "SELECT * FROM order WHERE ID = ?", id)

    // implementation removed
    return Order{}, errors.New("not implemented")
}
```

With the above changes in place, our tests are now entirely independent of each other, and there are no data races caused by monkey patching the global for each test.

Identifying Test-Induced Damage

In a 2014 blog post, David Heinemeier Hansson coined the term *test-induced damage* to describe detrimental changes to the code or software architecture for the sole purpose of testing. This is a very real problem that needs to get more attention. As we have seen in *Chapter 5—Optimizing for Code UX*, small changes can significantly improve our code's readability and maintainability. Unfortunately, the opposite is also true. Therefore, before making changes to our code to facilitate testing, we should ask ourselves how those changes will impact the code's UX and software architecture. When the result is detrimental, we must ask ourselves if these changes are necessary. Is there a better way to achieve the same outcome? And is there a way we could minimize the damage?

While many forms of test-induced damage exist, we will briefly introduce a few common examples.

Parameters or configuration that only exist for testing

There are situations where a value used in production is fixed but inconvenient for testing. A typical example of this is timeouts. Consider the following example:

```
const maxWaitTime = 3 * time.Second

type Client struct{}

func (c *Client) WaitForMessage(data chan *Message) (*Message, error) {
    select {
    case msg := <-data:
        return msg, nil

    case <-time.After(maxWaitTime):
        return nil, errors.New("timed out")
    }
}
```

We've hardcoded the timeout to three seconds, and in production, we are pleased with this implementation. However, if we were to construct a sad path test to test the timeout behavior, having the test take three seconds would be annoying and unnecessary. A natural response to this situation would be to add a parameter or config, but this then detracts from the code UX. This is especially true when this value is not supposed to be configurable.

To minimize this issue's cost, we can instead introduce a constructor and member variable and avoid adding a parameter like this:

```
const maxWaitTime = 3 * time.Second
```

```go
func NewClient() *Client {
    return &Client{
        waitTime: maxWaitTime,
    }
}

type Client struct {
    waitTime time.Duration
}

func (c *Client) WaitForMessage(data chan *Message) (*Message, error) {
    select {
    case msg := <-data:
        return msg, nil

    case <-time.After(c.waitTime):
        return nil, errors.New("timed out")
    }
}
```

In this way, we can test as needed, but the code UX remains the same. Another way to address this is to introduce a private constructor that has all of the configuration we want to provide using testing and have the public constructor call it with the appropriate default values.

Outputs that only exist for testing

In some situations, the outputs of a function or method do not include enough details to allow us to properly validate the behavior during testing. For example, let's say we have a function that consumes from a channel, validates the data, and silently drops anything that's invalid. There is no way for us to observe that the data was dropped. We could refactor to add some output for testing, but the callers of this code do not need this, so we would be compromising our UX again. Instead, we should use a test latch (see section earlier in this chapter) to address this situation to give ourselves an observable side-effect.

Another common manifestation of this problem is a function that returns an error, and yet all production usage ignores it, like this:

```go
_ = DoSomething()
```

This shows that the return value is unnecessary. The simplest solution is the same as the solution of unnecessary parameters or config; remove the output from the public API like this:

```
func DoSomething() {
    _ = doSomething()
}

func doSomething() error {
    // implementation removed
    return nil
}
```

Parameters that cause leaky abstractions

This problem is more of a software architecture issue than the others. Sometimes, a URL or database DSN is passed into the business logic code, the motivation being that the author wants to swap out these external dependencies during testing. The underlying issue here is not actually testing, but rather the architecture. The existence of the URL or DSN indicates our business logic has dependencies that should have been encapsulated and dependency injected.

Unfortunately, the solution here is a bunch of refactoring. We need to extract access to external dependencies into a separate object (or package) and then inject mocks for these dependencies. When we test the extracted code, the URLs and DSNs are logical configurations and, therefore, perfectly reasonable.

Publishing mocks in production code

As you know, any code that resides in a **_test.go** file is package private. Therefore, faced with the desire to reduce duplication, some folks will place their mocks in regular go files. **Please do not do this**. Publishing mocks introduces the risk of test code being used in production. Yes, this risk is minimal, but the potential costs of this mistake can be significant. If our production system was accidentally using the mocked version, it might look like it was working when it was not. Imagine if we accidentally used the mock code instead of the real code to charge customers' credit cards or keep track of the sales inventory; the costs of this mistake could be immense.

It is also important to remember that we should define interfaces that state what our code requires and not what it provides. As such, interfaces will generally be defined in the package they are used in and seldom imported. In cases where these interfaces are used by other packages, there is still no need to publish the mocks into production code; instead, we can add another **go generate** line that calls Mockery a second time, like this:

```
//go:generate mockery --name=Bank --case underscore --testonly --inpackage
//go:generate mockery --name=Bank --case underscore --testonly --outpkg "example" --output
"./internal/example"
type Bank interface {
    Charge(ctx context.Context, customerName string, amount int64) (string, error)
}
```

With this code in place, it will cost us nothing to generate multiple versions of the mocks and keep them in sync.

Excessive test coverage

Programmers and managers both love metrics. Sometimes, due to this love of metrics, it becomes a goal to have 100% test coverage. We must resist this temptation. We must remember that we are testing behavior and not the implementation.

We also must remember that every test has a cost to write, run, and maintain and that these costs should be measured against the value they bring. With a bit of experience, achieving our stated goal of ≥70% test coverage takes minimal effort. However, the amount of effort, —in the form of additional tests and refactoring—required to achieve 100% coverage is significant, and the return on investment is terrible. Consider the following simple function:

```
func UserAsJSON(name, address string, age int) ([]byte, error) {
    user := &User{
        Name:    name,
        Address: address,
        Age:     age,
    }

    payload, err := json.Marshal(user)
    if err != nil {
```

```
        return nil, fmt.Errorf("failed to convert User to JSON with err: %w", err)
    }

    return payload, nil
}
```

Even with the most straightforward happy path test, we instantly have 80% test coverage. Now ask yourself, how do we write a sad path test? How do we make **json.Marshal()** fail? To answer this question, we need knowledge of the internal implementation of that function. This is knowledge we probably don't have and don't need.

We could refactor our call to **json.Marshal()** into a global variable and then monkey patch it. Or we could refactor this function into a method and make the call to **json.Marshal()** a member variable and achieve the same. However, a better question here is, why do we need to? How do we benefit from all this effort and the resulting ugly code? Simply put, the costs here far outweigh the benefits.

This concept is the main takeaway from this section. For every decision we make regarding testing, we should contrast the cost with the benefits and try to come out ahead.

Make it Work, Make it Clean, and Then, Maybe, Make it Fast

Writing great code is hard. It is arguably impossible to do while doing anything else, like adding new behavior. The answer to this problem is to only worry about one thing at a time. When we are adding new behavior, we should worry only about that. We should temporarily put aside all concerns about performance, design principles, code UX, or any goals or ideals discussed in the previous chapters. Doing so allows us to focus solely on the problem at hand and not be hampered by anything else.

Once we have a working solution in place, as proven by our tests, then we should refactor to solve software design or code UX issues.

After any design and UX issues have been addressed, then and only then should we consider if we need to worry about performance.

Tests are an integral piece of this approach; first, they help us to prove the solution we are writing has the behavior we require. Then, this proof enables us to safely and efficiently refactor as we now have a far better idea of which patterns or ideals will fit the solution.

This is another reason our tests should focus on behavior rather than implementation. If our tests are too tightly coupled with the implementation, they will require refactoring when the implementation is changed—introducing risk and more work, which in turn may discourage us from refactoring.

We are paid to add behavior to our systems. Tests, software design, and code UX are unimportant to our users or the product managers requesting new behavior. This does not make them any less essential; it just means we need to use them as efficiently as possible. And the most efficient way to do this is to make it work, then make it clean, and then, maybe, make it fast.

Summary

Great unit tests can be incredibly valuable. They can enable us to be very efficient and effective. They are, however, also just a tool. When misused, unit tests can pose more of a burden than they should, even to the point of being detrimental.

By testing from the public API and focusing our testing on behavior, not implementation, we can avoid much of the potential unit testing costs and not inhibit our ability to refactor or add new features.

By paying close attention to our tests' quality, code UX, and resilience to changes, and avoiding test-induced damage, we can enjoy long-term value from our testing efforts.

We can produce great tests by selectively applying the collection of tricks, tools, and tactics we examined in this chapter. There are many more tricks out there, and I encourage you to seek them out or even invent your own and then share them back with our community.

At the end of the day, testing is not an activity we do because we have to but rather something we do because it helps us create better code with less effort.

Questions

1. Why do we write tests?

2. How much effort should we spend on testing?

3. How do unit tests vary from user acceptance or end-to-end tests?

4. Why are table-driven tests an effective pattern for testing?

5. What kinds of scenarios should we be testing?

6. Why should we focus on behavior and not implementation?

7. Why are the quality and code UX of our tests important?

8. How can we use tests to prove and fix bugs?

9. Why is 100% test coverage the wrong goal?

10. How can we apply the DRY principle to make tests easier to read and maintain?

Interlude

Firstly, I apologize for the interruption. I hope you have discovered numerous valuable and informative aspects of the book. This is an opportune moment for me to act like every other content creator and ask you to share your thoughts and honest feedback. Your insights not only help me as an author but also potential readers discover the true value of this book.

Our world is governed by algorithms, which are shaped by engagement. Please take a moment to post your review of this book on Amazon using **https://amzn.to/3VCGbkm** or the QR code below.

I really appreciate any help you can provide.

Yours sincerely,

Corey.

Chapter 7

Improving your Development
Productivity

Introduction

When we set out to improve our programming skills, we often focus on aspects like code style, software patterns, frameworks, or a better language understanding. We seldom consider the more fundamental issues like which tools we use to program, how we interact with these tools, or what we can do to be more productive. In this chapter, we dive deep into these fundamental issues and more.

The goal of this chapter is to inspire you to take a good look at how you program. It will give you the tools and techniques to program faster, be more consistent, make fewer mistakes, and get more out of your day.

The following topics will be covered in this chapter:

- Be Lazy
- Be Observant
- Be Introspective
- Be Adventurous
- Master Your Tooling
- Make Small Changes

Code

To get the most out of this chapter, you will need a recent copy (1.13+) of Go installed and your favorite IDE.

Full versions of all code examples and other related material can be found at **https://github.com/corsc/Beyond-Effective-Go/tree/master/Chapter07**.

Be Lazy

Of all the keys to being a productive developer, being lazy is, by far, the most useful. Being lazy doesn't mean not doing our job, or not delivering value; it means finding ways to do so with the least possible time and effort.

By being lazy, we are incentivized to drive up our efficiency and productivity, with which we can use the time saved to deliver even more value. This idea of doing more with less effort and fewer mistakes is prevalent throughout this chapter—but first, let's examine two, perhaps counterintuitive, examples.

Less is often better

As programmers, we instinctively think that writing more code is the answer to all problems. This is a trap.

The more code we have, the more time and effort we must spend maintaining that code. To avoid these maintenance costs, we should seek ways to reduce the code we must maintain. One way we can do this is to apply the *don't repeat yourself* (DRY) principle.

When applying the DRY principle, we aim to reduce the total amount of code by refactoring duplication. A word of warning: the DRY principle can be taken too literally. We do not need to remove all duplication. When making changes under this principle, we should also consider how these changes may impact other vital factors, like coupling and complexity.

Another effective way to reduce the amount of code is to remove features. This might be shocking, but consider this: most applications have more and more features added to them over time. Some features might stop being used. Some features might be only used by a tiny percentage of users. While the cost to develop these features has already been paid, maintaining them has ongoing costs; someone must understand the code for these features, the tests still need to be run and pass, and any dependencies need updating. These are the features we should be looking to remove.

Often, the decision to add or remove features is the product owner's responsibility, not ours as programmers. However, that doesn't mean we cannot propose this; we must put it from a business perspective. Product owners are focused on cost versus benefits, so we need to structure our proposal from this perspective. Our key assertion to the product owner is that all code incurs costs to maintain, whether it is being used by users or not. Therefore, when a feature has few (or no) users, it is not generating enough revenue and, therefore, has a lousy cost to benefit ratio.

Writing documentation can save time

This one is definitely counterintuitive. Writing and maintaining documentation takes time. However, we need to remember why we wrote the documentation in the first place. The purpose of documentation is to explain to others our decisions and why we believe they're the right ones.

This need to explain and justify decisions is perpetual; there will always be new members joining the team who need to understand the code. There will (hopefully) always be users. There will always be other stakeholders who want to understand the how and why of the application. Documentation allows these folks to self-serve these needs without taking engineering time away with meetings or email queries to achieve the same goal.

I am not suggesting that every single decision at all levels should be documented; quite the opposite. Like code, documentation should be kept to the minimum possible to achieve our goals. Sometimes, the need for particular documentation is predictable; for example, documentation that explains what an application is and does will always be needed, as is documentation for users, like API documentation.

An easy way to determine when more documentation is needed is to note the questions being asked and ask yourself: how likely is this question to be asked by someone else? When it is likely, then answer the question with documentation. Taking the time to write and maintain documentation makes you look professional and helps develop the ability to explain and justify your decisions to others.

There is another way that writing documentation can save us significant time: up-front planning. It does not matter if you use an RFC document or some other software planning document; the act of thinking through significant problems before writing any code enables us to make the best decisions. This is particularly true for decisions relating to system and software architecture. Such a document should justify the need for your proposed work and include decisions relating to cross-functional requirements, like instrumentation, security, availability, scalability, and data privacy. These factors are often overlooked and can add mess or complexity to our code.

Be Observant

Once we internalize the goal of being lazy and trying to achieve more with less effort, we can further this goal by being observant. Throughout our workday, many things can be made more efficient. The key is to be aware and motivated to do better.

While paying attention to your tasks, it is okay to allow yourself to become irritated. If a task is repetitive, slow, cumbersome, unnecessarily complicated, or otherwise sub-optimal, then get annoyed. Then, use the energy your annoyance gives you to fix it.

Let's look at three prevalent examples where our productivity can be improved.

Look for repeated tasks

We might not like to admit it, but there are activities we repeat every day and perhaps multiple times every day. Running tests, generating code, and submitting code for review are all tasks we do all day, every day. Often, these tasks can be made simpler and/or faster. These repeated tasks are great candidates for automation and custom tooling.

Assume we run the race detector over our tests before submitting our code for review. The commands for the whole process might look like this:

```
$ go test -race ./...
$ git add .
$ git commit
```

```
$ git push
```

This is a non-trivial amount of typing. Typos are going to happen. Consider what happens if we take the time to turn this list of commands into a script called **pr**. We could reduce this to:

```
$ pr
```

With this, we have reduced the potential for mistakes, improved our consistency, and made this process faster. Sure, these improvements are minor, but over time, these small improvements really add up.

This streamlining can be taken even further by having our scripts run automatically. For example, we could have put our race detection code as a git pre-commit hook; this would make it run automatically every time we commit. I find pre-commit hooks annoying, but some folks swear by them.

Another example of this streamlining, and my personal favorite, is to have the IDE configured to automatically format my code and fix the imports every time unit tests are run. With this, the code is always neat, and the imports are "automatically" resolved.

We will go through several optimizations like these in the *Master Your Tooling* section later in this chapter.

Look for common mistakes

No matter how good we are, we all make mistakes. In fact, often, the more senior we are, the higher the cost of our mistakes. When it comes to coding mistakes, our reaction should not be shame but rather inspiration. We should be inspired to consider why we made the mistake and what we can do to avoid repeating it. Some mistakes, like dead code, unused constants, or forgetting to check return errors, can be caught by adopting linters. Mistakes like out-of-date comments, the placement of interfaces, or misleading variable naming can only be caught as part of a code review.

Sometimes, the best response to the discovery of a common mistake is knowledge sharing. Writing and sharing a short article that outlines the mistake and how to address it is extremely valuable to both you and your peers.

Next time you notice a common mistake, let it inspire you into an action that will help eliminate or neutralize it.

Clean as you go

The phrase "Clean as you go" was drummed into me in my first job as a teenager working at the local McDonald's. Strangely enough, it is still pertinent to programming many years later. No codebase is perfect. Throughout our day, we will come across code that can be improved in one way or another. Depending on the size of the resulting change and our team's culture, we should either take the time to fix it now or make a note and come back and fix it later. As we have seen in previous chapters, small changes can lead to significant code UX improvements, and making these changes will improve the entire team's productivity. Performing these changes "as you go" ensures the quickest time to better code, and makes them feel less arduous or demanding. I should clarify the apparent conflict between this section and the *Make it Work, Make it Clean, and Then, Maybe, Make it Fast* section from Chapter 6. Here, I am talking about merge requests—we should add any "clean as you go" changes to the "Make it Clean" part of the process and send a single merge request, or add a cleaning-only supplementary merge request if the changes would make the first one too large.

Be Introspective

In the previous section, I encouraged you to notice issues as you are working; now, I am encouraging you to take this further. Occasionally, perhaps once a month, examine how you work and wonder: is there a better way? Ask yourself: are there ways to do the same work faster, easier, or with fewer errors? Is there anything that is slowing you down? What are you doing that is working well, and how can you do more of that?

These questions could lead to the adoption of new tools or adjustments to your (or your team's) development practices and processes. We may not always be able to set the team's development practices, but the issues are often invisible to management, and if they are not raised, they cannot be addressed.

Such introspection can lead to identifying issues in code style and structure or system architecture that must be addressed. We should also re-evaluate our previous decisions. We may now have better information or knowledge and can make better decisions. When this is the case, we must compare the cost of changing our decision, refactoring, and its long-term benefits against the ongoing cost of not refactoring.

Being introspective is a skill like any other; initially, you might find it helpful to schedule time to reflect. Eventually, you will find that it becomes part of your subconscious and will happen naturally. You will also find that this process is helpful when repeated as a team activity.

Be Adventurous

As programmers, we often need to solve complicated problems with incomplete information. How we respond to this can be anywhere on the spectrum between reckless abandon and meticulous caution. While meticulous caution will lead to better outcomes, it is also the slowest possible approach by a wide margin. To improve our productivity, we should look for ways to get closer to reckless abandon without introducing unnecessary mess or mistakes.

Use automated tests

The first and most valuable tool available to us is automated tests. As we have seen previously, we use tests to ensure our code's behavior is what we need. As such, they are a safety net for any additions or refactoring we might make. However, tests can also be used as an efficient way to discover and explore code. Assume you are new to a project: you could spend time reading every line of code to build up a mental model of what the application does, or you could write some tests. Tests allow you to efficiently form and prove assumptions about the code. They are the fastest way to build an understanding of the codebase. This same process can be used to efficiently debug reported bugs. Instead of reading code and hoping to find the error, it is much more efficient to construct a test (or tests) that proves the bug and helps localize it.

Plan, but just enough

One of the more common pieces of advice I offer mid-level engineers is to develop ways to become comfortable making decisions with incomplete information. It is very easy to spend a significant amount of time investigating, planning, researching, and debating the problems we are faced with. Sadly, this effort has diminishing returns. Now, I am not trying to suggest that we don't plan and just start coding. I am suggesting that the amount of time and effort we spend on planning the solution should be relative to the problem's size and complexity. For example, when starting a new application or service, we should write up a software plan or RFC document and have that peer-reviewed (sanity checked, really). Note: if you don't already have a company standard, I have included a sample RFC document format with this chapter's code. This planning process is intentionally not trivial; in some cases, it can actually be a little arduous but does force us to think through and discuss the problem.

After planning, it is essential to realize that the resulting plan is nothing more than a starting point. As you proceed with the implementation, you will gain a better understanding of the problem and an appreciation for the qualities and limitations of the chosen implementation. There is nothing wrong with leveraging this new knowledge and understanding to deviate from the plan; in fact, these changes are so common they can be expected.

Expect change

Beyond planning work before starting, another strategy for dealing with incomplete information is structuring your solution to allow decisions to change. Many implementation decisions can be changed with minimal impact by focusing on encapsulation, decoupling, and durable abstractions. With this lessened impact, we can refactor faster and with more confidence.

The underlying goal of the approaches discussed in this section is to gain confidence in the face of uncertainty: confidence that we are moving in the right direction, confidence that things won't break without us knowing, and confidence that we can cheaply change our minds later. This confidence will empower us to be adventurous and move faster.

Master Your Tooling

Now, we come to the most effective and most commonly overlooked strategy: mastery of our tools. As programmers, we spend a significant portion of our day coding. As such, the effectiveness of our chosen tools plays a significant part in our productivity. If we use a 10-year-old computer, every action we take will be slower than something newer. But it goes far deeper than that. Which tools we choose, how effectively we use the tools we use, and even how we interact with the computer itself can all improve or detract from our productivity. So, I implore you to spend time mastering the tools and your development environment, even if that means taking the time to build new tools for yourself.

A significant first step in this process is to minimize the use of your mouse. Every time you take your hand off the keyboard to grab the mouse, you lose time. Yes, we are talking about a second or two, but these seconds quickly add up. Taking the time to learn (and configure) keyboard shortcuts to replace the mouse will give you this time back.

The second step is to adopt a code formatter and let it do as much work as possible. While you are still figuring out what the implementation should look like, formatting is unimportant. Having your IDE automatically take care of the basic formatting and complete the imports saves a lot of time. A quick side note here: import completion is much more efficient when we use internal directories and unique package names. This is another reason to avoid using common package names like **errors**, **commons**, or **utils**.

The third step is to adopt a code linter. I've been in companies where linters were used as a stick with which to beat people; this is sad and completely misses the intent of linters. Adopting a linter in our personal work allows us to learn how to produce better code and gives us the fastest possible feedback. Linters should be used as automated code reviews. Using a linter is like having a programming buddy on your shoulder pointing out when you have made a mistake or could do better.

They should be configured to find issues that otherwise would have to be caught by a human during a thorough code review. As such, they are an opportunity for us, individual programmers, to learn how to write better code more efficiently and do so before spending our teammate's time in code review.

This is not to say all linters are created equal. There will be some lint checks that you and your team will disagree with; turn these checks off. These settings can and should change over time as you and your team improve and your collective tastes change.

My preferred Go linter is GolangCI-Lint (**https://golangci-lint.run/**), which is actually a lint aggregator. It supports about 50 linters, with more frequently added. The default configuration is excellent for getting you started quickly, but remember that your lint configuration should be based on your team's preferences. So, we should spend the time configuring the linter so that the only issues highlighted are the ones we want to fix. The moment we start ignoring the linter's output is the moment it goes from being a useful productivity tool to a waste of time.

With the mouse out of the way and a code formatter and linter taking care of the code's fundamentals, we have the basics covered. Now, we can ratchet up the productivity and look at ways to make our everyday tasks faster, simpler, and less error-prone.

Build tools that work for you

This section will introduce a series of bash scripts to perform daily Go programming tasks. Copying these scripts somewhere on your PATH will allow you to perform these tasks quickly, consistently, and without mistakes. These scripts use bash and were designed to be used on Mac OS X, but they could be converted to other platforms or, if you prefer, refactored into a makefile. All of the scripts in this section are included in the source code for this chapter.

Calculate unit test coverage

To quickly and efficiently calculate the unit test coverage of an entire project, I created a tool that recursively calls **go test -cover** and then combines the result (**https://github.com/corsc/go-tools/tree/master/package-coverage**). As this tool expanded, it became unwieldy to use, because there were so many command-line arguments. So, I now use the following script most of the time:

```
#!/bin/bash

set -o errexit
set -o pipefail

# Ensure the formatting of the source directory is consistent.
DIR=${1%...}
PKG_DIR=${DIR%/}/

# Import a regex with files to ignore and assign it to COVERAGE_EXCLUDE.
source ~/Applications/go-exclusions

# Calculate the go import path of the base package.
BASE_PKG=$(go list)
BASE_PKG=${BASE_PKG%/}/

# Calculate unit test coverage and highlight any packages under 70%.
#
# The settings we are using here are:
# -a = requests the tool to calculate the coverage, output it to the terminal, and clean up
afterwards.
# -i $COVERAGE_EXCLUDE = excludes some paths from coverage given the supplied
regular expression.
# -m 70 = sets the minimum coverage value to 70%. Any packages under this number will be
highlighted in red.
# -prefix $BASE_PKG = trims the BASE_PKG value from the start of all package names. This
makes the output easier to read.
# $PKG_DIR = specifies the base directory from which coverage will be calculated.
# ${@:2} = passes any additional flags used to call to this script to the call to the tool.
package-coverage -a -i $COVERAGE_EXCLUDE -m 70 -prefix $BASE_PKG ${@:2}
$PKG_DIR
```

When attempting to understand the coverage for a particular package, it can be better to use the HTML representation of test coverage; for this, I use the following script:

```
#!/bin/bash
```

```
set -e

# Ensure we specified a directory
if [ "$1" == "" ]; then
    echo "No input file. Usage: pcov-html ./your-package-dir/"
    exit 1
fi

# Clean up the input
DIR=${1%...}
PKG_DIR=${DIR%/}/
PKG_DIR=./${DIR#./}

# Calculate test coverage and open the HTML result
go test $PKG_DIR -coverprofile=$PKG_DIR/coverage.out ${@:1}
go tool cover -html=$PKG_DIR/coverage.out
rm $PKG_DIR/coverage.out
```

Perform race detection with tests

Another operation we should do every day is checking our code for race conditions. To speed up the typing of that command, we can use the following:

```
#!/bin/bash

# Ensure we specified a directory
if [ "$1" == "" ]; then
    echo "No input file. Usage: gtest ./your-package-dir/"
    exit 1
fi

# Run go test but exclude any vendor code
go test -race $(go list $1 | grep -v /vendor)
```

If you use the console to run tests, you might consider making another script like this without the **race** flag to cut down on typing and avoid race detection's performance cost.

Format code and imports

Perhaps the most common task we need to do is fixing the code's formatting and the imports. I don't use this script much directly, but instead, I have this set up to run every time I run my unit tests in the IDE. Here is the script:

```bash
#!/bin/bash

set +x

# Enable verbose debugging output by setting DBG_SCRIPTS to any value.
if [ -n "${DBG_SCRIPTS}" ]; then
    set -x
fi

set -o errexit
set -o pipefail

# Ensure we specify a directory.
if [ -z "$1" ]; then
    echo "Please supply a destination directory"
    exit 1
fi

# Ensure the formatting of the source directory is consistent.
DIR=${1%...}
PKG_DIR=${DIR%/}/

# Build a list of all Go files
DIRS=$(find $PKG_DIR -type f -name '*.go')

# Shortcut when no directories with Go files are found.
if [ -z "$DIRS" ]; then
    exit 0
fi

# Clean and simplify the code
gofmt -w -s -l $DIRS

# Fix imports
```

```
goimports -w -l $DIRS
```

As you can see, this script uses **gofmt** and **goimports**; if you prefer other tools for formatting and imports, then you can swap these out.

Generate/regenerate code

Regenerating code might be straightforward, but I like to follow it up with a call to the formatter to ensure everything is clean and consistent. Additionally, moving the call to **go generate** to the following script reduces my mistakes, and the script name is faster to type. Here is the script:

```
#!/bin/bash

set -o errexit
set -o pipefail

clear

# Enable verbose debugging output by setting DBG_SCRIPTS to any value.
if [ -n "${DBG_SCRIPTS}" ]; then
    set -x
fi

if [ -z "$1" ]; then
    # A specific directory was not supplied; use all changed directories.

    # Check changed dirs
    dirsToCheck=$(for f in $(git diff --name-only --diff-filter=d); do dirname $f; done | sort |
uniq)

    for d in $dirsToCheck; do
        # Regenerate the directory.
        go generate ./$d

        # Format generated code (call the formatting script).
        goclean ./$d
    done
```

```
      exit
fi


# Regenerate only the supplied directory.
go generate $1


# Format generated code (call the formatting script).
goclean $1
```

Generate the dependency graph

Creating the dependency graph is not something I find myself needing to do often; thus, I often find it hard to remember the exact sequence of commands. With this script, I don't have to bother:

```
#!/bin/bash

set -o errexit
set -o pipefail

# Note:
# This script should be run in the base directory of the project/service

# Required Tools
# go get github.com/kisielk/godepgraph
# brew install graphviz

# Inputs
#
# This cuts down on typing by allowing you to enter only the sub-directory you wish to graph, #
instead of the entire package

prefix="./"
PKG=${1#$prefix}

# Constants
#
# Save the file in the home directory (so it's easy to find)
DEST_FILE=~/depgraph.png
```

```
# Calculate the package in the current directory and assume this is the base or project
package
BASE_PKG=$(go list)
BASE_PKG_DELIMITED=$(echo $BASE_PKG | sed 's/\//\\\//g')

EXCLUSIONS="$EXCLUSIONS${GO_BASE_PKG}/vendor"

# Generate the dependency graph
godepgraph -s \
    -p "$EXCLUSIONS" \
    -o "$BASE_PKG" \
    $BASE_PKG/${PKG} |
    sed "s/$BASE_PKG_DELIMITED//g" | dot -Gsplines=true -Tpng -o $DEST_FILE

# Open the result in the default web browser (only works on OS X)
open $DEST_FILE
```

Ship it!

Perhaps the most valuable script (and the most complicated) is this final one. In this script, we perform all the checks on our code before committing and pushing the code. By using this script to ship code, we are ensuring consistent style and formatting for all of our code. This consistency not only ensures a better code UX but also results in smaller change sets. These smaller change sets mean less work for code reviewers and less code churn resulting from inconsistent formatting. Here is the script:

```
#!/bin/bash

set +x

# Enable verbose debugging output by setting DBG_SCRIPTS to any value.
if [ -n "${DBG_SCRIPTS}" ]; then
    set -x
fi

clear

# Define some standard exclusions to linting and code coverage checks
```

```
# and assign them to LINTER_EXCLUDE.
source ~/Applications/go-exclusions

# Build list of modified directories.
dirsToCheck=$(for f in $(git diff --name-only --diff-filter=d --merge-base HEAD); do dirname $f;
done | sort | uniq)

# Run standard checks and cleaning.
for d in $dirsToCheck; do
    # Ignore directories marked as excluded.
    skipLint=$(echo "/$d/" | grep -E "$LINTER_EXCLUDE")
    if [ $? -eq 0 ]; then
        echo "$d skipped due to LINTER_EXCLUDE"
        echo
        continue
    fi

    # Header to keep track.
    echo -e "\033[1;34mChecking: $d\033[0m"

    # Format code and fix imports.
    echo -e "\033[1;34mClean:\033[0m"
    if [ "$d" != "." ]; then
        goclean ./$d

        if [ $? -ne 0 ]; then
            exit -1
        fi
    fi

    # Run tests and race check.
    echo -e "\033[1;34mRace Tests:\033[0m"
    testResult=$(gotestr ./$d 2>&1)
    if [ $? -ne 0 ]; then
        testFailed=$(echo "$testResult" | grep "no Go files")
        if [ $? -ne 0 ]; then
            echo -e "$testResult"
            exit -1
        fi
    fi
```

```
        fi

        # Skip further checks when no changes were made.
        testsWereCached=$(echo "$testResult" | grep "(cached)")
        if [ $? -ne 0 ]; then
            # Perform lint checks
            echo -e "\033[1;34mLint:\033[0m"
            lintResult=$(golint ./$d 2>&1)
            if [ $? -ne 0 ]; then
                lintFailed=$(echo "$lintResult" | grep "no go files to analyze")
                if [ $? -ne 0 ]; then
                    echo -e "$lintResult"
                    exit -1
                fi
            fi

            # Enforce minimum coverage.
            echo -e "\033[1;34mCode Coverage Check:\033[0m"
            coverageResult=$(pcov $d -s 2>&1)
            if [ $? -ne 0 ]; then
                testFailed=$(echo "$testResult" | grep "no Go files")
                if [ $? -ne 0 ]; then
                    echo -e "$coverageResult"
                    exit -1
                else
                    echo -e "$coverageResult"
                fi
            fi
        else
            echo "skipped further checks as code was not changed since last run"
        fi

        echo
done

# Ship it!
read -p "Ship it? (y/n): " -n 1 choice
echo
```

```
if [ "$choice" == "y" ] || [ "$choice" == "Y" ]; then
    git add .
    git commit
    GIT_BRANCH=$(git rev-parse --abbrev-ref HEAD)
    git push --force-with-lease -u origin ${GIT_BRANCH}
fi
```

You will note this script calls the other scripts we have introduced and **golint**, which we did not mention previously. This script is included in the source code for this chapter and is similar to the others. It calls the **golanglint-ci** tool that we mentioned earlier.

We have discussed six different scripts in this section, but you will likely find more tasks that you frequently perform that would benefit from being wrapped in a script. This may include tasks with multiple steps, programs with multiple command-line arguments, or anything else you cannot trigger reliably and quickly. The key is to keep an eye out and then take the time to build and maintain the script. If writing scripts is not something you enjoy doing or if the task you are trying to complete has some pretty complicated logic (like parsing JSON or downloading files), then write Go programs. Executing other applications from inside a Go application is not as simple as scripts, but it is straightforward.

Master your IDE

Just as chefs spend time and effort to master their knives, programmers must spend the time and effort to master our most basic tool, our IDE.

Just as there is no "best knife" or one knife that can be used by all chefs in all situations, similarly, there is no IDE that works for all programmers in all situations. The best IDE for you is the one that enables you to most productively achieve your current goals. Currently, I use Goland from JetBrains (**https://www.jetbrains.com/go/**). In this section, I will highlight the features of Goland that offer significant productivity improvements and some commands, plugins, and keybindings that help me be productive. If you don't use Goland, I encourage you not to skip this section, not because I am trying to convert you, but because your IDE likely has similar features, plugins, or options you could leverage to be more productive.

Useful features

While Goland has many features, I want to highlight three that are integral to productivity. These are:

1. Context actions

2. The test runner

3. Live templates

Context actions

Context actions are very similar to autocomplete because different actions are offered at different times depending on the cursor's position and the code surrounding the cursor. For example, when the cursor is inside a struct that we are initializing, we are shown the following context action pop-up:

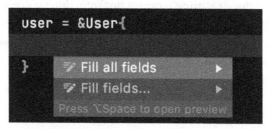

Figure 7.1—Context actions pop-up

As you can see, we are given the option to fill the fields of the struct. Selecting this option gives us:

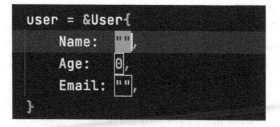

Figure 7.2—Fill all fields context action result

The IDE has added all of the field names and default zero values based on their type, thus giving us a very efficient way to populate our struct.As you might expect, the context menu has many other features beyond populating structs; for example, when there are mistakes or lint issues in the code, the context menu gives us:

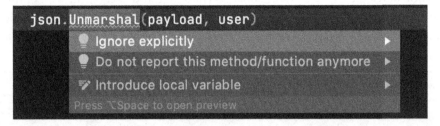

Figure 7.3—Issue context action pop-up

From this menu, we can apply quick fixes to resolve the issue. When we combine this feature with the keyboard shortcut for "Next Highlighted Error" (F2 on my Mac), we can quickly find and fix any issues with the current file.

There are many other context actions, all designed to make coding easier and faster; I encourage you to explore further.

The test runner

Whether you develop using test-driven development or not, you likely spend a lot of time running and waiting for tests. Therefore, it is imperative that we trigger our tests quickly and easily and that they run as fast as possible. In Goland, the first time we trigger the test runner (via keyboard shortcut or menu), we are presented with the following dialog:

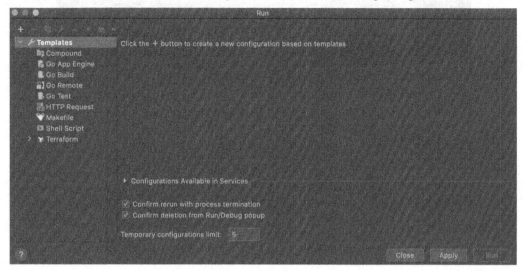

Figure 7.4—Run dialog

From this dialog, we choose *Go Test* from the left-hand side, and then we are presented with the following dialog:

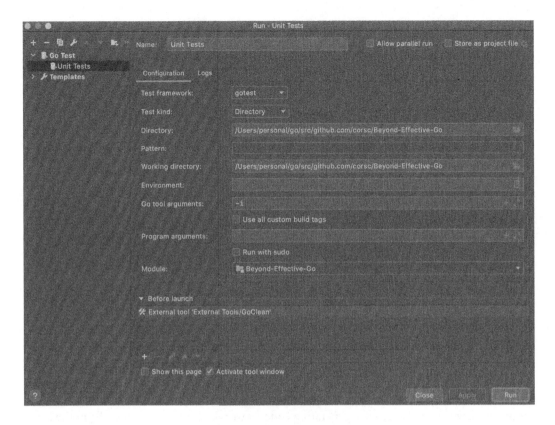

Figure 7.5—Run tests dialog

We will configure the various settings based on our project and preferences and then click *Run*. After this first configuration, we can run the tests without seeing this dialog. You might also have noticed I have configured an *External tool*. This tool is calling the code formatting script that we introduced earlier. This way, our code is formatted, and the imports are fixed automatically before the tests are run.

Here is the configuration for the external tool:

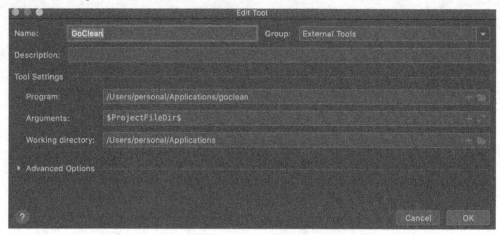

Figure 7.6—External tools dialog

Beyond the initial productivity improvement of being able to trigger the tests with a keyboard shortcut, being able to trigger formatting and imports will save you a bunch of time.

We can also use external tools without running tests to call our other scripts. This can be useful for other everyday operations, like generating code, as we will not have to switch from the IDE to a console.

Live templates

The last feature we are going to look at is *live templates*. This feature is a notable productivity improvement as it can significantly decrease the amount of typing we have to do, which in turn improves our consistency and reduces mistakes. They enable us to configure additional tab-completion options that we can use. For example, if we want to add a for/range loop to our code, with Live Templates, we can type **forr**, and then we will be presented with the following context menu:

Figure 7.7—Live template forr context menu

With this menu, we can press tab, and then we are presented with the following:

Figure 7.8—For-range live template

With this, we can quickly fill in the parts of the statement and move on to other things.

Goland has several handy templates built in, and you can also define your own. Once you are mindful of this feature, you will likely notice many occasions where you use the same code pattern. For example, one of the most common templates that I have created uses the live template named **cctx**, which expands into this:

```
ctx, cancel := context.WithTimeout(context.Background(), $TIMEOUT$ * time.Second)
defer cancel()
```

Note: the words surrounded by **$**, like **$TIMEOUT$** in the above example, are template variables. Goland allows for quick navigation between these variables with the tab key.

To allow me to forget the exact format of the **go:generate** command for Mockery, the Template named **mockery** expands into this:

```
//go:generate mockery --name=$INTERFACE_NAME$ --case underscore --testonly --
inpackage
```

If you are not familiar with generating mocks for testing using Mockery, there is *A very brief introduction* in Chapter 9.

I have found that there is a lot of duplication (and consistency) in my test code. The most common and valuable test-related live template I use generates the table-driven test skeleton from **tdt** into this:

```go
scenarios := []struct {
    desc          string
    in            $IN_TYPE$
    configureMocks func(*$MOCK_TYPE$)
    expected      $EXPECTED_TYPE$
    expectAnErr   bool
}{
    {
        desc:           "Happy path",
        in:             $IN$,
        configureMocks: func(*$MOCK_TYPE$) {
        },
        expected:       $EXPECTED$,
        expectAnErr:    false,
    },
}

for _, s := range scenarios {
    scenario := s
    t.Run(scenario.desc, func(t *testing.T) {
        t.Parallel()

        // inputs

        // mocks

        // call object under test
        result, resultErr := $METHOD$()

        // validation
        require.Equal(t, scenario.expectAnErr, resultErr != nil, "expect an error: %t err: %s",
scenario.expectAnErr, resultErr)
        assert.Equal(t, scenario.expected, result, "expected result")
    })
}
```

As you can see, this one saves a tonne of typing and mistakes.

I have included more of these templates in the source code for this chapter, and there are even more that you could create that would match your coding style and speed up your productivity.

Useful shortcuts

Continuing with our focus on coding faster, more consistently, and with fewer errors, learning and utilizing shortcut commands can significantly impact our overall productivity. Yes, I am again attempting to save the few seconds it takes to move our hand from the keyboard to the mouse, but you might be surprised just how often you perform this action throughout the day —and, as a result, just how much time you can save by using the keyboard instead. The following is a list of 10 Goland shortcuts you might not be aware of but will find helpful. I have also included the default MacOS keyboard shortcut and a short explanation for each.

1. **Open file (Command: ⇧⌘O)**—Opens the file dialog. This dialog allows you to select from a list of files that match what you have entered. Additionally, if you append a colon and a number, it will jump to that line number in the file, which can be very useful when combined with linter or test results.

2. **Go To Declaration or Usages (Command: ⌘B)**—This is perhaps my most used shortcut. When the cursor is on a variable, the cursor will jump to the creation of the variable. When the cursor is on the usage of a type, it will jump to the definition of that type. Inversely, when the cursor is on the creation of a variable or the definition of a type, it will show a list of all the usages of that variable or type.

3. **Find Usages (Command: ⌥F7)**—This command will show the complete list of all locations where a type or variable has been used. This can be useful during refactoring and investigating code.

4. **Show implementations (Command: ⌥⌘B)**—When we use the Go style of defining interfaces in the package they are used, it is less obvious where this interface has been implemented. This command generates a list of all implementations.

5. **Run tests (Command: ^⌥R or ^R)**—The first command allows us to select the test configuration we want to run, and the second will re-run the last test run.

6. **Switch focus**—These commands allow us to quickly switch between the IDE panes without using the mouse. They can also be used to show and hide these panes.

   a. **To Project (Command: ⌘1)**—Move focus to the file list.

   b. **Search Results (Command: ⌘3)**—Move focus to the search results list. This list could be the results of a search or other commands like *Find Usages*.

   c. **Test Results (Command: ⌘4)**—Move focus to the test results.

7. **Generate (Command: ⌘N)**—When focusing on the code pane, this command shows a context menu from which we can generate tests or implement an interface, both of which are very common actions.

8. **New Scratch File (Command: ⇧⌘N)**—Often, we need somewhere to store some text, a fragment of code, or a TODO list; instead of switching to a text editor or notepad application, we can use this command. It will open a file that's outside the current project (so we don't have to worry about SCM-related mess) but persistent so we won't accidentally lose it.

9. **Fold/Unfold (Command: ⌘.)**—Folding code can be a helpful way of hiding details we are not currently working on or utility functions that are seldom changed. This command toggles this code folding.

10. **Find Action (Command: ⇧⌘A)**—For many commands, there are no keyboard shortcuts assigned; we can, of course, assign our own. In the meantime, or if we forget the shortcuts, there is this command. This command opens a dialog from which we can search, find, and trigger other actions. This command is handy for triggering infrequent actions like *Resolve Conflicts* or *Split Screen*.

Like the previous section on features, there are far more commands available than those discussed here. I strongly encourage you to check the manual occasionally, configure your own custom shortcuts, and even investigate other ways to learn more commands (for example, the *Key Promoter* plugin coming up in the next section).

Useful plugins

There are a wealth of plugins for Golang, as with most IDEs. Often, plugins result from people like you and me wanting to code a little easier or faster. Therefore, we should take a look around the plugin marketplace every six months or so and see what is around.

There are three plugins that I would like to highlight to you. Perhaps surprisingly, two of them are not directly related to coding.

The first plugin is called *Key Promoter X* (**https://plugins.jetbrains.com/plugin/9792-key-promoter-x**) by Patrick Scheibe. This plugin is designed to help you learn the keyboard shortcuts available in Goland. It monitors when you use your mouse to navigate or trigger actions and then shows an unobtrusive dialog when the same action could have been done with a keyboard shortcut. This plugin is an easy and painless way to become a power user and avoid wasting time with the mouse.

The second plugin comes bundled with Goland and is called *IDE Features Trainer*. This plugin is also designed to help you master Goland. It provides quick and helpful lessons on everyday tasks like debugging, code completion, generating code, and refactoring.

The third plugin to mention is *Copilot* (**https://github.com/features/copilot**) by GitHub. With the explosion of large language models (LLMs), there has been a similar explosion in LLM-based coding helpers. For me, Copilot is currently the best of the bunch. Copilot works in a very similar manner to the live templates we have mentioned earlier. The main difference is that we don't have to define the templates in advance. Instead, it uses its language model to generate code based on the current context at the cursor. Copilot is not a tool that will do your work for you, but it can save you a lot of typing and time with frequently occurring things like generating formatted errors, test assertions, or error return blocks, or pulling data from a database. The most impressive feature has been that the more I used it, the more it adapted to my style.

The IDE we choose to use and our mastery of it significantly impact how productive we can be. It is worth the time to find an IDE that suits you and to find all the shortcuts, features, and plugins that can help you be more productive.

Master your environment

No matter how good our IDE is or how well we master it, there will always be tasks where the most efficient option is to drop into a shell. For example, despite Goland having support for Git built in, I prefer to do most Git-related actions in a shell.

In this section, I will share two ways to get more out of our time in a shell.

The first is the extension of an approach we have already seen, creating bash scripts to handle repeated, complicated actions, and the second is shell aliases.

Handy Git scripts

Most companies I have worked for use the short-lived branch approach to feature development. As such, I am frequently creating new Git branches and hopping between branches. This first script is used to start work on a new feature and looks like this:

```
#!/bin/bash

if [ -z "$1" ]; then
    echo "Usage: newfeature [branch name]"
    exit 1
fi

IS_CLEAN=$(git status --short | wc -l)
if [ ${IS_CLEAN} -ne 0 ]; then
    git stash
fi

git checkout master
git pull origin master
git checkout -b $1

if [ ${IS_CLEAN} -ne 0 ]; then
    git stash pop
fi
```

As you can see, it also stashes and unstashes any pending changes and downloads the latest master before starting a new branch. This becomes two fewer things to remember to do.

The second script expands the first and is used to jump between branches, allowing us to work on multiple features at once. Here is the script:

```bash
#!/bin/bash

set -o errexit
set -o pipefail

if [ -z "$1" ]; then
    echo "Usage: sw [branch name]"
    exit 1
fi

# Check if we need to stash and in-progress changes
IS_CLEAN=$(git status --short | wc -l)
if [ ${IS_CLEAN} -ne 0 ]; then
    git stash
fi

# Grab the latest
git checkout master
git pull origin master

# Rebase master into the work branch
git checkout $1
git rebase master

# Merge any stashed changes
if [ $IS_CLEAN -ne 0 ]; then
    git stash pop
fi
```

You will notice that we are changing from one branch to another towards the end of the script but downloading the latest master and rebasing our feature branch against that. It can be a little irritating to have to rebase before getting back to work on a feature branch, but I find it less annoying than thinking I am finished and then having to rebase before submitting my code for review.

Shell aliases

Shell aliases define custom shell commands that expand and call applications and other shell commands. They are perfect for replacing frequently used shell commands with something shorter and easier to type. For example, let's assume you use a shell to run your Go tests. Instead of using this command:

```
$ go test ./...
```

You could instead define an alias named **gt** and instead type:

```
$ gt
```

This is clearly much easier, faster, and less error-prone. Additionally, as it is known by the shell, we can leverage tab completion, although not in this particular case. To define an alias, we add the following line to your .bashrc (or similar) file:

```
alias gt='go test ./...'
```

As mentioned, I use my IDE to run tests and have custom scripts to handle the most common Go-related tasks. However, I do use the shell for interacting with Git. The following is a sample of the aliases that I use:

```
# Common Git-related actions
alias gs='git status '
alias ga='git add '
alias gc='git commit '
alias gd='git diff '
alias gco='git checkout '
alias gp='git pull '
alias grm='git rebase master '
alias gst='git stash '
alias grc='git rebase --continue '
alias grs='git rebase --skip '
alias gb='git branch '

# Call the sw script and switch to master branch
alias swm='sw master'
```

```
# Aliases to catch accidental mistakes
alias got='git '
alias gut='git '
```

There really is no limit to the aliases that you can define. The key is to be mindful of the tasks that you are performing daily and create useful, memorable, and unique aliases to make life easier.

Hopefully, you can see a consistent theme running through all of the sections under this *Master of Your Tooling* section; it is absolutely worth the time and effort to find, customize, and master the tools you use daily. We should seek out tools and tricks to make us faster, more consistent, or less error-prone.

Make Small Changes

In most companies, there is a ceremony related to the submission of code changes (often referred to as pull requests). With this ceremony comes additional work to get the code ready for submission and then a wait for review. Because of this extra work, programmers are instinctually incentivized to avoid it and, as a result, submit larger pull requests. However, we should instead borrow a mantra from the *continuous delivery* (CD) ideology: when something is painful, we should do it more often.

This concept has a few layers, so please bear with me. Firstly, the underlying idea from CD posits that if something is painful and we force ourselves to do it more, we become highly motivated to streamline this process. If getting code ready for submission and waiting for review is not trivial, optimizing it will be a big win for all developers all the time.

Secondly, when submitting large pull requests, we introduce a more significant burden for our peers. Larger pull requests are more burdensome, often more complicated, and, as a result, will take longer to review.

Finally, we should acknowledge the risks associated with making a large number of changes. If the team does not agree with the approach we have taken, we risk spending a lot of time on changes that will not be accepted.

And finally, if any problems are caused by the changes, it will likely take longer to find the cause, given that we would have to investigate more changes.

Most large problems in programming can be broken into a collection of smaller ones. We should always be mindful of the size and scope of the changes we have made and look for opportunities to submit our pull requests before they become too big. It may not be obvious, but we can merge new features without wiring them to the public API. In this way, they cannot cause us any trouble. Similarly, we can protect implementation changes with a feature flag (that is turned off). In both cases, the code is merged but cannot be used and does not add any risk.

Summary

In this chapter, we discussed many of the peripheral tasks and actions related to programming with the goal of being more productive.

We examined micro but frequent improvements, like replacing the mouse with keyboard shortcuts; we also examined potentially significant improvements, like using documentation and planning to avoid big mistakes and reduce the time needed to explain and justify decisions.

We introduced the idea that we should take stock of all the tasks we do throughout the day and look for ways to perform them faster or more reliably, or eradicate the need for them.

And finally, we discussed the importance of mastering the tools that we use: finding an IDE that suits us, using all of the IDE's features, plugins, and keyboard shortcuts to get the most out of it, constructing our own tools, and customizing the environment in which we work.

Many of the techniques introduced in this chapter might seem like extra work from a micro perspective, and they are. However, from a macro perspective, taking the time to learn new things and find or build more effective ways of achieving our goals are invaluable investments that will repay the time and effort many times over.

Questions

1. How can being lazy help us be productive?

2. Why is less code generally better than more code?

3. How can writing documentation save us time?

4. How can being observant and introspective help us find potential productivity improvements?

5. How can we be adventurous and not be unnecessarily risky?

6. Why is mastering the tools we use imperative?

7. What can we do when our tools could be more convenient or simple to use?

8. Why is it more desirable to make small sets of changes?

9. How can we submit, merge, and deploy changes that are not yet ready for the user?

Chapter 8

Examining Unusual Patterns for Go

Introduction

Let's take a step back for a moment and acknowledge how unusual Go is as a language. It is not really an object-oriented language, but, as we saw in Chapter 4, that does not stop us from adopting the object-oriented design patterns to great effect.

Similarly, Go is not a functional language, but, as we will see in this chapter, it does not stop us from adopting and benefiting from some of the functional programming patterns.

In this chapter, we will introduce functional programming and its concepts, and then anonymous functions and closures. We will then examine many fun things we can achieve with functions in Go. After these, we will take a quick look at futures: yet another approach that may not be, strictly speaking, a Go concept, but is possible.

By now, you are likely sensing a pattern; these concepts are unusual, at least from a Go perspective. Most of these typically are not found in the manual or beginners' Go text. These concepts and patterns have been included here to offer you an awareness of these concepts and approaches and broaden our understanding of what is possible. For this reason, we will round out the chapter with something unique to Go, a collection of struct-related tricks.

The following topics will be covered in this chapter:

- Functional Programming in Go
- Fun with Functions
- Implementing Futures
- Curious Struct Tricks

Code

To get the most out of this chapter, you will need a recent copy (1.13+) of Go installed and your favorite IDE.

Full versions of all code examples and other related material can be found at **https://github.com/corsc/Beyond-Effective-Go/tree/master/Chapter08**.

Functional Programming in Go

While Go is not a functional language, it does have many of the features required to program in a functional style. As such, it is possible to employ some of the patterns used in functional programming and leverage their benefits. But first, what is functional programming?

Functional programming (FP) is a programming style based on the three fundamental ideas:

- Mathematical or pure functions
- Immutability
- No implicit state

The first fundamental idea is mathematical or pure functions. At a fundamental level, mathematics defines a function as a relation or mapping between inputs and outputs. In mathematics, a function is considered a pure function when given the same inputs, the output is the same regardless of how many times it is called, and the function has no side effects (it doesn't, for example, change any non-local variables or any inputs passed by reference).

In programming, we often use a similar concept called *idempotency*. An idempotent function is one that can be called numerous times without any side effects beyond the first call. The difference between idempotent and pure functions is subtle but significant. A function that sums two numbers is pure because it will always give the same result when given the same inputs and there are no side-effects. However, if we took that same summing function and had it store the result in a global variable as well as returning the result, then it would no longer be a pure function but would still be an idempotent function.

We should take a brief detour and talk and refresh our understanding of idempotency. Consider the following code:

```go
func TimeRemaining(when time.Time) time.Duration {
    return when.Sub(time.Now())
}
```

This code is not idempotent because it depends on the result of **time.Now()**, and as such, every time we call it and provide the same input value, we will receive a different outcome. We can, however, implement a slightly different version that is idempotent, like this:

```
func TimeRemaining(when, now time.Time) time.Duration {
    return when.Sub(now)
}
```

This code is idempotent as every time we supply the same inputs, we will receive exactly the same output.

The second fundamental idea of FP is global immutability, which expands the principle of no data mutations or side effects from the pure function to the entire application. This means that once a variable is created, it cannot be changed; it is immutable.

When programmers come from an object-oriented background, this facet of FP is often the one that can take the most getting used to. It is, however, the facet that makes individual parts of FP code significantly more effortless to understand and debug than non-functional code. When a function cannot affect anything outside of itself or be affected by anything outside of itself, then the output of a function is always the same given the same inputs. Similarly, when a variable cannot change after it has been created, there is no need to trace the execution of a program to understand the contents of a variable; we only need to find its creation point.

The third fundamental idea of FP is that components have no implicit state. This is arguably an extension of the previous notion of no data mutations. It also has similar intentions. When objects have state (e.g., struct member variables) and that state can be changed, then to debug an instance of an object, we would have to trace all interactions with that object.

Now that we have our basic understanding of FP fundamental ideas, we can discuss some programming concepts related to FP and what that means in Go.

The concepts we will examine are:

- First-class and higher-order functions

- Recursion
- Currying and partial functions
- Immutability

First-class and higher-order functions

First-class functions are a language feature where you can assign functions to variables. Because functions can be variables, they can be passed as arguments or even returned as outputs from functions.

First-class functions are a necessary language feature when programming in a functional style, as constructing, composing, and passing around functions form the basis of FP.

Moving on to higher-order functions.: when a function takes one or more functions as inputs or returns a function as an output, then it is considered a *higher-order function*. The following code is a higher-order function:

```
func forEach(in []string, operation func(string) string) []string {
    out := make([]string, len(in))

    for index, thisString := range in {
        // apply transformation using the supplied operation
        result := operation(thisString)

        out[index] = result
    }

    return out
}
```

As you can see, this function iterates over the supplied slice of strings and calls the supplied **operation()** once for each item.

We can use this higher-order function by passing in other functions like these as inputs:

```go
func toUpper(in string) string {
    return strings.ToUpper(in)
}

func addPeriod(in string) string {
    return in + "."
}
```

You can see that the functions we are passing in are unaware of how they are used or being called as part of the loop iteration. They are relatively simple and, therefore, are very easy to write and test. You can also notice that these functions adhere to the ideas of no implicit state or data mutations; they are pure functions.

Recursion

Recursion is an execution loop that results from a function calling itself. Because FP-based languages do not allow for mutable data, recursion is used instead of loops, with the current state of the loop being passed as part of the recursive call.

In the previous example, we used a loop to apply our string operations to each item in the slice. We can achieve the same by replacing the loop with recursion, like this:

```go
func forEach(in []string, operation func(string) string) []string {
    return forE(in, 0, operation)
}

func forE(in []string, index int, operation func(string) string) []string {
    if index >= len(in) {
        return nil
    }

    // apply transformation using the supplied operation
    result := operation(in[index])

    return append([]string{result}, forE(in, index+1, operation)...)
}
```

With this change, our implementation takes a more functional style.

Now, consider what happens if our input slice is enormous, say one million items? For every function call, the Go runtime will create a frame on the stack. No matter how capable the machine we are running this on, it will eventually run out of memory.

In functional languages, the compiler can detect this recursion and perform a *tail-call optimization* (TCO). During a TCO, the runtime is aware that the call is recursive, and a new stack is not created for each function call, which prevents the recursion from creating memory problems. However, Go doesn't perform TCOs, so we're left with the million-frame stack. This is perhaps the main limiting factor in using a functional programming style with Go.

Currying and partial functions

Function currying is the process of breaking down a function that takes multiple inputs into a series of functions that take only one argument. For example, this function has multiple arguments:

```go
func Multiply(a, b int) int {
    return a * b
}
```

To curry this function, we need to decompose it into the following:

```go
func Multiply(a int) func(int) int {
    return func(b int) int {
        return a * b
    }
}
```

You can see that our **Multiply()** function now returns a function instead of an integer. The returned function is referred to as a *partial function*. To calculate our integer result, we will need to call the partial function in either of the following two formats:

```go
func ExampleMultiply_ShortForm() {
    result := Multiply(5)(3)

    // Output: 15
    fmt.Println(result)
}
```

```
func ExampleMultiply_LongForm() {
    multiply5 := Multiply(5)

    result := multiply5(3)

    // Output: 15
    fmt.Println(result)
}
```

But why did we do this? That's an excellent question, given our usual focus on code that is easy to read and given that while clever, our curried function is more complicated. The power of curried functions comes from their flexibility. Our **Multiply()** was perfect for two arguments, but what happens when we have three? How about a slice of arguments? In all of these scenarios, the curried function can be used unchanged.

Here's one more example to make sure we have mastered this concept. Take a close look at the following code. Is there anything wrong with it from an FP perspective?

```
func ExampleMultiply_notFP() {
    inputs := []int{1, 2, 3, 4, 5}

    var result int

    for index, thisValue := range inputs {
        if index == 0 {
            result = thisValue
            continue
        }

        result = Multiply(result, thisValue)
    }

    // Output: 120
    fmt.Println(result)
}
```

This code has no bugs, but it violates one of the fundamental ideas of functional programming: *no data mutations*. The **result** value changes as the loop executes.

Immutability

Immutability means that once a variable is defined, it cannot be changed.

Unfortunately for us, it is not easy to enforce immutability in Go as there are only so many places we can replace the **var** keyword with **const**. There are, however, some steps we can take to avoid mistakes caused by variables being mutable. The first is ensuring we pass all objects using copies rather than pointers. When we pass an object using a pointer, that variable can be mutated and, therefore, break our desire for immutability.

Similarly, we must also be careful when dealing with maps, slices, and arrays. These collections are all passed by reference. Take a look at the following function:

```go
func ToLower(in map[string]string) {
    for key := range in {
        in[key] = strings.ToLower(in[key])
    }
}
```

This function converts all map values to lowercase. There is nothing we can reasonably do to prevent this mutation; if we wished to protect ourselves from the mutation, the best we could do would be to copy the map before calling the function, and this is hardly ideal.

So why is immutability beneficial? When variables are immutable, your code has the following advantages:

- **Idempotent**—the results of a function call are the same no matter when or how often you call it.

- **Cachable**—when functions are idempotent, they are simple to cache.

- **Modular**—when code has no state and is only a series of functions, we can compose these functions together to achieve our larger goal.

- **Parallelization**—when functions are independent and stateless, they are straightforward to parallelize.

- **Concurrency**—because the functions are idempotent and variables are immutable, all of the inconveniences related to concurrent code, like race conditions and deadlock, are impossible. As a result, constructs like mutexes and semaphores are unnecessary.

As we have seen, while Go isn't a functional language, we can adopt a functional style with a few restrictions. The weakness in enforcing referential transparency, particularly with collections, is a source of risk but not a complete adoption killer. The lack of tail-call optimization is a more substantial issue that many open-source FP packages attempt to address.

There are numerous advantages to adopting an FP style, but it is likely that in many situations, it is just too different from what our other team members expect. That said, armed with an appreciation for the central concepts of functional programming, especially currying, first-class functions, and partial functions, enables us to achieve some interesting things with functions, as we will see in the next section.

Fun with functions

In this section, we will examine several more fun things we can do with functions in Go. Some you may have seen before, and some probably not. As with all the sections in this chapter, the goal is to load ourselves up with tricks and patterns in case we ever need them.

Understanding anonymous functions and closures

In the previous section, we described first-class functions as functions that could be assigned to variables and passed around like data. Because Go supports first-class functions, we can also use a related concept, anonymous functions. Anonymous functions are just like normal functions, except they do not have a name. Let's look at an example. The following is a normal function:

```
func DoWork() error {
    // implementation removed
    return nil
}
```

There's nothing special there. Let's refactor this into an anonymous function:

```
var DoWork = func() error {
    // implementation removed
    return nil
}
```

In this example, we have declared the function anonymously and assigned it to a variable called **DoWork()**. As you may have guessed, to the users of this function, the interaction is the same as a named function, and they would need to examine the code to be aware if this is an anonymous function or just a regular one. However, because our **DoWork()** function is now a variable, we can swap it out at runtime. This feature is called *monkey patching* and can be used during testing. For example, suppose we had a function that returned a database connection like this:

```
var (
    db     *sql.DB
    dbInit sync.Once
)

// GetDB will return a database connection
var GetDB = func() *sql.DB {
    // prevent the accidental creation of multiple db connection pools
    dbInit.Do(func() {
        db, _ = sql.Open("mysql", "user:password@/dbname")
    })

    return db
}
```

During our unit tests, we could swap this function for another that returned a mocked database instead.

One last thing to note about anonymous functions: they don't need to be assigned to global variables, as we have done here. They can be defined and used anywhere. In fact, you likely already use anonymous functions quite regularly when you use **defer** and call goroutines.

Now, let's move on to a special type of anonymous function called *closures*. A closure is an anonymous function that refers to variables outside the function's scope. By this, we don't just mean a function that accesses global variables; we don't need closures for that. Let's look at an example:

```go
func buildGreeting(name string) func() string {
    greeting := "Hello " + name + "."

    return func() string {
        out := greeting + " Nice to meet you!"
        return out
    }
}
```

As you can see, our **buildGreeting()** function returns a function that refers to the local variable **greeting**. This variable is outside the scope of the returned function. Because of this, the returned function is considered a closure. When we use the closure returned from the **buildGreeting()** function, something interesting happens:

```go
func Example_buildGreeting() {
    var greetSophia = buildGreeting("Sophia")

    fmt.Println(greetSophia())

    // Output: Hello Sophia. Nice to meet you!
}
```

Our closure **greetSophia** continues to access the **greeting** variable from the **buildGreeting()** scope even though that function has ended. We can leverage this fact to create closures that return different values based on how they were created, as we have done here or as we did in the partial functions earlier in the chapter. We can also use this fact to enable our closures to have state, as we will see in the following example:

```go
func buildTotaler() func(int) int {
    total := 0

    return func(in int) int {
        total += in
        return total
    }
}
```

In this example, we are building a closure that sums integers, and it uses the **total** variable to hold the current total of all calls to the closure.

We can use this closure like this:

```go
func Example_buildTotaler() {
    totaler := buildTotaler()

    _ = totaler(1)
    _ = totaler(2)
    _ = totaler(3)
    _ = totaler(4)
    result := totaler(5)

    // Output: 15
    fmt.Printf("%d", result)
}
```

You can see that the **total** value is updated by each call, and the current total is maintained between requests. We could have achieved the same outcome using a global variable to maintain the state between calls. However, this would open the possibility of other code or instances of this closure accessing that variable. With our closures, the data is completely isolated and protected from any unexpected access.

Now that we have a better handle on anonymous functions and closures and what they offer us, we can look into some of the fantastic things we can do with functions in Go.

Function-based patterns

In this section, we will look at five exciting patterns we can achieve with Go. They are:

- Replacing abstract methods
- Implementing middleware
- Functional options
- Decorating functions to satisfy an interface
- Function chaining

While these are not patterns in the traditional software design pattern sense, they are general solutions to requirements that regularly pop up in our Go programs.

Replacing abstract methods

If, like me, you come from an object-oriented background, you will be familiar with abstract classes and abstract methods. Abstract methods are methods attached to an abstract class, but the implementation is left to the concrete class that extends the abstract class. This is perhaps easier to see as an example. Take a look at the following object diagram:

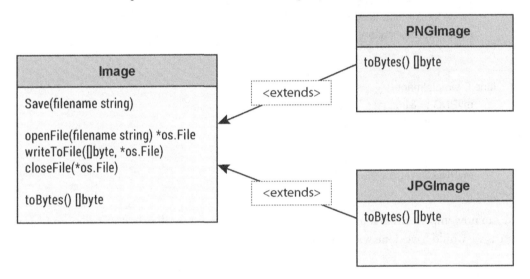

Figure 8.1—Abstract Object example

In the above diagram, we have an abstract type called **Image**. All of its private methods except **toBytes()** have been implemented as part of the Image type, and **toBytes()** has been defined as an abstract method. We have two classes, **PNGImage** and **JPGImage**, which extend **Image** and implement our abstract method. But why was it implemented in this way? In this example, the logic for loading, writing, and closing the file is the same regardless of the encoding. So, instead of duplicating that logic, we put it in one place, a concrete method in the abstract class, and shared it.

While abstract classes and methods are unavailable to us in Go, we can still achieve the same goals in Go and even do so without using composition. We implement the shared code in a struct and replace the abstract method with a member variable that is an anonymous function like this:

```
type Image struct {
    toBytes func() []byte
}

func (i *Image) Save(filename string) {
    destination := i.openFile(filename)
    data := i.toBytes()
    i.writeToFile(data, destination)
    i.closeFile(destination)
}

func ExampleImage() {
    myPNG := &Image{
        toBytes: pngEncoder,
    }

    myPNG.Save("my-file.png")
}
```

We can now implement as many encoders as we need without duplicating the common logic, just as we would have done with an abstract class and method.

Implementing middleware

Middleware is very similar to the previous pattern and perhaps more common in Go, particularly when building HTTP handlers. Let's assume you want to log every request or track the processing time. While it is possible to include this code everywhere it is needed, it is more effective to introduce a self-contained function that can act independently of other processing. This is referred to as middleware. Consider the following code:

```
func Usage() {
    listHandler := http.HandlerFunc(ListUsersHandler)
    http.Handle("/", listHandler)
    http.ListenAndServe(":8080", nil)
}
```

```go
func ListUsersHandler(resp http.ResponseWriter, req *http.Request) {
    start := time.Now()

    users := loadAllUsers()

    payload, _ := json.Marshal(users)
    _, _ = resp.Write(payload)

    log.Printf("Time taken: %s", time.Since(start))
}
```

You can see that we are tracking how long the processing of the request takes by recording the start time and calculating the difference when the function finishes. We can extract the tracking code and create a function that creates closures that perform the tracking and call the supplied HTTP handler. After applying this pattern to our example, we have:

```go
func Usage() {
    listHandler := http.HandlerFunc(ListUsersHandler)
    http.Handle("/", trackRequest(listHandler))
    http.ListenAndServe(":8080", nil)
}

func ListUsersHandler(resp http.ResponseWriter, req *http.Request) {
    users := loadAllUsers()

    payload, _ := json.Marshal(users)
    _, _ = resp.Write(payload)
}

func trackRequest(handler func(http.ResponseWriter, *http.Request)) http.Handler {
    return http.HandlerFunc(func(resp http.ResponseWriter, req *http.Request) {
        start := time.Now()

        handler(resp, req)

        log.Printf("Time taken: %s", time.Since(start))
    })
}
```

In the code above, we are wrapping our original handler in the closure created by our middleware and passing that to the **http.Handle()** function to register it to the default HTTP server.

We use this pattern to embellish our HTTP handlers with many things, including logging, authentication, and input validation. The pattern is not restricted to HTTP handlers either; it can be used in any situation where we need to swap out the code from the middle of a function and keep the shared start and/or end code.

Functional options

Sometimes, especially when writing general-purpose packages, we are left with an API with too much configuration. Take a look at the following code, which serves as a constructor for a StatsD client:

```
func NewStatsDClient(host string, port int, sampleRate int, sendBuffer int, validateKeys bool,
tags []string) *StatsClient {
    return &StatsClient{
        // implementation removed
    }
}
```

You can see that we have many configuration inputs, and because of this, the user experience of this function is terrible—particularly as several of these values will only be used by a few users. For the sake of the few users that need these options, everyone must suffer. We could move all of the configuration to a struct, and then our function would become:

```
func NewStatsDClient(config *Config) *StatsClient {
    return &StatsClient{
        // implementation removed
    }
}

type Config struct {
    host        string
    port        int
    sampleRate int
    sendBuffer  int
    validateKeys bool
```

```
        tags        []string
}
```

This approach is acceptable, and we would even be able to expand the struct to accommodate more configuration as we needed to, but what happens if we want to do more than provide configuration to our constructor? What happens if we want to include calculation or validation? This is where the *functional options* pattern comes in.

With this pattern, we can clean up our constructor API, include calculation and validation of the config in tidy little functions, and not restrict our ability to extend as needed. This is how it works. First, we must examine our config and determine if it is required. For the sake of argument, let's assume, in our example, that the **host** value is required. Because of this, we should leave it as a parameter to the constructor, ensuring that it is always supplied. For all of the optional configuration, we can use functional options. We do this by first defining a custom type like this:

```
type Option func(*StatsClient)
```

This **Option** type is not actually necessary, but it does make the code a lot cleaner. It is a function that takes a pointer to the **StatsClient** that we will configure as an input. Now, we can implement our functional options using the same function signature as our **Option** type, like this:

```
func Port(port int) Option {
        return func(client *StatsClient) {
                // validate and set port
                if port <= 0 {
                        port = defaultPort
                }
                client.port = port
        }
}
```

There are two aspects of this function to notice. The first is that we are creating a closure that includes the configuration that we passed to it. The second is that although the **Port()** function is a public function, it is accessing and setting the private member variable **port**. With this function, we have given users of this package controlled access to private member variables, which is far safer and cleaner than making the member variable public.

With this pattern, we can now add as many functional options as we need to support all of our different users' needs without detracting from the usability or giving users unnecessary access to implementation details.

For the final step, we need to update our constructor to accept a variadic number of options and to apply all supplied options to the client before returning it, like so:

```
func NewStatsDClient(host string, options ...Option) *StatsClient {
    client := &StatsClient{
        host: host,
    }

    // apply options
    for _, option := range options {
        option(client)
    }

    return client
}
```

With our new constructor in place, we have ensured that the required configuration is provided and made all other configuration optional.

Decorating functions to satisfy an interface

Have you ever had a function that was perfect, right up until the moment that you needed to use it in a place that needed an interface? Often, such functions are already in use or part of code we do not own, such as the standard library. Sometimes, it is just more convenient to write code as functions instead of structs and methods. A widespread example of this second situation is HTTP handlers. For both situations, there is a simple and elegant solution: decoration. For our example, we are going to use the **http.Handler** from the standard library, but we can do this in our own packages in the same way. Firstly, let's look at the interface we need:

```
type Handler interface {
    ServeHTTP(resp ResponseWriter, req *Request)
}
```

Compare this interface above with the function that we have:

```
func SayHelloHandler(resp http.ResponseWriter, req *http.Request) {
    _, _ = resp.Write([]byte(`Hello World!`))
}
```

You can see that, in this case, the **SayHelloHandler()** function and **Handler**'s **ServeHTTP()** method parameters are the same. This is not necessary, but it does make our life a little simpler. Our first step is to define a custom type with the same signature as the **SayHelloHandler()** we already have, like this:

```
type MyHandlerFunc func(resp http.ResponseWriter, req *http.Request)
```

We can now decorate this type with the method or methods to fulfill the **Handler**'s interface definition. In this example, because the function **SayHelloHandler()** and **Handler**'s **ServeHTTP()** method signatures are identical, the implementation merely calls the function and passes through the supplied arguments. If the signatures differed, we would need to add some data conversions. Here is the implementation of **http.Handler** that we have decorated our function with:

```
type MyHandlerFunc func(resp http.ResponseWriter, req *http.Request)

func (m MyHandlerFunc) ServeHTTP(resp http.ResponseWriter, req *http.Request) {
    m(resp, req)
}
```

As you can see, we have attached a method to the custom type we defined. Our **ServeHTTP()** method simply calls our original function defined by **MyHandlerFunc**. With this in place, we can cast our **SayHelloHandler()** function into a variable of type **MyHandlerFunc** and because the **MyHandlerFunc** type satisfies the **http.Handler** interface we can use it as a HTTP handler in an HTTP server like this:

```
var myHandler http.Handler = MyHandlerFunc(SayHelloHandler)

http.Handle("/", myHandler)
http.ListenAndServe(":8080", nil)
```

With this, we have cast our original **SayHelloHandler()** function into our custom type **MyHandlerFunc** so that we could attach methods to the our custom type and have it satisfy the **http.Handler** interface without any changes to the original function, which can be especially useful in cases where we cannot change the original function.

Function chaining

The final pattern we will examine is a more traditional functional programming pattern, *function chaining*. We use function chaining to apply a series of transforms to an input so that the output of one function is the input of the next. This is the same idea as method chaining, which we can use on objects—except with functions. Let's dig into an example. Say we have a channel of data transfer objects (DTOs), and we want to transform and filter this data. First, we need to define our DTO format like this:

```
type User struct {
    ID      int64
    Name string
    Age    int64
    Email string
}
```

Nothing surprising there. Now, we will define a custom type for the chained functions we will use to perform the operations on our data. This is not strictly necessary, but it makes the code read much nicer and doesn't cost us anything. Here is our custom type:

```
type ChainedFunction func(in <-chan *User) <-chan *User
```

As you can see, we have a read-only channel of data and output a write-only one. The channel directions here are also purely for code readability. The critical thing to notice is that the input and output are the same type. For function chaining to work, the data types didn't have to be channels; they could have been any type as long the input and output types are the same.

Now, we can define some transform and filtering functions. In the sample code for the chapter, there are three, but for brevity, let's look at these two:

```
func ProperCaseName(in <-chan *User) <-chan *User {
    out := make(chan *User)

    go func() {
        defer close(out)

        for user := range in {
            user.Name = strings.ToTitle(user.Name)

            out <- user
```

```
        }
    }()

    return out
}

func EmailIsValid(in <-chan *User) <-chan *User {
    out := make(chan *User)

    go func() {
        defer close(out)

        for user := range in {
            _, err := mail.ParseAddress(user.Email)
            if err != nil {
                continue
            }

            out <- user
        }
    }()

    return out
}
```

In the first function, **ProperCaseName()**, we transform the data by applying **strings.ToTitle()** to the **Name** value. In the second function, **EmailIsValid()**, we filter the data to only those with a valid email address. These are simple examples, and there are a vast number of these types of functions we could write, the only real restriction being the input and output format. In our particular example, the key factor to call out is channel management; we use unbuffered channels, iterate over the input channel until it is closed, and close the channel we have created when the incoming channel is closed. All of this ensures we don't have any panics and the caller controls our goroutines and channels.

With our chained functions in place, we can now wrap it all together with a controlling function like this:

```go
func TransformAndFilter(in <-chan *User, chainedFunctions ...ChainedFunction) []*User {
    for _, chainedFunc := range chainedFunctions {
        in = chainedFunc(in)
    }

    var results []*User

    for user := range in {
        results = append(results, user)
    }

    return results
}
```

In this function, we apply all of the chained functions to the supplied data channel and then collate the results into a slice. The pivotal line here is **in = chainedFunc(in)**—you will notice that when we are calling the chained functions we are using the same channel for input and output. By doing so, we are using the output of one chained function as the input to the next. Here is an example where we use all of this code together:

```go
func TestFunctionChaining(t *testing.T) {
    // Inputs
    data := make(chan *User, 3)
    data <- fred
    data <- john
    data <- paul

    // Close the channel to signal the end of the data
    close(data)

    // Perform transforms and filtering
    results := TransformAndFilter(data, AgeOver20, ProperCaseName, EmailIsValid)

    assert.Equal(t, 1, len(results))
}
```

If you would like more details, please refer to the code for this chapter.

Now that we have examined some of the unusual things we can do with functions in Go, we can move on to another pattern you may be familiar with from other languages: futures.

Implementing Futures

In programming, *futures* are a software construction technique where a function returns an object that serves as a proxy for the actual result rather than the result itself. This proxy provides access to the value that will eventually become available.

Futures are often used when the calculation of the result is time-consuming and we wish to achieve some level of parallelism. So, how do we implement this pattern in Go? Firstly, we need to borrow from our work with closures earlier in the chapter and create a closure. This time, our closure will contain a mutex and the result value, as you can see here:

```
func doWorkFuture(in int64) func() int64 {
    var result int64
    mutex := &sync.Mutex{}
    mutex.Lock()

    // start goroutine to calculate/fetch the value asynchronously
    go doTimeConsumingWork(mutex, &result, in)

    return func() int64 {
        // this function cannot return until the value has been calculated
        mutex.Lock()
        defer mutex.Unlock()

        return result
    }
}
```

We share the **mutex** and **result** value between the closure we create and the goroutine performing the time-consuming operation. Now let's look at the code for the time-consuming operation:

```
func doTimeConsumingWork(mutex *sync.Mutex, result *int64, in int64) {
    defer mutex.Unlock()
```

```
        // do something that takes a while
        <-time.After(1 * time.Second)

        // assign the result of the calculation/fetch
        *result = int64(1000 + in)
    }
```

There are two key parts to this function. The first is the **defer** with which we are unlocking the **mutex**. This will, in turn, allow reading of the **result** from the closure. The second important part is the assignment of the result. In this example, it is a hard-coded value, but it would generally be the data fetched from a remote system or the result of some extensive calculation. Finally, the usage of our future code:

```
func Example() {
    futureA := doWorkFuture(123)
    futureB := doWorkFuture(456)

    // other code

    valueA := futureA()
    valueB := futureB()

    // Output: Receive future value: 1123
    // Receive future value: 1456
    fmt.Printf("Receive future value: %d\n", valueA)
    fmt.Printf("Receive future value: %d\n", valueB)
}
```

The takeaway from our usage code is this: our **doWorkFuture()** will return immediately, but the calculation will continue concurrently. If we were to read the value of the future immediately, then our code would block, and the code would become synchronous and the use of futures pointless.

In this example, we have implemented futures in a manner very similar to how we might do it in a functional language, but how about doing so in a more Go style?

Implementing futures the Go way

In our previous implementation, we employed a closure that included the result value and a synchronization primitive, namely a mutex, to signal when the value could be read. However, in Go, we have something that combines these concepts into a single, easy-to-use package: you guessed it—channels. To implement the future pattern with a channel, we first start with a buffered channel with a buffer size of 1, like so:

```go
func doWorkFuture(in int64) <-chan int64 {
    result := make(chan int64, 1)

    // start goroutine to calculate/fetch the value asynchronously
    go doTimeConsumingWork(result, in)

    return result
}

func doTimeConsumingWork(result chan<- int64, in int64) {
    // do something that takes a while
    <-time.After(1 * time.Second)

    // assign the result of the calculation/fetch
    result <- 1000 + in
}
```

The channel provides both the ability to pass and store the data and a synchronization point. Now, when our **doTimeConsumingWork()** is complete, we can simply write the value to the channel and be done. Now for the usage pattern for our channel-based approach:

```go
func Example() {
    futureA := doWorkFuture(123)
    futureB := doWorkFuture(456)

    // other code

    valueA := <-futureA
    valueB := <-futureB

    // Output: Receive future value: 1123
    // Receive future value: 1456
```

```
    fmt.Printf("Receive future value: %d\n", valueA)
    fmt.Printf("Receive future value: %d\n", valueB)
}
```

As you can see, the result is very similar to the previous approach and is fairly straightforward channel-based code.

With both function-based and channel-based futures available, you may wonder why this pattern is not more prevalent in Go code. Sadly, there are some considerations that come along with this pattern.

Considerations surrounding futures

There are three considerations we must keep in mind before using either of our futures patterns in Go:

1. The channel-based implementation differs slightly from other languages because we can only access the value once. Once we have read the value from the channel, we cannot do so again.

2. The function-based implementation can be called multiple times; however, the usage of closures, while legal Go code, is unusual. As such, it may not be well understood by others in your team or users you may have.

3. The power of futures is that they offer a handy way to implement concurrency. However, when they form part of an API, users are forced to use them, even when they don't need or want concurrency. In these cases, the usage of futures results in poor usability and wasted resources.

4. It is often better to leave futures out of the API itself and instead let users wrap the API in futures as they need.

As we have seen, futures are another unusual pattern that we can selectively apply to our Go projects. Next, we will round off this chapter of unusual patterns with some curious things we can achieve with structs.

Curious Struct Tricks

Let's round out our chapter of unusual patterns with some uniquely Go tricks related to structs. In this section, we will look into:

- Empty structs

- Anonymous structs

- noCopy

Unlike the other patterns in this chapter, these are small tricks that, once mastered, you are likely to use pretty regularly.

Empty structs

Empty structs are precisely what you think they are. You may have even used them before without realizing it. This is an empty struct:

```
type emptyStruct struct{}
```

That's right, an empty struct is a struct that contains no member variables. Because they contain no data, they have no size, as you can see here:

```
func Example() {
    var myEmptyStruct = emptyStruct{}

    // Output: 0 bytes
    fmt.Printf("%d bytes", unsafe.Sizeof(myEmptyStruct))
}
```

It is this lack of size that we can leverage to our benefit.

We will first examine replacing potentially expensive loop iterations with map lookup. For example, suppose we have a type **StringCollection** that contains a slice of strings, an **Add()** function that can append another slice of strings to it, and a **Match()** function that finds matches between the strings in the **StringCollection** and another slice of strings. We can change this:

```go
type StringCollection struct {
    data []string
}

func (s *StringCollection) Match(in []string) []string {
    var out []string

    for _, thisIn := range in {
        for _, thisItem := range s.data {
            if thisItem == thisIn {
                out = append(out, thisItem)
            }
        }
    }

    return out
}

func (s *StringCollection) Add(in []string) {
    for _, thisIn := range in {
        s.data = append(s.data, thisIn)
    }
}
```

to this:

```go
type StringCollection struct {
    data   []string
    index map[string]struct{}
}

func (s *StringCollection) Match(in []string) []string {
    var out []string

    for _, thisIn := range in {
        _, found := s.index[thisIn]
        if found {
            out = append(out, thisIn)
        }
    }
```

```
        return out
}

func (s *StringCollection) Add(in []string) {
    for _, thisIn := range in {
        s.data = append(s.data, thisIn)
        s.index[thisIn] = struct{}{}
    }
}
```

Because we're using a map, **Match()** only needs to run a single loop, not a loop within a loop. And, as our empty struct has no size, the cost of that map is limited to only the size of the keys.

We can also implement a semaphore using channels and an empty struct. In this case, the reason for using empty structs is twofold: firstly, the low cost of empty structs, and secondly, to convey a lack of relevance. This might seem strange, but in the semaphores, the type and values of the channel are irrelevant; only the amount of data matters. You can find an example of implementing a semaphore using a channel in the source code for the first book in this series (in the same Git repository) under **Chapter02/04_semaphores/01_limit_pending/**).

We can leverage these same concepts when adding signal channels to our code. Imagine you have a worker pool, and you want to be able to signal the workers to exit. Our worker creation might look like this:

```
func NewWorkerPool(total int) *WorkerPool {
    workerPool := &WorkerPool{
        shutdownCh: make(chan struct{}),
    }

    for x := 0; x < total; x++ {
        go doWork(workerPool.shutdownCh)
    }

    return workerPool
}
```

Above, we create a signal channel and then pass that channel to all of the goroutine workers. Inside of the workers, we do the work and wait to receive a signal from the **shutdownCh** like this:

```
func doWork(shutdownCh chan struct{}) {
    for {
        select {
        case <-shutdownCh:
            // quit
            return

        default:
        }

        // do work - implementation remove
    }
}
```

With all of the pieces in place, we can now shut down all of the workers by merely closing the channel as we have in this method:

```
func (w *WorkerPool) Shutdown() {
    close(w.shutdownCh)
}
```

As you saw in the code, the data type and contents of the channel did not matter, so in this case, using an empty struct was the cheapest option.

Anonymous structs

Anonymous structs are structs that are defined inline and, as such, have no name. They are defined like this:

```
carrot := struct {
    Variety          string
    WhenToPlant      []time.Month
    Spacing          int
    WeeksTilHarvest int
}{
    Variety:          "Atomic Red",
```

```
        WhenToPlant:      []time.Month{time.January, time.February, time.November,
    time.December},
            Spacing:          10,
            WeeksTilHarvest: 18,
        }
```

As you can see, we are defining the struct and populating it at the same time. This may seem weird or inefficient, but it can be helpful when we do not need to reuse the struct or pass it around. For example, it can be advantageous when dealing with Go's built-in template engines. Both the **html/template** and **text/template** packages expect data to be passed into the template engine as a struct, and often, that struct has no use anywhere else. Take, for example, the following code:

```
    welcomeSource := `
<html>
    <body>
        Hello {{ .Name }}.<br />
        It has been {{ .Days }} since your last login.<br />
        You have {{ .Messages }} unread messages.<br />
    </body>
</html>
`
    results := &bytes.Buffer{}

    data := struct {
        Name      string
        Days      int
        Messages int
    }{
        Name:     "John",
        Days:     7,
        Messages: 2,
    }

    welcomeTemplate, err := template.New("welcome").Parse(welcomeSource)
```

This structure is very tightly coupled to the resulting HTML page we are generating and, as such, would make a poor choice to use anywhere else. By using an anonymous struct, we ensure that it cannot be used anywhere else, and it is defined alongside its usage, so we don't suffer any readability loss from the lack of a name.

noCopy

Our last struct trick is not a type of struct but, instead, something we can do with our structs to ensure they are used as they are intended. When working with structs that implement concepts like caches, worker pools, or dictionaries, it is often vital to ensure that instances of these structs are not accidentally passed by value and copied. Not only does such copying often result in an unnecessary strain on memory and the garbage collector, but it would often lead to unexpected results (for example, if you later change the original and your copy doesn't change). To achieve this, we leverage a **go vet** feature that ensures that no object that implements the **sync.Locker** interface is passed by value. The **sync.Locker** interface looks like this:

```
type Locker interface {
    Lock()
    Unlock()
}
```

We could add these methods to our struct, but this would pollute the public API of our struct, and therefore, a cleaner option is to create a private empty struct like this:

```
type noCopy struct{}

func (*noCopy) Lock() {}

func (*noCopy) Unlock() {}
```

We can now embed our **noCopy** struct into any struct we like without polluting the API, as you can see here:

```
type Cache struct {
    // implementation removed

    noCopy
}
```

It is important to note that naming our empty struct **noCopy** is not necessary, but it does add to the readability of our code.

Summary

In this chapter, we have looked at a collection of unusual things we can achieve with Go. We started by examining the functional programming paradigm and discovered that while Go is not a functional language, many FP patterns and advantages remain available. In particular, Go's support for first-class functions, partial functions, and currying can make for some unusual but rather interesting Go code.

We followed this up by exploring anonymous functions and closures. We saw how closures can be used to allow functions to have and maintain state.

We then examined a series of interesting patterns that we can implement using functions, including how to use them as you might use abstract methods from other languages, how to implement middleware, how to clean up an API with functional options, and how to decorate a function to enable it to satisfy an interface.

After that, we introduced futures, another concept founded in functional programming. We saw how we could implement this pattern not only using functions but using channels as well.

Finally, we looked at a few unusual but advantageous patterns we can apply to structs, including both empty and anonymous structs.

Questions

1. What are the three fundamental ideas of functional programming?
2. Why do we have to be careful when using recursion in Go as compared to pure functional programming languages?
3. What are the advantages of referentially transparent code?
4. How does the middleware pattern work and why would we want to use it?
5. When using the functional options pattern, how do we determine which config should be constructor parameters and which moved to functional options?

6. How can we decorate a function so it can be used as an interface?

7. Why would we want to use futures?

8. How do channel-based Go futures differ from those in other languages?

9. When would we use empty structs?

10. Why would we want to use anonymous structs?

Chapter 9

Metaprogramming with Go

Introduction

Artisans like carpenters, blacksmiths, and even chefs will create tools that make life easier; we programmers should not be any different. Metaprogramming is the approach by which we can achieve this. As we have seen in previous chapters, there are many opportunities for us to be more efficient, more productive, and improve our work quality. This chapter will examine some techniques we can apply to create programs and tools for ourselves to achieve our goals more effectively.

We will start this chapter by looking into using our engineering tools, like PagerDuty, GitHub, or Slack, more effectively by integrating with their APIs. In many cases, these services have more features than we realize, and with automation, it is possible to save ourselves a bunch of time and inconsistencies.

We will then examine how to use Go to call and coordinate other applications in ways that allow us to achieve more with less effort.

We will then round out the chapter by briefly exploring the code generation tools provided by Go's standard library. I describe this section as brief because the sky is the limit when it comes to code generation. Once you have learned to use this particular hammer, you will be surprised how many problems look like a nail.

The following topics will be covered in this chapter:

- Integrating with APIs
- Using Go to Coordinate Other Programs
- Code Generation in Action

Code

To get the most out of this chapter, you will need a recent copy (1.13+) of Go installed and your favorite IDE.

Full versions of all code examples and other related material can be found at **https://github.com/corsc/Beyond-Effective-Go/tree/master/Chapter09**.

Integrating with APIs

The first type of metaprogramming we will look at is API integrations. As an experienced Go developer, there is a pretty good chance that you have already done this kind of thing before. However, you may not have considered doing so to improve your (or your team's) productivity. All of the Platform as a Service (PaaS), Software as a Service (SaaS), and other tools that we use every day have APIs that we can leverage to improve our consistency and productivity.

Services like Google Cloud Platform (GCP), Amazon AWS, Datadog, Slack, GitHub, and PagerDuty all have APIs that allow you to achieve the same outcomes as you already do via click-ops. While we don't want or need to automate all of our interactions with these services, there are many opportunities for us to gain from doing so. There are three typical scenarios where we will often find this beneficial:

1. For tasks that we do very often (e.g., once a day or more).

2. For tedious or complex tasks that we expect to do for an extended period.

3. For situations where combining two or more systems together gives us benefits we otherwise wouldn't have.

Let's take a brief look at these scenarios and identify some examples and possible integrations.

Firstly, let's look at adding reviewers to a merge request; this is an excellent example of a tedious and frequent task. Let's say that every time you open a new merge request, you have to manually add your team members as reviewers so that they will be notified. The cost of this might not seem much, say 30 seconds, but I would argue that this time is wasted.

Assuming we have experience interacting with APIs with Go, then creating a small application that calls the appropriate API to add our team members to the merge request should not take much time. Such an application doesn't need to be clever; for example, we could hardcode our team members rather than load them from somewhere. Similarly, the application doesn't even need the most outstanding code quality in the world; it is likely only we will see the code. The less time we spend on making the application, the faster we will see a benefit compared to continuing to do this manually.

Secondly, we can automate tedious or complex tasks that we expect to do for an extended period. A typical example of this is onboarding new members to the team. While this task is often done by an IT department and not left to us programmers, this doesn't mean we can't help here. Onboarding a new member to the team often involves creating new accounts on a bunch of different PaaS and SaaS tools and services and setting the correct permissions. It might even involve requesting access permissions to internal systems and resources. The tedious nature of this task, coupled with the fact that we only do it occasionally, makes it very easy to make mistakes and forget parts of it. If we were to take the time to integrate with the appropriate APIs and automate this task, we would avoid the monotony and ensure we don't make any mistakes. The code can also serve as an accurate documentation of the onboarding process.

Thirdly, we can use APIs in situations where the data exists in one system but needs to be used in another. The previous examples had team membership as part of the contextual data. This kind of situation comes up a lot, whether granting permissions to a database or adding people to an on-call schedule. Let's assume your team uses a service like PagerDuty to schedule and manage the on-call responsibilities for a service. To configure a tool like this, we first need to create a mapping between the service and the team members who can be on call. This data likely already exists in a company directory or as code ownership settings, meaning we could extract it automatically. Now that the schedule is up and running, ask yourself: wouldn't it be nice if it automatically updated itself to respect when people are on leave? Calendar services, like Google Calendar, have APIs that allow us to query for this type of information. We can then use our coding skills to combine these two APIs and make an app that ensures our on-call schedule never includes someone who isn't available.

The source code for this chapter includes three examples of API integrations. You will find this code at **https://github.com/corsc/Beyond-Effective-Go/tree/master/ Chapter09/01_api_integrations/examples_apps**.

API integration example

Let's work through an API integration example to reinforce the concepts from this section. If you are an experienced backend developer, this will likely be familiar to you, and you might want to skip to the next section.

For our example, we will create a tiny application that integrates with PagerDuty. In case you are not familiar with it, PagerDuty is a service that manages on-call schedules and notifies the appropriate on-call person when an incident occurs.

First, let's step back and consider what we are creating and why. When working with PagerDuty, it is imperative that the on-call person or persons are quickly and reliably notified of an incident. As such, PagerDuty offers various notification methods, including email, phone calls, SMS, and push notifications. However, when people create an account on PagerDuty, it is not always apparent to users that they should configure most, if not all, of these methods. For this reason, the app we will build will check that all users have configured their account as needed.

With that in mind, we can sketch a rough software architecture for our application by identifying the needed features. We are going to need some code that:

- Fetches current user settings from the PagerDuty API
- Compares the current settings with the required settings
- Outputs the result of the comparison

After mapping these components visually, we will likely end up with a package structure that looks like this:

Figure 9.1—API integration application structure

Now that we know roughly where we are going, let's examine the critical, unusual, and interesting parts of the solution.

Calling the PagerDuty API

When starting a project, I often start with the unknown or unfamiliar components first, as this unfamiliarity is the most significant source of risk. If there are no unfamiliar components, I would start with the most critical parts. In our example, these are the same thing. We first need to determine how to call the API: specifically, what authentication we need to use and what other headers might be needed. To achieve this, we consult the documentation at **https://developer.pagerduty.com/docs/**. From the documentation, we learn that we need to sign up for an authentication token and then include **Authentication**, **Accept**, and **Content-Type** headers in all requests. Searching the documentation deeper, we find the endpoint for retrieving user information at **https://api.pagerduty.com/users/{id}** and discover that we need to specifically request that the contact methods be included in the response. Putting all this together, we can build our request like this:

```
func (u *UsersAPI) buildRequest(ctx context.Context) (*http.Request, error) {
    params := &url.Values{}
    params.Set("include[]", "contact_methods")

    uri := u.apiBaseURL+"/users?"+params.Encode()

    req, err := http.NewRequestWithContext(ctx, "GET", uri, http.NoBody)
    if err != nil {
        return nil, err
    }
```

```
    req.Header.Set("Authorization", "Token token="+u.apiKey)
    req.Header.Set("Accept", "application/vnd.pagerduty+json;version=2")
    req.Header.Set("Content-Type", "application/json")

    return req, nil
}
```

You may notice from the code above that we have used a context when making the request. This allows us to set a timeout on the entire process, which will ensure that our program will always end, no matter what happens with the internet or the server we are calling. You may also notice that we have set the **apiKey** and **apiBaseURL** as member variables of the **UsersAPI** struct we are building. This handy trick allows us to swap these values out during testing. Hint: there are tests accompanying this code in the source for this chapter; please check them out.

Handling the API response

Now that we have a response from the API, which is a JSON payload, we will need to interrogate and convert the response to Go objects to make it useful. Firstly, let's convert the HTTP response body to a Go object:

```
decoder := json.NewDecoder(resp.Body)

apiResp := &apiResponse{}
err = decoder.Decode(apiResp)
if err != nil {
    return nil, err
}
```

So far, this is pretty straightforward. However, what we will do next will have a significant impact on the maintainability of our app. This is a quick and dirty tool that we are unlikely to be expanding, so we can use that as an excuse to cut some corners, but let's discuss the best way to do this anyway. Firstly, let's look at the **apiResponse** struct:

```
type apiResponse struct {
    Users []*users `json:"users"`
}

type users struct {
    ID          string          `json:"id"`
    Name        string          `json:"name"`
```

```
        Email           string        `json:"email"`
        ContactMethods []*contactMethod `json:"contact_methods"`
}


type contactMethod struct {
        Type    string
        Address string
}
```

While this format is self-explanatory, there is a better format for our purposes. Additionally, the PagerDuty API owns this format, and we have no control over it. If they want to change this format, it will impact us; the only question is how much. If we encapsulate this format and any associated logic inside this package, then the rest of our app will be largely immune to any changes in the API.

So, if we are going to change this format to something we define, what format and which fields do the users of our package need? Users of this package will want a list of the current settings and some basic information about the user. They may also need the user's unique ID to link to the PagerDuty website or use a different API to interact with the user. With these ideas in mind, the most straightforward output format would be:

```
type User struct {
        // User details
        ID      string
        Name    string
        Email   string

        // Current settings
        EmailIsSet bool
        PhoneIsSet bool
        SMSIsSet  bool
        PushIsSet bool
}
```

Now, by converting the API response format to our format, our package has better usability and a good level of encapsulation, giving us better maintainability. There isn't anything remarkable about the conversion logic, so I will not include it here.

Configuration and the command line

The next significant piece of the solution we should take a look at is accepting command-line configuration. This is not something we often see with backend applications, and the code is a little unusual. When using our application, we can pass command-line flags like this:

```
$ ./pd-user-check -email=true -sms=true -phone=true -push=true
```

In the above command, we enable checks for all notification types. Part of the beauty of configuring our application this way is that all of this configuration is optional. As the application developer, we can and should define "reasonable defaults" for this configuration. We should set this default configuration to the settings we believe most people use, thus making it easier for our users to use the application. To accept command-line config, we first need to define some variables to accept the config, like this:

```
var (
    onlyErrors bool

    requireEmail  bool
    requireSMS    bool
    requirePhone bool
    requirePush   bool
)
```

With our config variables in place, we can then use the **flag** package to parse the command-line arguments like this:

```
flag.BoolVar(&onlyErrors, "errors", true, "print only those users with invalid settings")
flag.BoolVar(&requireEmail, "email", true, "require Email setting")
flag.BoolVar(&requireSMS, "sms", false, "require SMS setting")
flag.BoolVar(&requirePhone, "phone", true, "require Phone setting")
flag.BoolVar(&requirePush, "push", false, "require Push setting")
flag.Parse()
```

To expand on the parameters of the **flag.BoolVar()** method: for the first parameter, we pass a pointer to the destination of the configuration that we created earlier. The second parameter is the command line flag name; you can see these in the command-line example from earlier. The third is the default value—those reasonable defaults we discussed—and the last parameter is the description. This description is displayed to users when calling the application with the **help** flag. Finally, after defining all of the config, we call **flag.Parse()** to trigger the actual parsing of the command line arguments and populate the config. In this example, all of our config options are boolean variables, but the **flag** package supports most basic types and some interesting ones, like **flag.DurationVar()**. It should be sufficient for a small amount of simple configuration; beyond that, we will need to adopt something more substantial, like file-based configuration.

Validation and reporting

Our validation logic for this application simply compares the user settings with the configuration; this is pretty straightforward, so we can skip over it. As always, if you are curious, it is in the companion source code.

The last interesting piece is how the results are printed to the terminal. We could use various methods to write to the terminal, but in this case, I recommend using **fmt.Fprintf()**. This method gives us the power of **Printf()** formatting and allows us to write the output to any **io.Writer** implementation. This means we can use the same code to write to a file, a logger, **os.Stdout**, **os.Stderr**, or even a buffer so we could check the output in a test. For our example, we have an **io.Writer** as a member variable, essentially deferring the decision of where to write the output to the users of this package. Writing code in this way gives us more flexibility and also makes it less likely we will need to make a large bunch of changes if we change our mind. We could even make the destination a configuration option controlled in **main()** very easily.

The other reason the **Printf()** family of functions is a good option for output from applications like this is the ability to pad values when inserting them into the template. Firstly, let's look at our output functions:

```go
type Printer struct {
    logger io.Writer
}

func (p *Printer) outputHeader() {
    _, _ = fmt.Fprintf(p.logger, "%-40s %-60s %-8s %-8s %-8s %-8s\n","Name", "Email
Address", "Email", "Phone", "SMS", "Push")
    _, _ =
fmt.Fprint(p.logger,"-------------------------------------------------------------------------------------------------
------------------------------------------------\n")
}
```

```
func (p *Printer) outputLine(user *User) {
    _, _ = fmt.Fprintf(p.logger, "%-40s %-60s %-8t %-8t %-8t %-8t\n",user.Name, user.Email,
user.EmailIsSet, user.PhoneIsSet, user.SMSIsSet, user.PushIsSet)
}
```

The above code shows that our **Printf()** format has values like **%-40s**. This format indicates we are using a string value (the **s** component), that we want to pad the value to a minimum of 40 characters wide, and the **-** sign indicates the padding should be at the end of the value. If our value exceeds 40 characters, it will overshoot the column we are trying to create and make the output look broken, but beyond that restriction, this method is a rapid and easy way to build neat terminal output.

Wrapping up

This tool is an excellent example of using a service's API to get more out of the service that has been provided. It is also an ideal example of the potential trap and appeal of solving our problems with small apps like this. While the cost of creating this tool is low, it is not worth it if we only have 5 staff. However, if we have 100+ staff, then taking the time to build the app can really make a difference. Additionally, we could expand this app: for example, to automatically email or message users to ask them to complete the setup. The question is, is it worth the effort?

Many, if not most, services we use now include APIs; with some imagination and effort, you can build some amazing things and significantly improve your consistency and productivity.

Using Go to Coordinate Other Programs

In *Chapter 7—Improving your Development Productivity*, we introduced the idea of keeping an eye out for repeated tasks and building ourselves handy shortcuts via scripts and shell aliases; here, we are going to take that a step further and use the output of command-line tools as the input to others. This is often done using the shell and shell tools, but in this case, we are using Go so that we don't have to learn new skills.

For our example, we will reduce the time it takes to verify our code changes before submitting them for review by running the unit tests for only the packages we have changed. Yes, this has some risks, and other packages may have been impacted by the changes; however, if our code is loosely coupled and well encapsulated, such incidents will be infrequent. Additionally, the CI process will run all of the tests, so we only run the risk of a failed build during submission and cannot hurt our users. The steps of our application will be as follows:

1. Call the source code manager (i.e., Git) to determine which files we have modified.

2. Build a list of the modified packages (directories).

3. Filter out the directories we don't want to test, like vendored code.

4. Run **go test** for all modified packages.

First, we need some code to get the list of modified files. We will do this by using the **exec** package to call Git and capture the output:

```go
func (c *Coordinator) getChanges(ctx context.Context, dir string) ([]byte, error) {
    // Ask Git for a list of all of the files we have changed.
    cmd := exec.CommandContext(ctx, "git", "diff", "--name-only", "-M100%", "master")

    // run the command in the supplied directory
    cmd.Dir = dir

    // use the current Environment
    cmd.Env = os.Environ()

    output, err := cmd.CombinedOutput()
    if err != nil {
        return nil, fmt.Errorf("failed to retrieve changes from Git with err: %w", err)
    }

    return output, nil
}
```

When building personal productivity tools, the **exec** package is your friend. Beyond the issue of having to supply the command as a series of strings, which could be simpler, it is otherwise a straightforward way of calling applications and capturing the results. In the example above, we capture the response from Git as a byte slice, which we will use as the input to the next step.

Now, we take our byte slice, clean it up a bit, convert it to a string, and then split it into lines. This will give us a slice of strings that contains one record per file that has been changed:

```go
func (c *Coordinator) buildListOfChangedPackages(changeList []byte) ([]string, error) {
    input := strings.TrimSpace(string(changeList))
    if input == "" {
        // short cut when there are no changes
        return nil, errNoChanges
    }

    // convert Git's output to a series of lines
    lines := strings.Split(input, "\n")

    var output []string
    dedupe := map[string]struct{}{}

    // convert the lines to directories and deduplicate
    for _, line := range lines {
        pkg := filepath.Dir(line)

        _, found := dedupe[pkg]
        if found {
            continue
        }

        dedupe[pkg] = struct{}{}
        output = append(output, pkg)
    }

    return output, nil
}
```

The code above is standard. There are only two aspects that I would call out as tricks you may wish to adopt if you are not already doing so. First, the initial check and shortcut. Without this, we would have to add an empty string check inside the loop because **strings.Split()** will always return at least one value, whereas the current structure is more explicit. However, it was mainly included here as a performance improvement. As a habit, I would save unnecessary processing by doing as little processing as possible, and a simple string comparison is significantly less costly than almost all other processing we do. In this app, it won't make a noticeable difference, but it's a good habit. Second, deduplication using a map. While creating a map for this purpose might seem like a waste of memory, creating a map is cheaper than recursively searching a slice, which is another common implementation of deduplication. Looking up items in a map is CPU efficient and more than makes up for any garbage collection cost caused by the map.

For the next step, we will use a regular expression to filter out some packages we don't want to test, like **testdata** and **vendor**. I have not included the code here because it is pretty predictable, but it is available in the chapter's source code if you are interested.

Moving on, we will use the **exec** package two more times. First, we need to get the base directory of the Git repository. We will get this from Git itself using the following code:

```
cmd := exec.CommandContext(ctx, "git", "rev-parse", "--show-toplevel")
```

We need this base directory because all of the paths returned by Git are relative to that, and in the next step when we want to run the tests, we will need to build the complete path. This brings us, finally, to the key function, running the tests on the changed directories:

```
func (c *Coordinator) runTests(ctx context.Context, baseDir string, pkgs []string) {
    for _, pkgDir := range pkgs {
        // Ask Git for a list of all of the files we have changed.
        cmd := exec.CommandContext(ctx, "go", "test", "-v", ".")

        // run the command in the supplied directory
        cmd.Dir = path.Join(baseDir, pkgDir)

        // use the current Environment
        cmd.Env = os.Environ()

        // ignore errors so that test errors do not break this code
        output, _ := cmd.CombinedOutput()

        _, _ = fmt.Fprint(os.Stdout, string(output))
    }
}
```

As you can see, the code here follows the same pattern as the other uses of the **exec** package. The only key difference here is that we ignore the errors from **go test**. We are doing this because test failures will result in a non-zero result code, which in turn causes **exec.Command** to return an error, which would break the loop.

As you have seen in this section, we can get more out of apps with a little bit of code than we could by using them directly. This is yet another example of the Unix philosophy in action, taking small components and composing them into something bigger and better. My challenge for you is to look at your day-to-day actions and look for places where you are calling a series of apps or using the result of the first app to influence the second. One prevalent example of this is preparing code for submission. You should run the code formatter, then if that passed, run **go test**, then run the linter, and so on. Making an app that does these in sequence from a single command might not seem like a huge win, but that slight time-saving, UX improvement, and reduction in mental burden will compound very quickly.

Code Generation in Action

Code generation is the most effective way to create and maintain a lot of code fast. Generated code should be high-quality, predictable, and require minimal effort to maintain. It is not infallible; we cannot use it to solve all problems, but it becomes a valuable part of your skill set once mastered. In this section, we briefly introduce Go's code generation support and then build ourselves a simple code generator by introducing a few parts of the Go standard library you may not have seen before.

A very brief introduction

To use Go's code generation features, the first thing to learn is a special comment that defines what we need to generate. The following is an example of such a comment:

```
//go:generate mockery --name=UserLoader --case=underscore --testonly --inpackage
type UserLoader interface {
    LoadByID(ctx context.Context, userID int64) (*User, error)
}
```

In the above example, you will notice no space between the start of the comment and the **go:generate** section. This lack of space tells the Go tooling that it is a comment meant for tooling, not humans. The **go:generate** signifies that this is a generation comment, the first parameter, **mockery**, indicates the code generation tool that Go generate should call, and the rest of the comment is the configuration for the tool. In this case, we ask Mockery (**https://github.com/vektra/mockery**) to generate a test mock for our interface. The comment is not required to be next to the interface, but it is a good convention. With the comment in place, we can now use Go to generate the code using the command:

```
$ go generate ./...
```

The style of this command will be familiar to you as it follows the same format as **go test** and the other Go tooling.

Before we dive deeper into code generation, we should note that the official Go documentation states that all generated code should be stored in our source code repository. This ensures the builds are repeatable and makes it easier for users to obtain and use our code, as they don't have to worry about obtaining and using the generator.

Code generation example

Let's work on an example to explore the idea of code generation. Earlier, we mentioned Mockery, a tool that generates test mocks from interfaces. Let's do something similar for our example: we will generate test stubs from interfaces. To achieve this, we will first need to be able to "see" the code like Go does. For this, we will delve into the Go *abstract syntax tree* (AST). After that, we will use Go's **text/template** package to generate the code.

Go's AST

Go's abstract syntax tree (AST) is a tree-based representation of the code's syntax. Working with the AST can be pretty daunting at first because the model of the code using the AST can be very different from the mental model of the code we have as programmers. I am afraid I don't have any magic tricks to help overcome this difficulty other than to say: explore slowly and fake it until you make it. It will start making more sense as you spend more time playing with the AST and related tools. One quick and easy way to get started is to use an online Go AST viewer like **https://shogo82148.github.io/goast-viewer/**.

Anyway, on to our example. Let's first define the interface we are going to use as an input to our stub generator like this:

```
type UserLoader interface {
    LoadByID(ctx context.Context, userID int64) (*User, error)
}
```

There is nothing surprising or unusual about our **UserLoader** interface. Let's see how we can use AST tools to see the code how the computer sees it. First, we need to parse the code:

```
fs := token.NewFileSet()

parsedFile, err := parser.ParseFile(fs, filename, nil, 0)
if err != nil {
    return nil, err
}
```

After successfully parsing the code, we are left with an ***ast.File** that contains the details of our code. After putting our example file into the Go AST viewer, the result looks like this:

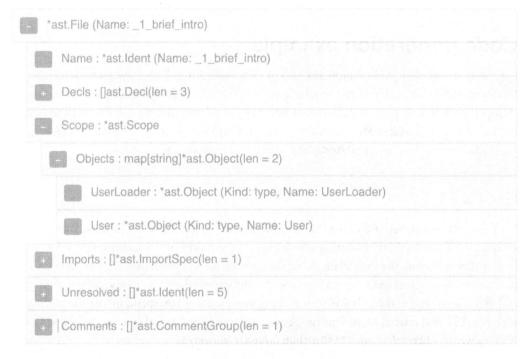

Figure 9.2—AST visualization

In this image, you can see our ***ast.File** object. The first object under the File is an ***ast.Ident**, which represents the first identifier in the code. The first **Ident** found by the parser was the package definition. After that, the parser has broken down our code into a slice of declarations, a slice of imports, a slice of comments, and a few other bits and pieces. For our purposes, all we are interested in is the slice of declarations because this contains the top-level declarations inside this file, which includes any interfaces. To find all of the interfaces, we will loop through the slice of declarations and skip over any declaration that is not a generic declaration (***ast.GenDecl**) like this:

```go
// Loop over all top-level declarations
for _, decl := range parsedFile.Decls {
    generalDecl, ok := decl.(*ast.GenDecl)
    if !ok {
        // Skip anything that isn't a generic declaration.
        // Generic declarations include imports, constants, types or variable
        // declarations.
        continue
    }
```

The above code reduces the code we need to search to only specifications, which gets us down to imports, constants, types, and variables. We need to further filter this down to just types and then filter the list of types down to just interfaces like this:

```go
// Loop over the specifications of the declaration
for _, spec := range generalDecl.Specs {
    typeSpec, ok := spec.(*ast.TypeSpec)
    if !ok {
        // Skip anything that isn't a type declaration.
        continue
    }

    interfaceDefinition, ok := typeSpec.Type.(*ast.InterfaceType)
    if !ok {
        // Skip anything that isn't an interface declaration
        continue
    }
```

After all that looping and filtering, we finally arrived at an object that defines an interface and can now extract the details. First, we extract the name:

```go
// Extract the details
outputInterface := &Interface{
    Name: typeSpec.Name.Name,
```

```
    }
```

Then we loop through the slice of methods and extract their details:

```
for _, method := range interfaceDefinition.Methods.List {
    if len(method.Names) == 0 {
        continue
    }

    funcType, ok := method.Type.(*ast.FuncType)
    if !ok {
        // Skip anything that isn't an interface method
        continue
    }

    outputMethod := &Method{
        Name: method.Names[0].Name,
    }

    outputMethod.Inputs = parseFieldList(funcType.Params)
    outputMethod.Outputs = parseFieldList(funcType.Results)

    outputInterface.Methods = append(outputInterface.Methods, outputMethod)
}
```

You will notice in the code above that we are extracting the parameters and the results of the method using **parseFieldList()**. Here is the implementation:

```
func parseFieldList(fieldList *ast.FieldList) []*Param {
    var out []*Param

    // iterate over input and output params
    for _, param := range fieldList.List {
        paramType := extractParamType(param.Type)

        if len(param.Names) == 0 {
            out = append(out, &Param{
                Name: "",
                Type: paramType,
            })
```

```
            continue
        }

    for _, paramName := range param.Names {
        out = append(out, &Param{
            Name: paramName.Name,
            Type: paramType,
        })
    }
}

return out
}
```

The implementation of this method follows the same pattern as the previous ones, looping over the list and filtering out the pieces that we aren't interested in. Perhaps the only surprising aspect of the code above is the second loop over the **param.Names**. This is because Go syntax allows you to skip the type definitions in parameters and outputs when the type is duplicated —for example, code like this: **func add(x, y int) int**—so when **parseFieldList()** has extracted a type, it then needs to loop over the names of all the parameters with that type To complete the picture, the last function we need to look at is this:

```
func extractParamType(param ast.Expr) string {
    switch concreteType := param.(type) {
    case *ast.SelectorExpr:
        return getNameFromIdent(concreteType.X.(*ast.Ident)) + "." +
getNameFromIdent(concreteType.Sel)

    case *ast.StarExpr:
        return "*" + extractParamType(concreteType.X)

    case *ast.Ident:
        return getNameFromIdent(concreteType)

    default:
        fmt.Printf("missing handler for type: %t", concreteType)
        return ""
    }
}
```

This code extracts the type definitions from the objects and converts them back into a string. When working with the AST, we end up with a lot of code that looks like this—type switch statements—plus some recursion. It can be challenging to build a clear mental model of the AST objects, due to this and all these unfamiliar types. It is best to take it slow, work through the layers from top to bottom, and investigate the AST types as you encounter them.

After all that processing, we have converted the AST version of the code into a more straightforward set of structs that we can pass to the template for code generation, for which we will use Go's **text/template** package.

Go's text/template package

The **text/template** package and its sister package **html/template** provide an extremely convenient way to generate data-driven content. The packages' features include formatting, execution flow control, sub-templates, and the ability to define custom formatting and content generation functions.

The following is a small example of **text/template** code:

```
func SimpleTemplate() (string, error) {
    templateContent := "Good morning {{ .Name }}.\nThe current time is: {{ .Time }}"

    tmpl, err := template.New("example").Parse(templateContent)
    if err != nil {
        return "", err
    }

    data := map[string]interface{}{
        "Name": "Craig",
        "Time":  time.Date(2000, 2, 1, 2, 3, 4, 5, time.UTC).Format(time.RFC3339),
    }

    destination := &bytes.Buffer{}
    err = tmpl.Execute(destination, data)
    if err != nil {
        return "", err
    }
```

```
        return destination.String(), nil
}
```

In this example, you can see that we have defined the template as a string and added some curly braces **{{ }}** to indicate where we want to insert the data. These braces are also used for all of the other template logic. You will also notice that we have parsed the template and then used it; a handy performance improvement is to parse the template once and reuse it with different input data and destination writers. The last feature of this code to notice is that we could pass data into the template execution and then dereference the data by using the dot operator. In this example, we have used a map to hold the data, but we can also use structs. Using structs is often more useful because we can traverse the struct hierarchy using this same dereferencing method, for example: **{{ .User.Name }}** would give us the **Name** field of the **User** object.

If you want to learn all the ins and outs of the **text/template** package, I encourage you to check out the package documentation at **https://pkg.go.dev/text/template**. I will not introduce all the features or replicate that documentation here, but instead, I will show you how to use it and highlight the exciting aspects in the next section.

Putting it all together

Let's return to our test stub generator project. When generating code with **text/template** I find it best to start by manually writing the code I want to generate and turning this into a test. The main reason is that the template can become complicated and complex to read. Additionally, manually writing the code first ensures that the resulting generated code has good quality. Firstly, let's reexamine the interface for which we want to generate a test stub:

```
type UserLoader interface {
        LoadByID(ctx context.Context, userID int64) (*user.User, error)
}
```

A test stub for this interface looks like this:

```
package loader

type StubUserLoader struct {}

func (s *StubUserLoader) LoadByID(ctx context.Context, userID int64) (*user.User, error) {
        return &user.User{}, nil
```

```
}
```

As you can see, we have created a struct using the name of the interface and prefixed it with Stub. You will also notice that we have set the return values for a "happy path" result, namely a copy of the **user.User** and a **nil** error. We have also included the package definition; we will need this in our template because we are generating a new file and not adding it to an existing one. Now that we know our destination, we can write the rest of the code to generate the stub and to test that that generated code is correct:

```go
func TestStubGenerator_Generate(t *testing.T) {
    filename := "testdata/input_interface.go"

    generator := &StubGenerator{}
    result, err := generator.Generate(filename, "UserLoader")
    require.NoError(t, err)

    assert.Equal(t, expectedStubResult, result)
}

var expectedStubResult = `
package loader

type StubUserLoader struct {}

func (s *StubUserLoader) LoadByID(ctx context.Context, userID int64) (*user.User, error) {
    return &user.User{}, nil
}
`
```

To get this to compile, we've defined a **StubGenerator** struct, supplied it with an input file containing the **UserLoader** interface, and given it the name of the interface we want to stub. We've also defined the outputs as a string and an error. While writing the resulting generated code to a file is our long-term goal, that would make it more troublesome while building the code generator, so our **Generate()** method returns a string (**result**) and we will save the generated code to a file somewhere else later.

To start implementing our code generator, the first thing we need to do is load and parse the input file and search for the interface provided as an input:

```go
func (s *StubGenerator) Generate(filename, targetInterface string) (string, error) {
    interfaces, err := s.parseSource(filename)
    if err != nil {
        return "", err
    }

    for _, thisInterface := range interfaces {
        if thisInterface.Name == targetInterface {
            return s.generate(thisInterface)
        }
    }

    return "", fmt.Errorf("supplied file does not include the interface %s", targetInterface)
}
```

For our initial implementation, we can initialize and use the **text/template** engine as we have before:

```go
func (s *StubGenerator) generate(thisInterface *Interface) (string, error) {
    output := &bytes.Buffer{}

    data := &templateData{
        Interface: thisInterface,
    }

    tmpl := template.New("generator")

    _, err := tmpl.Parse(stubTemplate)
    if err != nil {
        return "", err
    }

    err = tmpl.Execute(output, data)
    if err != nil {
        return "", err
    }

    return output.String(), nil
}
```

There are only two differences between this implementation and our earlier example. We have swapped out the map of input data for a custom struct, and we have extracted the template into a global variable. The ***Interface** variable we use here as an input parameter is the data transfer object (DTO) we generated in the *Go's AST* section earlier. You will remember that it contains the interface's name, a list of its methods, and their inputs and outputs. We didn't need to move the template to a global variable, but we have done this to make it easier to read and maintain the code and the template separately.

For the last piece of the puzzle, let's copy the expected output from our test to the template variable:

```
var stubTemplate = `
package loader

type StubUserLoader struct {}

func (s *StubUserLoader) LoadByID(ctx context.Context, userID int64) (*user.User, error) {
    return &user.User{}, nil
}
`
```

Running our tests will now pass and we can start iterating and filling in the template. The first and easiest thing to start with is the package statement. We can replace the package name with a variable from our input data, which makes our template:

```
var stubTemplate = `
package {{ .Interface.PackageName }}

type StubUserLoader struct {}

func (s *StubUserLoader) LoadByID(ctx context.Context, userID int64) (*user.User, error) {
    return &user.User{}, nil
}
`
```

In our new package line, we have replaced the package's name with the data we provided to the template generator. The fragment **{{ .Interface.PackageName }}** is equivalent to **fmt.Print(data.Interface.PackageName)** and is the primary method of injecting data into our template output. We can apply the same approach to replace the name of the interface, giving us:

```
var stubTemplate = `
package {{ .Interface.PackageName }}

type Stub{{ .Interface.Name }} struct {}

func (s *Stub{{ .Interface.Name }}) LoadByID(ctx context.Context, userID int64) (*user.User, error) {
    return &user.User{}, nil
}
`
```

Now we need to iterate over all of the methods of our source interface and add them to our output. We do this using the **{{ range }}** operator, like this:

```
var stubTemplate = `
package {{ .Interface.PackageName }}

type Stub{{ .Interface.Name }} struct {}

{{ range .Interface.Methods -}}
func (s *Stub{{ $.Interface.Name }}) LoadByID(ctx context.Context, userID int64) (*user.User, error) {
    return &user.User{}, nil
}
{{ end -}}
`
```

In this version of the template, we have made two notable changes. First we have added **{{ range .Interface.Methods -}}**. This causes the template engine to iterate over the **data.Interface.Methods** variable. To balance this loop, we have also added a **{{ end -}}** to the end of the template; this fragment marks the end of the template block that we will output for each method. The other notable change was to add a dollar sign to this fragment: **func (s *Stub{{ $.Interface.Name }})**. The dollar sign is necessary because while inside the loop, the dot changes scope from the top-level **data** variable to the loop iteration item. When we need to access data outside of the loop item, we need to use **$**.

You may have also noticed that we added some minus operators ("-") next to some of the curly brackets. These tell the template engine to remove all whitespace between this curly brace and the next code element. These are often unnecessary but can be very useful to allow us to format the template more readably and still achieve the desired output.

The next part of the code we will tackle is the method parameters. We will introduce another loop to do this, but this time, we will use a different format. Here is the updated template:

```
var stubTemplate = `
package {{ .Interface.PackageName }}

type Stub{{ .Interface.Name }} struct {}

{{ range .Interface.Methods -}}
func (s *Stub{{ $.Interface.Name }}) LoadByID(
    {{ range $index, $param := .Inputs }}
        {{- $param.Name }} {{ $param.Type }},
    {{ end -}}
) (*user.User, error) {
    return &user.User{}, nil
}
{{ end -}}
`
```

As you can see, this time we have explicitly defined a variable name for both the loop index and the loop item. When we run this version of the generator, we get the following output:

```
package loader

type StubUserLoader struct {}

func (s *StubUserLoader) LoadByID(
    ctx context.Context,
    userID int64,
    ) (*user.User, error) {
    return &user.User{}, nil
}
```

This code isn't very nice, but it did help us avoid one sticky problem: we need commas between all the variables but not after the last one. Let's now introduce some template functions to allow us to handle these commas in a better way. The template library allows us to use some built-in functions, like **len**, **print**, **html**, and **js**, and it also allows us to define our own custom functions. In this case, we are going to do both. First, we will use the built-in **len** function to know how many items are in the slice we are iterating and then we will define a function called **isNotLast**. Here is that function:

```go
func isNotLast(len int, index int, insert string) string {
    if (len - 1) == index {
        return ""
    }
    return insert
}
```

This function takes a length (e.g. of a slice), an index, and a string (e.g. ", "). It will return the supplied string whenever the current index is not equal to the length minus one. As we use this with slices, it will output the supplied string in all cases except for the last item of the slice.

Before we can use this function in our template, we first need to map it into the template generator. To do this, we need to update the initialization of our template to:

```go
tmpl := template.New("generator")

tmpl.Funcs(template.FuncMap{
    "isNotLast": isNotLast,
})

_, err := tmpl.Parse(stubTemplate)
```

Now we have everything in place, we can use the functions in our template:

```go
var stubTemplate = `
package {{ .Interface.PackageName }}

type Stub{{ .Interface.Name }} struct {}

{{ range .Interface.Methods -}}
func (s *Stub{{ $.Interface.Name }}) {{ .Name }}(
    {{- $len := len .Inputs }}
    {{- range $index, $param := .Inputs }}
        {{- $param.Name }} {{ $param.Type }} {{- isNotLast $len $index ", " }}
    {{- end -}}
) (*user.User, error) {
```

```
        return &user.User{}, nil
    }
{{ end -}}
`
```

You will notice that we've introduced more formatting of the template and more uses of the minus operator (-) to account for the formatting. Without this, the template would be getting very hard to read.

Our next step is to apply the same approach to the method outputs. There is nothing new or different so we show it here. For our last step, we need to deal with the **return** statement. As you can guess, we will need to use another loop and we will need to use our **isNotLast** function again but we will also need to introduce another custom function that can give us the "stub value". Such a function will likely grow as the use of our generator grows, but an initial implementation looks like this:

```
func stubValue(typeName string) string {
    switch {
    case strings.HasPrefix(typeName, "int"):
        return "0"

    case strings.HasPrefix(typeName, "float"):
        return "0"

    case typeName == "bool":
        return "false"

    case typeName == "string":
        return `""`

    case typeName == "error":
        return "nil"

    case strings.HasPrefix(typeName, "*"):
        return "&" + strings.TrimPrefix(typeName, "*") + "{}"

    default:
        return typeName + "{}"
    }
```

}

In this function, we've added zero values for the base types, int, float, and string. We've also made all error types return **nil** and returned the default instantiation of any object types. After we add this function to our template generator, our final template looks like this:

```
var stubTemplate = `
package {{ .Interface.PackageName }}

type Stub{{ .Interface.Name }} struct {}

{{ range .Interface.Methods -}}
func (s *Stub{{ $.Interface.Name }}) {{ .Name }}(
    {{- $len := len .Inputs }}
    {{- range $index, $param := .Inputs }}
        {{- $param.Name }} {{ $param.Type }} {{- isNotLast $len $index ", " }}
    {{- end -}}
) (
    {{- $len := len .Inputs }}
    {{- range $index, $result := .Outputs }}
        {{- $result.Name }} {{- $result.Type }} {{- isNotLast $len $index ", " }}
    {{- end -}}
) {
    return {{ $len := len .Inputs }}
    {{- range $index, $result := .Outputs }}
        {{- stubValue $result.Type }} {{- isNotLast $len $index ", " }}
    {{- end }}
}
{{ end -}}
`
```

Now that we have all the pieces in place, you can see that the result is quite complicated, but building it incrementally, as we have done, got us there without too much trouble.

Final thoughts on code generation

Code generation is a great tool to have in your bag. It is important to remember that it is not the right solution for every problem. Code generation is great for situations where we have multiple implementations or versions of something dependent on some information available prior to compile time. For example, you could generate code for interacting with a database, based on a struct that contains the complete table information, or generate test skeletons from a method signature, or generate HTTP handlers from a struct with JSON tags.

It is essential to not overuse generation; there will be cases where it is better to use the strategy or template design patterns instead of generating lots of code. In some cases, switching to generics is a better choice. Generics are better for smaller applications, like individual methods or functions. As a general approach, I would copy and paste for the second (first copy) version and wait to see if the problem needs a more complicated solution. When it proves that it does, I will refactor by trying design patterns, generics, and code generation.

When you do use code generation as the solution, please remember that this code still needs to be read by humans; as such, it should be consistently and cleanly formatted, and it should be clearly marked as generated, so they are not tempted to edit it. To achieve this, you can use a prominent **// @generated** comment at the top of the file or name the file in a unique but consistent way. I use **z_[file name].go**, this is not a format I have seen used for anything else and it also ensures that the generated files are always at the bottom of any file list. Please also remember that Go's community guidelines for generated code state that generated code should be checked into source control management, and the generation of these files should be ad hoc and not part of the build pipeline. Both actions ensure the code and app are predictable and consistent for all stakeholders.

Summary

The most important aspect to remember when using metaprogramming is that the goal is to save yourself time. Building and maintaining tools takes time and can be intoxicating. We must be mindful to ensure that the time we spend on the tool is less than the time we save by its existence. We could always add more features or improvements to these tools, but we should ask ourselves if they are worth adding. If automation saves us 30 seconds, how long can we spend building the automation? It depends on how often we use it; let's look at some raw numbers:

How often we use it	How long we can spend building (over 5 years)
50 times / day	4 weeks
5 times / day	3 days
Daily	12 hours
Weekly	2 hours
Monthly	30 minutes
Yearly	2 minutes

These effects multiply if we can share the automation with other developers and teams. Also, these numbers do not account for any costs lost due to mistakes or inconsistencies without automation.

Another compelling argument for metaprogramming is that we can gain many benefits by integrating multiple services and data sources. For example, if we maintained an LDAP mapping of users to their teams and teams to the resources they owned, we could use this data to configure all of our services, like GitHub, GitLab, Jira, PagerDuty, Datadog, etc. Doing so could save significant manual work and improve our overall system security. Another data source that is very valuable is calendars, like Google Calendar. Calendars have a wealth of information that folks must maintain anyway; integrating our tools with them makes that maintenance even more valuable.

Just as a blacksmith may make themselves a hammer or pair of tongs before making something more complicated, so can we, programmers, do the same. Go is the perfect language to call APIs and other applications and weave them together to make something predictable and productive. And most importantly, we have the skills and familiarity to do it easily and quickly.

Questions

1. Why do SaaS and PaaS providers provide developer APIs?

2. Are there any useful ways to integrate two or more SaaS or PaaS tools you use regularly to gain productivity?

3. After learning about code generation, have you noticed places in your codebase that were copied/pasted that could have been done with code generation?

4. Should we test the generated code?

Postface

Firstly, I want to express my sincere gratitude for your commitment and effort in reaching this point. Your dedication to our shared vocation is commendable. Many in our field need to devote more time to understanding the how and why of writing code, and your efforts are a shining example.

Embarking on the path of developing great software and becoming an exceptional programmer is not just a professional journey, but a personal one filled with immense potential for growth. I encourage you to revisit the Effective Go article, this book, and any other content on software patterns, clean code, or the craft of software construction. Each time you do, you'll uncover new nuances and deepen your understanding, thereby enhancing your skills and knowledge, and ultimately, your personal and professional journey.

I hope you found value in this book, which provides practical insights and strategies for improving your software development skills. If you haven't already, please take a moment to help me by leaving an honest review on Amazon using **https://amzn.to/3VCGbkm** or the QR code below or by discussing this book with your colleagues.

Happy Coding!

More From This Author

If you're interested in being notified and early access to any other books or articles that I am working on, join my Google Group @ **https://groups.google.com/g/coreys-writing-early-access-team**. It's low-traffic and spam-free.

Beyond Effective Go - Part 1

Part 1 focuses on achieving high-performance code. You will learn which aspects of your application or code to focus on and when. You will have a suite of tools, software patterns, and recipes at your disposal to make your life easier. After reading, you will:

- Understand the differences between Concurrency and Parallelism.

- Identify and avoid concurrency issues like deadlock, starvation, livelock, and data races.

- Understand the various concurrency interaction patterns and be able to apply the one that best fits the problem at hand.

- Take a deep dive into Go's concurrency primitives and be able to apply them expertly but also avoid many of their gotchas.

- Be able to diagnose concurrency and performance issues using Go's profiler, execution tracing, and benchmarking tools.

- Be able to identify when code needs optimizing, what needs optimizing and how.

- Have a catalog of concurrency and performance patterns that you can quickly apply to your projects.

Hands-On Dependency Injection in Go

Hands-On Dependency Injection in Go takes you on a journey, teaching you about refactoring existing code to adopt dependency injection (DI) using various methods available in Go.

Of the six methods introduced in this book, some are conventional, such as constructor or method injection, and some unconventional, such as just-in-time or config injection.

Each method is explained in detail, focusing on its strengths and weaknesses, followed by a step-by-step example of how to apply it.

You will learn how to leverage DI to transform code into something simple and flexible with plenty of examples. You will also discover how to generate and leverage the dependency graph to spot and eliminate issues.

Throughout the book, you will learn to leverage DI in combination with test stubs and mocks to test otherwise tricky or impossible scenarios.

Hands-On Dependency Injection in Go takes a pragmatic approach and focuses heavily on the code, user experience, and how to achieve long-term benefits through incremental changes.

This book is for you if you wish to produce clean, loosely coupled code that is inherently easier to test.

Articles and links to other content

Find more content, links to other books, and resources at **www.coreyscott.dev**

Index

A

a little copying vs. a little dependency, 8, 116, 118

abstract class, 253–254

abstract method, 13, 252–254, 273

abstract object, 253

abstract syntax tree, 291

abstract type, 12, 253

Accept interfaces and return structs, 14, 29, 72

accepting an interface, 14–15

adapter, 34, 42–45, 47. *See also Adapter pattern*

Adapter pattern, 42–43, 47. *See also adapter*

anonymous composition, 12

anonymous function, 153, 249–250, 254

anonymous functions, 240, 249–250, 252, 273

anonymous struct, 267, 270–271, 273–274

API integration, 278–281

application config, 35

assertion library, 89, 158–159

AST, 291–296, 300

automated tests, 125, 209

B

BDD (Behavior-Driven Development), 135

benchmarking, 184

benchmarking concurrent code, 184

boolean arguments, 104

build tools, 212

C

cache, 35, 115, 130, 189, 248, 272

case statement, 37, 58

CD, 235. *See also Continuous Delivery*

clarity, 50, 52–54, 62, 65, 69, 93, 119

clean as you go, 208

closure, 106–107, 142, 144, 154–155, 158, 161–163, 177, 180, 240, 249–252, 255–257, 263–266, 273

code clarity, 53–54, 119

code generation, 139, 142, 276, 290–291, 296, 305–306, 308

code maintainability, 9

code readability, 260

code to interfaces and not implementations, 14

code usability, 50, 52

code user experience, 52. *See also code UX*

code UX, 49–50, 52, 54, 56, 58–60, 62, 64, 66, 68, 70, 72, 74, 76, 78, 80, 82, 84, 86, 88, 90, 92, 94, 96, 98, 100, 102, 104, 106, 108, 110, 112, 114, 116–119, 156, 171, 190–192, 195–197, 208, 218. *See also UX*

coding faster, 229

cognitive complexity, 88

cohesion, 9–10, 47

comment test, 20

common mistakes, 207

common package, 116, 211

communication, 52–54, 73, 75, 118

composable, 4

composition, 12–14, 254

Made in the USA
Monee, IL
13 April 2025